TARGET YOUR MATHS

Year 5

Stephen Pearce

Elmwood Education

First published 2014 by
Elmwood Education
Unit 5 Mallow Park
Watchmead
Welwyn Garden City
Herts. AL7 1GX
Tel. 01707 333232

© Stephen Pearce
The moral rights of the authors have been asserted.
Database right Elmwood Education (maker)

ISBN 9781 906 622 299

Numerical answers are published in a separate book.

Typeset and illustrated by Tech-Set Ltd., Gateshead, Tyne and Wear.

PREFACE

Target your Maths has been written for pupils in Year 5 and their teachers.

The intention of the book is to provide teachers with material to teach the statutory requirements set out in the Year 5 Programme of Study for Mathematics in the renewed 2014 National Curriculum Framework

In the renewed Framework the Year 5 Programme of Study has been organised into eight domains or sub-domains.

Number – number and place value
Number – addition and subtraction
Number – multiplication and division
Number – fractions (including decimals and percentages)
Measurement
Geometry – properties of shape
Geometry – position and direction
Statistics

The structure of **Target your Maths 5** corresponds to that of the Year 5 Programme of Study. There is also a Review section at the end of the book.

All the statutory requirements of the Year 5 Programme of Study are covered in **Target your Maths 5**. Appendix I of the Teacher's Answer Book matches the statutory requirements and some essential non-statutory guidance with the relevant pages in this book. Most requirements are covered by more than one page. The author believes it is important that teachers have ample material from which to select.

Each single or double page lesson in this book is divided into four sections:

Introduction: the learning intention expressed as a target and, where necessary, clearly worked examples.

Section A: activities based upon work previously covered. This generally matches the requirements for Year 4 pupils. This section can be used to remind children of work previously covered, as well as providing material for the less confident child.

Section B: activities based upon the requirements for Year 5 pupils. Most children should be able to work successfully at this level.

Section C: activities providing extension material for the faster workers and for those who need to be moved quickly onto more challenging tasks. The work in this section generally matches the requirements for Year 6 pupils. Problems in Section C can also provide useful material for discussion in the plenary session.

The correspondence of the three sections A–C to the requirements for different year groups provides a simple, manageable structure for planning differentiated activities and for both the formal and informal assessment of children's progress. The commonality of the content pitched at different levels also allows for progression within the lesson. Children acquiring confidence at one level find they can successfully complete activities at the next level.

There is, of course, no set path through either the Year 5 Programme of Study or **Target your Maths 5** but teachers may find Appendices II and III in the Teacher's Answer Book useful for planning purposes. In these tables one possible approach is given to the planning of the curriculum throughout the year.

In Appendix II the **Target your Maths** pages for each domain are organised into a three term school year. In Appendix III the work for each term is arranged into twelve blocks, each approximately corresponding to one week's work. For the sake of simplicity blocks are generally based upon one domain only.

The structure as set out in Appendices II and III enables teachers to develop concepts progressively throughout the year and provides pupils with frequent opportunities to consolidate previous learning.

The author is indebted to many colleagues who have assisted him in this work. He is particularly grateful to Sharon Granville and Davina Tunkel for their invaluable advice and assistance.

Stephen Pearce

CONTENTS

	Page
NUMBER	
Numbers	2
Ordering Numbers	4
Place Value of Digits	5
Counting in 100s, 1000s, 10 000s	6
Rounding	7
Negative Numbers	8
Roman Numerals	10
ADDITION AND SUBTRACTION	
Mental Addition/Subtraction – 1	12
Mental Addition/Subtraction – 2	13
Mental Strategies +/−	14
Written Method For Addition	15
Written Method For Subtraction	16
Written Method +/−	17
Using Rounding To Estimate	18
Using Rounding To Check	19
Number Problems +/−	20
Multi-step Problems +/−	21
Arithmagons – Puzzles	22
Magic Squares – Puzzles	23
MULTIPLICATION AND DIVISION	
Multiples	24
Common Factors	25
Prime Numbers	26
Prime Factors	27
×/÷ Problems – Mental Methods	28
Multiplication Facts – 1	29
Multiplication Facts – 2	30
Multiplication Facts – 3	31
Mental Strategies ×/÷	32
Multiplying/Dividing by 10, 100, 1000	33
Square Numbers	34
Square and Cube Numbers	35
Written Method For Multiplication – 1	36
Written Method For Multiplication – 2	37
Long Multiplication – 1	38
Long Multiplication – 2	39
Written Multiplication Review	40
Written Method For Division – 1	41

	Page
Written Method For Division – 2	42
Written Method For Division – 3	43
Rounding Remainders – 1	44
Rounding Remainders – 2	45
Rounding Remainders – 3	46
Remainders As Fractions/Decimals	47
Written Method For ×/÷	48
Missing Number/Word Problems	49
Word Problems (1-/2-step)	50
Word Problems (2-step)	51
Find The Numbers	52
FRACTIONS	
Equivalent Fractions	53
Comparing Fractions – 1	54
Comparing Fractions – 2	55
Mixed Numbers	56
Improper Fractions	57
Addition/Subtraction of Fractions – 1	58
Addition/Subtraction of Fractions – 2	59
Addition/Subtraction of Fractions – 3	60
Fractions of Numbers	61
Fraction Problems	62
Multiplying Fractions	63
Fractions of Amounts	64
Decimals and Fractions	65
Decimal Fractions	66
Rounding Decimals	68
Comparing Decimals	69
Ordering Decimals	70
Mental +/− of Decimals	71
Counting in Fractions	72
Counting in Decimals	73
Counting in Decimals/Fractions	74
Decimal Number Puzzles	75
Addition of Decimals – 1	76
Addition of Decimals – 2	77
Subtraction of Decimals – 1	78
Subtraction of Decimals – 2	79
Percentages	80
Fractions, Decimals and Percentages	82
Percentages of Amounts	83

MEASUREMENT

Converting Metric Units – 1	84
Converting Metric Units – 2	85
Imperial Units – 1	86
Imperial Units – 2	87
Length Problems	88
Weight Problems	89
Capacity Problems	90
Area and Perimeter – 1	91
Area and Perimeter – 2	92
Comparing Areas	94
Area – Scale Drawings	96
Volume	98
Units of Time	100
Measures – Mental +/−	101
Measures – ×/÷ by 10, 100, 1000	102
Measures – Mental ×/÷	103
Addition of Measures	104
Subtraction of Measures	105
+/− of Measures	106
Mental Calculations – Measures	107
Word Problems – Measures	108
Addition Pyramids – Puzzles	109

GEOMETRY

Quarter, Half and Whole Turns	110
Comparing Angles	111
Measuring Angles	112
Angles and Straight Lines	116
Drawing Angles	118
Properties of Rectangles	119
Constructing Quadrilaterals	120
Diagonals and Quadrilaterals	121
Three-Dimensional Shapes	122
Regular and Irregular Polygons	124
Reflections – 1	125
Reflections – 2	126
Multiplication Pyramids – Puzzles	128
Translations – 1	129
Translations – 2	130

STATISTICS

Line Graphs – 1	132
Line Graphs – 2	134
Frequency Tables	136
Interpreting Tables – 1	138
Interpreting Tables – 2	140
Timetables – 1	142
Timetables – 2	143

REVIEW PAGES

Number	144
Fractions, Decimals, Percentages	145
Measures	146
Shapes	147
Mental Tests	148

TARGET   To read and write numbers to one million.

Numbers are made up from digits.

There are ten digits, 0 1 2 3 4 5 6 7 8 and 9.

158 is a three-digit number, 1583 is a four-digit number, and so on.

The way we read a digit depends upon its place in the number.

4926 is four thousand nine hundred and twenty-six.

49 263 is forty-nine thousand two hundred and sixty-three.

492 637 is four hundred and ninety-two thousand six hundred and thirty-seven.

1 492 637 is one million four hundred and ninety-two thousand six hundred and thirty-seven.

TAKE CARE when a number has zeros in it.

2091 is two thousand and ninety-one.

30 508 is thirty thousand five hundred and eight.

107 004 is one hundred and seven thousand and four.

A

1 Copy the table, writing each area in figures.

UK County	Area (km²)
East Sussex	one thousand seven hundred and ninety-one
Suffolk	three thousand eight hundred
Northumberland	five thousand and thirteen
Merseyside	six hundred and forty-five
Cumbria	six thousand seven hundred and sixty-seven
Cambridgeshire	three thousand three hundred and ninety
South Ayrshire	one thousand two hundred and two
West Yorkshire	two thousand and twenty-nine
Aberdeenshire	six thousand three hundred and eighteen
Conwy	one thousand one hundred and thirty

2 These figures also show the areas of UK counties. Write each area in words.

a) Powys   5204 km²
b) Nottinghamshire   2159 km²
c) Somerset   4170 km²
d) Lincolnshire   6959 km²
e) North Yorkshire   8608 km²
f) Berkshire   1262 km²

g) Isle of Wight   380 km²
h) Argyll and Bute   6930 km²
i) County Durham   2721 km²
j) Norfolk   5371 km²
k) Lancashire   3075 km²
l) Devon   6707 km²

B

1 Copy the table, writing each population in figures.

UK City	Population
Chester	seventy-seven thousand and forty
York	one hundred and ninety-five thousand four hundred
Glasgow	five hundred and ninety-two thousand eight hundred and twenty
Coventry	three hundred and nine thousand eight hundred and six
Bath	eighty-four thousand and five
Leeds	seven hundred and seventy thousand nine hundred
Wells	ten thousand four hundred and two
Belfast	two hundred and sixty-seven thousand five hundred

2 Write the population of each of these UK cities in words.

a)	Salisbury	50 000	f)	Cardiff	341 054
b)	Hull	258 700	g)	Derry	85 016
c)	Edinburgh	486 120	h)	Sheffield	534 500
d)	Ely	15 102	i)	Gloucester	123 205
e)	Manchester	502 000	j)	Birmingham	1 000 000

C

1 This table shows the number of passengers passing through some UK airports in one year. Copy the table, writing each number in figures.

Airport	Total Passengers
Heathrow	seventy million
Belfast	four million, sixteen thousand one hundred and seventy
Leeds Bradford	two million seven hundred and fifty thousand and nine
Edinburgh	eight million six hundred thousand seven hundred and fifteen
Cardiff	one million four hundred and four thousand six hundred
Liverpool	five million thirteen thousand nine hundred
Gatwick	thirty-one million three hundred and seventy-five thousand
Manchester	seventeen million seven hundred and sixty thousand

2 Write the population of each city in words.

a)	Mumbai	12 500 000	f)	Hong Kong	7 108 000
b)	New York	8 244 900	g)	Sydney	3 749 902
c)	Auckland	504 830	h)	Rio de Janerio	6 323 037
d)	Cairo	6 758 581	i)	Shanghai	17 836 000
e)	Moscow	11 551 000	j)	Los Angeles	3 819 702

TARGET   To compare and order numbers.

Example

Arrange 138 256, 172 635 and 83 562 in ascending order.

Look at the highest value digits first. If they are the same look at the next highest value.

The correct order is 83 562, 138 256, 172 635.

	100 000	100 000	80 000
	↑	↑	↑
	138 256	172 635	83 562
	↓	↓	↓
	30 000	70 000	3000

A

Put these numbers in order, starting with the smallest.

1. 2167   1726   1672   2176
2. 3459   3945   3549   3594
3. 1875   1758   1857   1785
4. 6932   6392   6239   6923
5. 4867   4687   4678   4786

Copy and complete.

6. 263 + ☐ = 563
7. 6150 − ☐ = 2150
8. 1379 + ☐ = 1879
9. 4428 − ☐ = 2428
10. 2911 + ☐ = 2991

11. 6307 + ☐ = 9307
12. 9445 − ☐ = 9045
13. 2814 + ☐ = 2874
14. 5036 − ☐ = 36
15. 3322 + ☐ = 3672

B

Put these numbers in ascending order.

1. 5492   4529   5249   4925
2. 16 738   16 873   16 837   17 386
3. 41 982   114 892   42 189   121 498
4. 35 358   35 835   35 385   35 583
5. 121 210   122 011   121 102   120 212

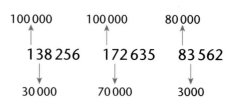

Target Maths 4A
S A C

Mental Maths . Test 2
B 2 . Test 3

C

Work out the number that is halfway between each pair of numbers.

1. 5600 ←——→ 6200
2. 710 000 ←——→ 800 000
3. 13 650 ←——→ 13 750
4. 212 900 ←——→ 213 500
5. 5 960 000 ←——→ 6 040 000
6. 126 000 ←——→ 135 000

7. Use these digits once each.

   (4   1   7   9   2   5   8   4)

   Make two different 4-digit numbers which give:

   a) the largest possible total
   b) the smallest possible total
   c) the largest possible difference
   d) the smallest possible difference

TARGET To determine the value of each digit in a number.

The value of a digit depends upon its position
in the number.

Example 2 754 863

M	HTh	TTh	Th	H	T	U
2	7	5	4	8	6	3

50 000	800	700 000
↑	↑	↑
2 754 863	2 754 863	2 754 863

A

Copy and complete by writing the missing number in the box.

1. 587 = 500 + ☐ + 7
2. 1326 = 1000 + ☐ + 20 + 6
3. 4615 = 4000 + 600 + 10 + ☐
4. 2471 = ☐ + 400 + 70 + 1
5. 734 = ☐ + 30 + 4
6. 3168 = 3000 + 100 + ☐ + 8

7. 6893 = ☐ + 800 + 90 + 3
8. 1256 = 1000 + 200 + 50 + ☐
9. 8942 = 8000 + ☐ + 40 + 2
10. 5319 = ☐ + 300 + 10 + 9
11. 7675 = 7000 + 600 + ☐ + 5
12. 2524 = 2000 + ☐ + 20 + 4

B

Write down the value of the digit underlined.

1. 5<u>3</u>17
2. 824<u>9</u>
3. 72<u>0</u>36
4. 19<u>24</u>1
5. 16<u>5</u>913
6. 346<u>8</u>95
7. 2<u>1</u>31 072
8. 1 45<u>5</u> 724
9. 3 0<u>7</u>3 568
10. 1 504 1<u>3</u>0
11. 5 4<u>2</u>7 459
12. 882 9<u>8</u>1
13. 2 690 31<u>5</u>
14. 4 2<u>6</u>8 293
15. 3 7<u>6</u>0 642

Add 3000 to:
16. 24 780
17. 15 296
18. 356 417

Add 20 000 to:
19. 16 593
20. 805 128
21. 46

Take 400 from:
22. 104 475
23. 639 543
24. 37 862

Take 200 000 from:
25. 739 160
26. 624 088
27. 251 793

C

Write the answers only.

1. 274 291 + 5000
2. 1 520 318 + 30 000
3. 1 736 496 − 6000
4. 2 299 178 − 40 000
5. 3 560 420 + 200 000
6. 883 562 − 600 000
7. 31 517 + 2 000 000
8. 2 624 190 − 4000
9. 6 800 370 − 3 000 000

Add 400 000 to:
10. 2 739 415
11. 816 480
12. 372

Add 2 300 000 to:
13. 95
14. 7524
15. 1 008 500

Take 5000 from:
16. 31 466
17. 2 123 907
18. 400 632

Take 110 000 from:
19. 539 802
20. 2 465 179
21. 1 508 368

TARGET To count on or back in steps of 100, 1000 and 10 000.

Examples

Count on four 100s from 70 830.

70 830   70 930   71 030   71 130   71 230

Count back five tens from 4936.

4936   4926   4916   4906   4896   4886

Count on 3000 from 127 416.

127 416   128 416   129 416   130 416

Count back 400 from 108 327.

108 327   108 227   108 127   108 027   107 927

A

Count on in 10s.

1. 70 from 2465
2. 50 from 5293
3. 90 from 1987
4. 60 from 6152

Count back in 10s.

5. 80 from 7414
6. 50 from 8381
7. 90 from 3669
8. 70 from 5196

Count on in 100s.

9. 600 from 5943
10. 400 from 7608
11. 700 from 1721
12. 900 from 6250

Count back in 100s.

13. 700 from 5474
14. 400 from 8232
15. 800 from 4797
16. 500 from 9185

B

Count on

1. six 100s from 63 870
2. nine 100s from 28 749
3. five 100s from 116 526
4. eight 1000s from 93 318
5. four 1000s from 251 934
6. seven 1000s from 72 552
7. five 10 000s from 447 681
8. nine 10 000s from 839 403
9. eight 10 000s from 80 767

Count back

10. four 100s from 65 328
11. seven 100s from 289 275
12. six 100s from 73 439
13. nine 1000s from 102 161
14. five 1000s from 94 505
15. eight 1000s from 326 314
16. six 10 000s from 416 920
17. nine 10 000s from 857 075
18. seven 10 000s from 704 819

C

Start at 1 396 419.
Count on

1. eight 100 000s
2. five millions
3. nine 1000s
4. seven 10 000s

Start at 7 613 085.
Count back

5. six millions
6. eight 1000s
7. seven 100 000s
8. five 10 000s

What number did I start from?

9. I count on 80 000 and reach 2 719 340.
10. I count back 4 000 000 and reach 8 267 189.
11. I count on 500 000 and reach 2 045 713.
12. I count back 60 000 and reach 4 371 596.
13. I count on 7000 and reach 5 903 420.
14. I count back 900 000 and reach 3 561 084.

TARGET To round numbers to the nearest 10, 100, 1000, 10 000 or 100 000

If rounding:
to the nearest 10, look at the units column
to the nearest 100, look at the 10s column
to the nearest 1000, look at the 100s column
and so on
5 or more, round up
Less than 5, round down

Example
Round 358 472:

to the nearest 10	→	358 470
to the nearest 100	→	358 500
to the nearest 1000	→	358 000
to the nearest 10 000	→	360 000
to the nearest 100 000	→	400 000

A

Round to the nearest 10.

1 253
2 697
3 129
4 461
5 575
6 4382
7 1718
8 3234
9 2945
10 5806

Round to the nearest 100.

11 368
12 241
13 773
14 135
15 917
16 3864
17 2526
18 9489
19 1652
20 8085

Round to the nearest:
a) 10   b) 100.

21 3572
22 2825
23 7439
24 4714
25 6157
26 8348
27 5093
28 9265
29 1681
30 7976

B

Round to the nearest:

(10)	(100)	(1000)	(10 000)	(100 000)
1 4628	7 3818	13 21 930	19 63 742	25 872 000
2 7173	8 47 072	14 53 285	20 96 280	26 647 926
3 25 385	9 15 360	15 15 817	21 51 863	27 380 138
4 38 706	10 30 249	16 169 542	22 209 000	28 154 071
5 106 242	11 572 651	17 330 496	23 672 590	29 935 295
6 391 959	12 180 434	18 476 700	24 895 014	30 561 302

C

Round to the nearest:
a) 10   b) 100.

1 75 338
2 10 843
3 104 096
4 832 525
5 3 543 277

Round to the nearest:
a) 100   b) 100 000.

6 362 740
7 219 265
8 545 508
9 173 491
10 497 080
11 1 821 934
12 5 984 360
13 4 606 192
14 7 938 504
15 2 050 800

Round to the nearest:
a) 100 000   b) 1 000 000.

16 1 683 000
17 5 461 750
18 2 839 067
19 3 270 200
20 7 954 003

TARGET To count forwards and backwards through zero and to interpret negative numbers in context.

Negative numbers
Below zero
Have a minus sign

Positive numbers
Above zero

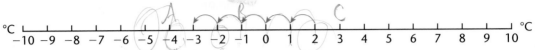

°C ⌐———————————————————————————————————┐ °C
−10 −9 −8 −7 −6 −5 −4 −3 −2 −1 0 1 2 3 4 5 6 7 8 9 10

We often use negative numbers in the context of temperature.

Example   The temperature is 2°C. It falls 5°C.
What is the new temperature?   Answer −3°C

A

Use the number line above.

1 Count on 3 from −8

2 Count on 6 from −10

3 Count on 4 from −1

4 Count on 6 from −4

5 Count on 4 from −3

6 Count on 3 from −5

7 Count on 7 from −7

8 Count on 8 from −2

9 Count on 5 from −6

10 Count on 10 from −3

11 Count on 6 from −8

12 Count on 9 from −5

Copy and complete by filling in the boxes.

13 −5   −4   □   □   □   □   1   □   3   □   5

14 □   □   −6   −4   □   0   □   □   6   □   10

15 □   □   3   2   □   □   −1   −2   □   −4   □

16 10   □   □   □   2   0   −2   □   □   □   −10

Look at the scale.

17 What temperatures are shown by the letters?

18 Which letter shows the coldest temperature?

19 Give the difference in temperature between:

   a) A and B

   b) B and C

   c) A and C

20 What would the temperature be if it was:

   a) at B and rose 5°   c) at A and rose 6°

   b) at B and fell 4°   d) at C and fell 5°.

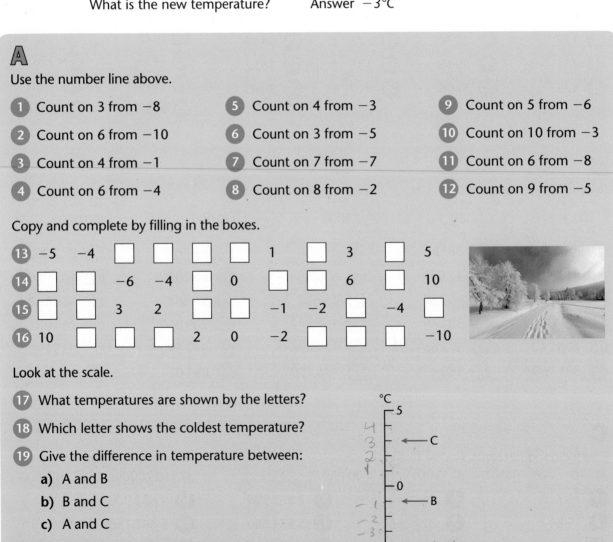

B

Use the number line on page 8.

1. Count on 7 from -9
2. Count on 6 from -3
3. Count on 10 from -6
4. Count on 8 from -1
5. Count back 5 from 2
6. Count back 12 from 8
7. Count back 7 from 0
8. Count back 6 from 5

Copy and complete the sequences.

9. 4 3 2 1 □ □ □
10. -5 -4 -3 -2 □ □ □
11. □ □ □ -2 -4 -6 -8
12. 6 4 □ □ □ -4 -6
13. -10 -8 □ □ □ 0 2
14. 9 7 5 3 □ □ □

15. What temperatures are shown by the letters?

16. Give the difference in temperature between:
    a) A and C
    b) B and D
    c) B and C
    d) A and D

17. What would the temperature be if it was:
    a) at A and rose 10°
    b) at B and rose 5°
    c) at C and fell 10°?

Put > or < in each box.

18. 0 □ -2
19. -5 □ 5
20. -4 □ 3
21. -1 □ -2
22. 0 □ 1
23. -2 □ -8
24. -1 □ 0
25. 7 □ -9

C

Find the difference between:

1. -2 and -5
2. -7 and 1
3. 4 and -1
4. -1 and 9
5. -6 and -1
6. 0 and -3
7. 2 and -4
8. -5 and 4.

Put these numbers in order, smallest first.

9. 1 -3 2 0 -5
10. 2 4 -1 -3 1
11. 0 2 -4 -1 3
12. 1 -5 0 -2 5

Copy and complete these tables showing changes in temperature.

13.

Sunday	Change	Monday
-2°C	$+4$°C	
1°C	-3°C	
0°C	-5°C	
3°C	-4°C	
-5°C	$+3$°C	
-3°C	$+5$°C	

14.

Sunday	Change	Monday
3°C		-3°C
-4°C		-1°C
-1°C		5°C
5°C		-7°C
0°C		-4°C
-6°C		3°C

TARGET   To read Roman numerals to 1000.

The Ancient Romans used letters to stand for numbers. Roman numerals were used in Europe until they were replaced by the Arabic numbers we use today. However, Roman numerals are still used for some things, such as the names of kings and queens or on some clock faces.

Letter	Values
I	1
V	5
X	10
L	50
C	100
D	500
M	1000

Rules For Forming Numbers

1. Repeated numbers are added. V, L and D are never repeated. Only repeat a number three times.
   Example   CCC = 100 + 100 + 100 = 300

2. Larger value first means add.
   Example   CXXVI = 100 + 10 + 10 + 5 + 1 = 126

3. Smaller value first means subtract.
   Example   CMXC = 1000 − 100 + 100 − 10 = 990

   a) Only subtract one number from another.
      Example   80 is LXXX not XXC (50 + 30 not 100 − 20)

   b) Only subtract I, X and C, not V, L or D.
      Example   450 is CDL not LD (400 + 50 not 500 − 50)

   c) Only subtract the nearest value out of I, X and C.
      Example   490 is CDXC not XD (400 + 90 not 500 − 10)

A

Write as Arabic numbers.

1. VII
2. XXVIII
3. XLIV
4. XC
5. XXXV
6. LXXII
7. LIX
8. XLVI
9. LXVIII
10. XCIV
11. XIX
12. LXXXI
13. XLIII
14. XXIV
15. LXXVII
16. XCVI

Write as Roman numerals.

17. 39
18. 40
19. 93
20. 54
21. 69
22. 91
23. 85
24. 48
25. 76
26. 37
27. 26
28. 45
29. 63
30. 12
31. 99

Roman numerals are sometimes used on gravestones and memorials. Copy the name and age at which each of these famous people died, changing the age to Roman numerals.

32. Abraham Lincoln   56
33. Elvis Presley   42
34. Lewis Carroll   65
35. Isaac Newton   84
36. Joan of Arc   19
37. Winston Churchill   90
38. Leonardo da Vinci   67
39. Wolfgang Amadeus Mozart   35
40. Charlie Chaplin   88
41. William Shakespeare   52

B

Write in Arabic numbers.

1. CXLVII
2. CDIX
3. DCCCLX
4. CCXXVIII
5. CCCXCII
6. CMLXXIV
7. DCCLII
8. DXLI
9. DCXXIX
10. CXCVII
11. DCCCXVI
12. CDLV
13. DCCLXXX
14. CCCXIV
15. CMXXXIII
16. CCLXXXIX

Write in Roman numerals.

17. 322
18. 995
19. 503
20. 264
21. 649
22. 117
23. 471
24. 756
25. 808
26. 384
27. 525
28. 198
29. 942
30. 434
31. 879

Write these dates as they would have been written by Anglo-Saxon historians, in Roman numerals.

32. AD 43 — Romans invade Britain.
33. AD 126 — Hadrian's Wall completed.
34. AD 180 — Romans defeated in Scotland.
35. AD 410 — Romans leave Britain.
36. AD 597 — St. Augustine brings Christianity to Britain.
37. AD 604 — St. Paul's Cathedral built in London.
38. AD 793 — First Viking raids.
39. AD 878 — Alfred the Great burns the cakes and defeats the Danes.
40. AD 1066 — Battle of Hastings

C

Roman numerals are often used on gravestones and memorials.
Change the dates of the following monarchs' reigns to Arabic numbers.

1. William I — MLXVI to MLXXXVII
2. Richard I — MCLXXXIX to MCXCIX
3. Edward I — MCCLXXII to MCCCVII
4. Henry V — MCDXIII to MCDXXII
5. Henry VIII — MDIX to MDXLVII
6. Elizabeth I — MDLVIII to MDCIII
7. Charles I — MDCXXV to MDCXLIX
8. George III — MDCCLX to MDCCCXX
9. Victoria I — MDCCCXXXVII to MCMI
10. George VI — MCMXXXVI to MCMLII

At the end of a film, the year it was made is shown in Roman numerals.
Write the year these films were made in Roman numerals.

11. Up 2009
12. ET 1982
13. Mary Poppins 1964
14. Snow White and the Seven Dwarfs 1937
15. Winnie the Pooh 2011
16. Sleeping Beauty 1959
17. Toy Story 1995
18. Bedknobs and Broomsticks 1971
19. Finding Nemo 2003
20. Bambi 1942
21. Write the date of the year in which you were born.

TARGET   To practise adding and subtracting large numbers mentally.

A

Write the answer only.

1. 35 + 47
2. 58 + 36
3. 27 + 58
4. 46 + 25
5. 73 + 19
6. 39 + 34

7. 92 − 26
8. 75 − 48
9. 53 − 35
10. 84 − 47
11. 61 − 38
12. 90 − 54

13. 85 + 49
14. 68 + 54
15. 96 + 78
16. 54 + 56
17. 79 + 67
18. 87 + 34

19. 126 − 39
20. 151 − 76
21. 105 − 67
22. 132 − 83
23. 114 − 49
24. 143 − 56

B

Write the answer only.

1. 157 + 27
2. 324 + 68
3. 419 + 46
4. 172 − 55
5. 293 − 49
6. 580 − 28

Copy and complete.

7. 76 + ☐ = 162
8. ☐ − 58 = 57
9. ☐ + 59 = 153
10. 142 − ☐ = 75
11. 67 + ☐ = 112
12. ☐ − 74 = 49

Write the answer only.

13. 840 + 570
14. 5900 + 9500
15. 233 000 − 67 000
16. 102 000 − 48 000
17. 6500 + 7500
18. 97 000 + 89 000
19. 1210 − 840
20. 16 000 − 7500
21. 73 000 + 98 000
22. 480 + 670
23. 512 − 340
24. 145 000 − 89 000

C

Write the answer only.

1. 275 + 46
2. 893 + 97
3. 231 − 59
4. 613 − 78
5. 356 + 74
6. 464 + 89
7. 340 − 92
8. 706 − 37
9. 388 + 22
10. 977 + 36
11. 854 − 68
12. 420 − 51

Copy and complete.

13. 690 + ☐ = 1670
14. ☐ + 4700 = 120 000
15. 16 200 − ☐ = 8900
16. ☐ − 5700 = 4600
17. 55 000 + ☐ = 141 000
18. ☐ + 690 = 1460
19. 124 000 − ☐ = 78 000
20. ☐ − 6500 = 4800
21. 72 000 + ☐ = 151 000
22. ☐ + 9800 = 13 300
23. 1440 − ☐ = 750
24. ☐ − 370 000 = 930 000

TARGET To use an understanding of place value to add and subtract large numbers mentally.

A
Write the answer only.

1. 2035 + 50
2. 1647 + 8000
3. 1500 + 309
4. 204 + 5210

5. 7281 − 4000
6. 4940 − 700
7. 2168 − 160
8. 3524 − 3004

9. 2275 + 600
10. 4198 + 2000
11. 34 + 7406
12. 8053 + 710

13. 1750 − 30
14. 6304 − 5000
15. 3827 − 27
16. 8195 − 1005

17. 3904 + 7000
18. 6515 + 400
19. 2040 + 357
20. 880 + 5200

21. 4755 − 200
22. 3286 − 80
23. 1279 − 209
24. 6358 − 6050

B
Write the answer only.

1. 170 250 + 40 000
2. 45 394 + 8000
3. 231 816 + 25 000
4. 4020 + 144 138

5. 376 190 + 200 000
6. 29 845 + 600
7. 2070 + 416 394
8. 158 109 + 55 000

9. 119 465 + 6000
10. 800 000 + 295 832
11. 64 100 + 1700
12. 400 020 + 538 297

13. 85 964 − 500
14. 302 519 − 70 000
15. 777 280 − 106 000
16. 128 366 − 2030

17. 407 852 − 300
18. 561 379 − 500 000
19. 60 307 − 40 050
20. 204 000 − 200 005

21. 83 483 − 5000
22. 600 744 − 40 000
23. 999 999 − 300 700
24. 100 256 − 60 010

C
Write the answer only.

1. 2 581 629 + 920 000
2. 373 950 + 7500
3. 2 446 183 + 4 006 000
4. 725 094 + 300 008

5. 135 237 − 78 000
6. 6 167 409 − 3 800 000
7. 341 872 − 60 900
8. 1 859 240 − 703

9. 272 605 + 80 900
10. 3 914 028 + 5 700 000
11. 4060 + 698 351
12. 600 050 + 403 799

13. 382 574 − 4900
14. 1 366 286 − 807 000
15. 7 542 132 − 2 080 000
16. 817 400 − 9050

17. 5 438 063 + 1 900 000
18. 270 547 + 40 070
19. 3 529 715 + 802 000
20. 386 248 + 5006

21. 63 482 − 4700
22. 8 157 391 − 160 000
23. 84 606 − 9009
24. 10 910 820 − 4 000 600

TARGET To develop strategies to +/− numbers mentally.

Examples

Partitioning	Near Doubles	Counting Up	+/− Multiples of 10 and Adjust
$227 - 74$	$25 + 27$	$603 - 387$	$245 - 78$
$227 - 70 - 4$	$(25 \times 2) + 2$	$387 \rightarrow 400 = 13$	$245 - 80 + 2$
$157 - 4$	$50 + 2$	$400 \rightarrow 603 = 203$	$165 + 2$
Answer *153*	Answer *52*	Answer *216*	Answer *167*

A

Write the answer only.

1. $36 + 27$
2. $48 + 35$
3. $67 + 24$
4. $79 - 43$
5. $96 - 51$
6. $84 - 37$

7. $11 + 12$
8. $24 + 25$
9. $13 + 14$
10. $22 + 23$
11. $14 + 15$
12. $31 + 32$

13. $84 - 68$
14. $301 - 194$
15. $2000 - 1987$
16. $52 - 24$
17. $705 - 589$
18. $6000 - 5988$

19. $28 + 55$
20. $86 + 69$
21. $94 + 38$
22. $77 - 29$
23. $145 - 61$
24. $113 - 42$

B

Write the answer only.

1. $348 + 46$
2. $615 + 37$
3. $229 + 53$
4. $476 - 58$
5. $523 - 46$
6. $341 - 65$

7. $25 + 26$
8. $15 + 17$
9. $35 + 36$
10. $45 + 44$
11. $35 + 33$
12. $45 + 47$

13. $404 - 196$
14. $807 - 484$
15. $513 - 291$
16. $6000 - 3986$
17. $9006 - 2979$
18. $7000 - 6382$

19. $373 + 61$
20. $825 + 79$
21. $517 + 98$
22. $6134 - 2002$
23. $4529 - 2996$
24. $7863 - 1995$

C

Write the answer only.

1. $247 - \boxed{} = 65$
2. $362 - \boxed{} = 128$
3. $516 - \boxed{} = 74$
4. $\boxed{} - 143 = 385$
5. $\boxed{} - 138 = 477$
6. $\boxed{} - 174 = 656$

7. $3.6 + 3.7 = \boxed{}$
8. $4.8 + 4.7 = \boxed{}$
9. $2.7 + \boxed{} = 5.6$
10. $5.8 + \boxed{} = 11.4$
11. $6.7 + \boxed{} = 13.3$
12. $4.6 + \boxed{} = 9.3$

13. $537 - \boxed{} = 392$
14. $851 - \boxed{} = 484$
15. $624 - \boxed{} = 377$
16. $4001 - \boxed{} = 1898$
17. $7005 - \boxed{} = 2973$
18. $9004 - \boxed{} = 4966$

19. $\boxed{} + 202 = 651$
20. $\boxed{} - 397 = 936$
21. $\boxed{} + 1984 = 5368$
22. $\boxed{} + 398 = 624$
23. $\boxed{} - 504 = 875$
24. $\boxed{} + 4021 = 9759$

TARGET To use a formal written method to add whole numbers.

Examples

```
   3764            58 290          427 385
 +2568          + 47 843        +392 749
 ------          --------        --------
   6332           106 133         820 134
   1 1 1           1 1  1         1 1 1  1 1
```

A

Copy and complete.

1 1638
+ 854

7 4716
+1452

2 2475
+1369

8 3298
+1638

3 4853
+2526

9 5847
+2925

4 3167
+ 748

10 6585
+2367

5 6929
+1549

11 4932
+1648

6 5384
+4276

12 5479
+2194

13 There are 4629 trees in a wood. 3785 saplings are planted. How many trees are there now in the wood?

14 A hotel has 5973 guests in the summer and 1468 in the rest of the year. How many guests does it have in the year altogether?

B

Copy and complete.

1 43 675
+15 859

7 13 819
+ 7 685

2 37 649
+14 631

8 76 543
+15 389

3 58 595
+25 274

9 45 968
+11 679

4 26 828
+13 457

10 24 736
+17 364

5 49 274
+34 797

11 37 857
+36 588

6 65 936
+25 349

12 48 625
+23 497

13 In one year a museum has 53 964 visitors. This total increases by 17 485 in the next year. How many people visit the museum in the second year?

14 In the first week of a sale a shop takes £39 058 and in the second week, £21 975. What are the takings for the two weeks combined?

C

Set out as in the examples.

1 367 657 + 145 897

2 295 738 + 245 984

3 549 546 + 372 855

4 298 399 + 145 786

5 467 838 + 349 372

6 679 473 + 265 989

7 363 756 + 346 476

8 556 967 + 24 976

9 798 298 + 176 838

10 685 685 + 349 375

11 427 396 + 157 249

12 594 149 + 446 562

13 During the week 481 975 passengers arrive at Terminal 1 of an airport and 265 328 arrive at Terminal 2. How many passengers arrive at the airport altogether?

14 On Friday 609 387 copies of a newspaper are sold. On Saturday sales go up by 131 695. How many copies of the paper are sold on Saturday?

TARGET To use a formal written method to subtract whole numbers.

Examples

Borrowing when there is a 0 in the next column. e.g. 4307 − 1648

```
  7 11  1 2 1
  8 2  7 3 0
− 2 6  8 2 4
  5 5  9 0 6
```

Exchange one 100 for ten 10s and then one 10 for ten units.

```
    3 12 9 1
    4 3 0 7
  − 1 6 4 8
    2 6 5 9
```

or exchange one of thirty 10s for ten units.

```
    3 12 9 1
    4 3 0 7
  − 1 6 4 8
    2 6 5 9
```

A

Copy and complete.

1. 2763
   − 1435

2. 4518
   − 3556

3. 3950
   − 1442

4. 7426
   − 3762

5. 8871
   − 6923

6. 5542
   − 2298

7. 6085
   − 3537

8. 9663
   − 5484

9. 8357
   − 2792

10. 7290
   − 2467

11. 6427
   − 2519

12. 9205
   − 3863

13. There are 5620 geese in a river. 4573 fly off. How many are left?

14. Len has £8164. He spends £1926. How much does he have left?

B

Copy and complete.

1. 25 846
   − 12 475

2. 19 523
   − 7 398

3. 40 750
   − 35 383

4. 28 259
   − 10 748

5. 81 605
   − 54 397

6. 40 384
   − 21 655

7. 73 541
   − 15 646

8. 97 190
   − 47 329

9. 66 042
   − 27 565

10. 81 418
   − 32 683

11. 72 164
   − 26 708

12. 50 825
   − 31 869

13. Raina has £94 037 in her savings account. She takes out £14 749. How much is left in the account?

14. A supermarket chain employs 35 194 people full time and 18 758 people part time. How many more employees are full time than part time?

C

Set out as in the example.

1. 122 940 − 13 472

2. 536 017 − 329 643

3. 851 329 − 257 082

4. 374 806 − 209 877

5. 945 293 − 762 597

6. 203 468 − 139 470

7. 710 534 − 555 168

8. 486 052 − 336 174

9. 659 615 − 567 839

10. 832 041 − 787 956

11. 547 216 − 265 928

12. 920 370 − 536 514

13. During their relegation season a Premiership club has a total of 613 527 spectators at their home games. In the next season attendances fall by 164 849. How many spectators attend home matches in the second season?

14. A company makes 761 409 jars of jam and 568 705 jars of marmalade. How many fewer jars of marmalade than jam are made?

TARGET To add and subtract whole numbers using written methods.

Examples

$$\begin{array}{r} 84\ 759 \\ +\ 25\ 963 \\ \hline 110\ 722 \\ \hline \end{array}$$
          1 1 1 1

         8 11 14 10 1
$$\begin{array}{r} 9\!\!\!\;2\ \,5\!\!\!\;1\!\!\!\;3 \\ -\ 17\ 548 \\ \hline 74\ 965 \\ \hline \end{array}$$

A

Copy and complete.

1 2748
   + 1875

2 4583
   + 1679

3 5469
   + 3537

4 3795
   + 1648

5 6857
   + 2379

6 4674
   + 2956

7 3453
   − 1947

8 5215
   − 2340

9 9491
   − 6626

10 4106
    − 1893

11 7342
    − 3587

12 6530
    − 1745

13 North Yorkshire has an area of 8309 km². South Yorkshire's area is 1560 km². How much larger is the more northerly county?

B

Copy and complete.

1 29 756
   + 26 245

2 56 945
   + 27 382

3 37 567
   + 21 964

4 48 378
   + 39 776

5 25 693
   + 15 858

6 63 859
   + 16 432

7 85 144
   − 32 375

8 32 317
   − 28 698

9 64 523
   − 48 549

10 71 431
    − 52 485

11 93 250
    − 34 593

12 46 365
    − 36 398

13 During the year 32 786 fiction and 18 259 non-fiction books are bought from a shop. How many books are bought altogether?

14 A warehouse has 63 170 sacks of potatoes in stock. 29 485 sacks are dispatched. How many sacks are left?

C

Set out as in the example.

1 166 594 + 93 889

2 305 737 + 299 390

3 578 479 + 412 791

4 243 685 + 188 556

5 459 368 + 249 767

6 387 846 + 316 858

7 424 512 − 236 678

8 343 354 − 156 759

9 602 635 − 236 797

10 833 128 − 548 199

11 590 243 − 496 475

12 911 570 − 256 992

13 A store has takings of £639 827 in a week. During the next week takings rise by £275 984. What are the store's takings in the second week?

14 The population of Longport is 726 540. The population of Bridgeford is 559 856. How many more people live in Longport than Bridgeford?

TARGET To practise using rounding to estimate.

Examples

3762 + 2945
rounds to
3800 + 2900 = 6700

Answer ≈ 6700

935 − 386
rounds to
940 − 390 = 550

Answer ≈ 550

319 × 3
rounds to
320 × 3 = 960

Answer ≈ 960

2357 ÷ 8
rounds to
2400 ÷ 8 = 300

Answer ≈ 300

(≈ means 'is approximately equal to')

A

Round to the nearest 10 and estimate.

1 323 + 147
2 458 + 291
3 269 − 153
4 617 − 387

Round to the nearest 100 and estimate.

5 5253 + 2728
6 6540 + 1592
7 4406 − 2639
8 8764 − 3285

Round to the nearest 10 and estimate.

9 57 × 3
10 92 × 5
11 46 × 8
12 68 × 6

13 372 ÷ 4
14 279 ÷ 7
15 115 ÷ 2
16 648 ÷ 9

B

Round to the nearest 10 and estimate.

1 766 + 439
2 1392 + 248
3 926 − 481
4 2649 − 374

Round to the nearest 100 and estimate.

5 7432 + 5648
6 11 756 + 4671
7 7964 − 2353
8 35 627 − 3885

Round the first number to the nearest 10 and estimate.

9 128 × 7
10 153 × 6
11 657 ÷ 3
12 962 ÷ 8

Round the first number to the nearest 100 and estimate.

13 2739 × 4
14 3194 × 9
15 5972 ÷ 5
16 4751 ÷ 6

C

Round to the nearest 10 and estimate.

1 1673 + 756
2 2478 + 1229
3 3634 − 946
4 5248 − 1697

Round to the nearest 100 and estimate.

5 18 856 + 4330
6 23 514 + 15 467
7 28 062 − 3773
8 32 685 − 14 368

Round both numbers to the nearest 10 and estimate.

9 1536 × 29
10 2671 × 18
11 1392 × 43
12 465 × 47

Estimate by rounding the first number to the nearest:

(10)   (100)

13 883 ÷ 7   15 10 574 ÷ 8
14 1275 ÷ 9   16 13 629 ÷ 12

TARGET To use rounding to check answers to calculations.

Examples

487 − 259
rounds to
490 − 260 = 230

Answer ≈ *230*

5264 + 4935
rounds to
5300 + 4900 = 10 200

Answer ≈ *10 200*

1472 × 6
rounds to
1500 × 6 = 9000

Answer ≈ *9000*

3154 ÷ 4
rounds to
3200 ÷ 4 = 800

Answer ≈ *800*

(≈ means '*is approximately equal to*')

A

Round to the nearest 10.

1 34
6 63
2 57
7 98
3 25
8 36
4 82
9 71
5 49
10 85

Round to the nearest 100.

11 183
16 749
12 535
17 361
13 274
18 827
14 651
19 294
15 418
20 952

Round to the nearest 10 and estimate.

21 35 + 22
22 24 + 17
23 67 − 31
24 54 − 23

Round to the nearest 100 and estimate.

25 641 + 183
26 358 + 219
27 573 − 145
28 926 − 467

B

Round to the nearest 10, estimate and then work out. Check your answer.

1 163 + 126
2 345 + 174
3 422 − 178
4 869 − 253

5 178 × 2
6 153 × 6
7 185 ÷ 3
8 252 ÷ 8

Round to the nearest 100, estimate and then work out. Check your answer.

9 2795 + 2473
10 4317 + 1582
11 5174 − 3358
12 7526 − 1914

13 1384 × 4
14 1526 × 7
15 2635 ÷ 5
16 6770 ÷ 9

C

Choose the correct answer and then work out to check.

1 52·76 + 28·49

   a) 80·15   c) 81·25
   b) 80·25   d) 82·15

2 63·18 − 39·62

   a) 23·46   c) 24·46
   b) 23·56   d) 24·56

Copy and complete.

3 5 ☐ 9·5 + 364· ☐ = 944·2
4 8 ☐ ·53 − 17·8 ☐ = 64·69
5 641· ☐ − 3 ☐ 2·9 = 278·7
6 46·6 ☐ + 2 ☐ ·87 = 72·55

Estimate and then work out. Check your answer.

7 345·3 + 181·9
8 678·2 + 257·5
9 45·27 + 39·35
10 56·61 + 46·48
11 721·8 − 249·2
12 954·6 − 373·7
13 63·29 − 18·73
14 81·81 − 47·54

TARGET   To solve number problems involving addition and subtraction.

A

1. Find two numbers with:

   a) a total of 100 and a difference of 50

   b) a total of 100 and a difference of 26

   c) a total of 200 and a difference of 72.

2. I think of a number.
   I add 78.
   I take 126.
   The answer is 236.
   What is my number?

3. I think of a number.
   I take 63.
   I add 82.
   The answer is 174.
   What is my number?

Copy and complete by writing the missing digits in the boxes.

4. 6☐ + ☐5 = 97

5. ☐8 + 4☐ = 126

6. 9☐ + ☐3 = 147

7. ☐5 + 2☐ = 112

8. 7☐ − ☐3 = 33

9. 1☐3 − 5☐ = 65

10. 13☐ − ☐9 = 95

11. 1☐2 − 8☐ = 74

B

1. Find two numbers with:

   a) a total of 500 and a difference of 156

   b) a total of 1000 and a difference of 338

   c) a total of 150 and a difference of 54.

2. I think of a number.
   I subtract 247.
   I add 385.
   The answer is 619.
   What is my number?

3. I think of a number.
   I add 176.
   I subtract 493.
   The answer is 648.
   What is my number?

Copy and complete.

4.
```
   ☐ 4 ☐
 + 1 ☐ 8
 ───────
   3 7 5
```

5.
```
   4 ☐ 9
 + ☐ 6 ☐
 ───────
   8 2 4
```

6.
```
   ☐ 7 ☐
 − 2 ☐ 9
 ───────
   6 1 2
```

7.
```
   5 ☐ 8
 − ☐ 7 ☐
 ───────
   3 4 2
```

C

1. Find two numbers with:

   a) a total of 10 000 and a difference of 2186

   b) a total of 2500 and a difference of 718

   c) a total of 318 and a difference of 132.

2. I think of a number.
   I add 1628.
   I subtract 847.
   The answer is 2356.
   What is my number?

3. I think of a number.
   I subtract 793.
   I add 1428.
   The answer is 4175.
   What is my number?

Copy and complete.

4.
```
   ☐ 5 ☐ 7
 + 1 ☐ 9 ☐
 ─────────
   3 9 4 3
```

5.
```
   3 ☐ 6 ☐
 + ☐ 5 ☐ 9
 ─────────
   6 3 1 1
```

6.
```
   ☐ 7 ☐ 1
 − 1 ☐ 2 ☐
 ─────────
   3 8 1 3
```

7.
```
   8 ☐ 9 ☐
 − ☐ 3 ☐ 7
 ─────────
   2 9 0 6
```

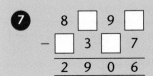

TARGET   To solve addition and subtraction multi-step problems.

Example

A library has 7917 fiction books and 2468 fewer non-fiction books. There are 4708 books in the children's section. How many books are there in the adult section?

1. Find the number of non-fiction books.
2. Find the total number of books in the library.
3. Find the number of adult section books.

Answer   *There are 8658 books in the adult section.*

1	2	3
8 101		0 12 1 5 1
7 9 X 7	7 917	X 3 3 6 6
− 2468	+ 5 449	− 4 708
5449	13 366	8 658

A

1. There are 113 children in Year 5. 58 are boys. 36 of the girls are in the choir. How many of the Year 5 girls are not in the choir?

2. One tin has 84 biscuits. Another has 48. Ninety-seven are eaten. How many are left?

3. In an orchard there are 168 apple trees, 126 pear trees and 75 cherry trees. How many trees are there in the orchard altogether?

4. There are 260 children and 87 fewer adults in a cinema. How many people are in the audience altogether?

5. A farmer has 157 brown cows and 183 black and white cows. 251 of the cows have been milked. How many have not been milked?

B

1. Elroy's book has 407 pages. He is on page 186. He reads another 59 pages. How many pages are left?

2. Seventy-four fewer children come to school by car than walk. 211 walk. 65 come in other ways. How many children go to the school?

3. George has 739 stamps in two albums. 294 are in his blue album and he has 158 British stamps in his red album. How many foreign stamps are there in his red album?

4. A supermarket has 1350 bottles of milk for sale. There are 169 more green top than red top bottles. 465 of the bottles are red top. How many blue top bottles are for sale?

C

1. In an election 32 736 people vote. 14 485 vote for the winner and 13 726 for the candidate in second place. How many people vote for the only other candidate?

2. Jocelyn has £8376 in her bank account. In the next month she takes out £4595 for a new car and a further £1806. Her salary of £2649 is paid in. How much is in her account at the end of the month?

3. In one month a supermarket sells 5847 cans of tomato soup, 3734 cans of vegetable soup and 2485 cans of chicken soup. The combined sales of these three varieties is 3728 greater than the total sales of all the other varieties of soup. How many cans of soup were sold during the month altogether?

TARGET   To solve number puzzles involving addition and subtraction.

In these triangular arithmagons the pair of numbers at the end of each side are added together to give the number between them.

Example

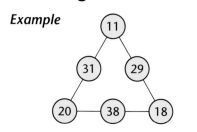

11 + 18 = 29
18 + 20 = 38
20 + 11 = 31

Find the missing numbers in these arithmagons.

A

1
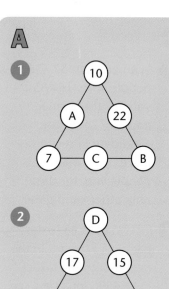

2

3
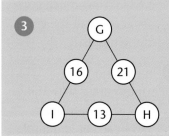

4
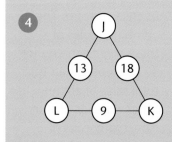

B

1
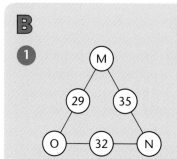

2
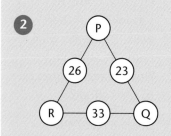

3
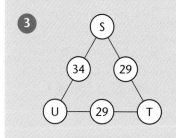

4
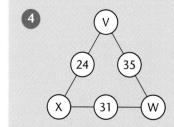

C

1
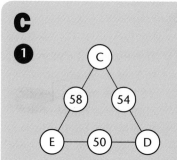

2
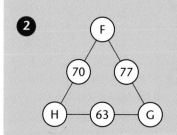

3
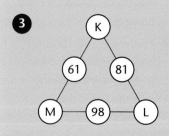

4
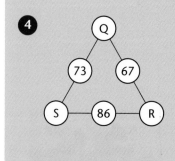

TARGET To solve number puzzles involving addition and subtraction.

In a magic square the sum of each row, column and diagonal is the same.

21	10	17
12	16	20
15	22	11

Example

Row	15 + 22 + 11 = 48
Column	10 + 16 + 22 = 48
Diagonal	11 + 16 + 21 = 48

Copy and complete the following magic squares.

A

1

3		5
	8	
		13

2

		14
10	9	17

3

	3	
	15	
	27	5

4

22	21	14
		27

5

		18
	22	
26	6	

B

1

	17		3
11		9	
	10	13	
16		2	15

2

9			7
6	15	1	12
	10		
		11	2

3

21		16	
8	15	13	
		6	17
	9	19	

4

6	19		5
		11	
	12		10
18		4	17

C

1

2		4
	1	
−2		

2

0	3	−6
4		

3

−2		
	−3	−7
		−4

4

		−1
		4
	2	−3

5

−7		
	−2	
	−10	3

TARGET   To identify multiples.

A multiple of a number can be divided by that number without leaving a remainder.

Example

$24 \div 6 = 4$ $56 \div 6 = 9 \text{ r } 2$ $120 \div 6 = 20$ $3000 \div 6 = 500$

24, 120 and 3000 are multiples of six. 56 is not a multiple of six.

A

Write down the first six multiples of:

1   3   3   6

2   4   4   9.

Write Yes or No.

5   Is 78 a multiple of 2?

6   Is 25 a multiple of 3?

7   Is 48 a multiple of 4?

8   Is 95 a multiple of 5?

9   Is 130 a multiple of 10?

10   Is 56 a multiple of 6?

11   Is 56 a multiple of 7?

12   Is 56 a multiple of 8?

Which number should not be in the box?

13
| Multiples of 5 |
| 65, 130, 151, 115 |

14
| Multiples of 7 |
| 74, 63, 140, 56 |

15
| Multiples of 8 |
| 64, 88, 72, 84 |

16
| Multiples of 9 |
| 45, 39, 72, 108 |

B

Write down the first six multiples of:

1   7   3   15

2   12   4   99.

Write True or False.

5   48 is a multiple of 3.

6   152 is a multiple of 5.

7   42 is a multiple of 4.

8   72 is a multiple of 6.

9   91 is a multiple of 7.

10   104 is a multiple of 8.

11   109 is a multiple of 9.

12   111 is a multiple of 11.

13   140 is a multiple of 20.

14   510 is a multiple of 50.

15   250 is a multiple of 100.

16   360 is a multiple of 12.

Write down:

17   the 20th multiple of 8

18   the 4th multiple of 19

19   the 13th multiple of 12

20   the 5th multiple of 22.

C

1   Make up a rule for recognising multiples of:

   a) 2   b) 10   c) 5.

A number is a multiple of 3 if the sum of its digits is divisible by 3.
Multiples of 3 which are even are also multiples of 6.

Examples

$8 + 7 + 3 = 18$
(divisible by 3)
387 is a multiple of 3
378 is a multiple of 3 and 6

2   Which of these numbers are multiples of:

   a) 3   b) 6?

| 534   267   463   948 |
| 715   882   171 |

3   Use these digits.

      2   3   5   7   8

Make up as many three-digit and four-digit multiples of 6 as you can.

4   Investigate the 2 digit and 3 digit multiples of 9. What do you notice?

TARGET To find all the factors of a number and common factors of two numbers.

Factors are numbers that divide exactly into another number.

Two or more numbers may have common factors as well as 1.
The largest of these is the highest common factor.

Examples
Factors of 12   1, 2, 3, 4, 6, 12
Factors of 30   1, 2, 3, 5, 6, 10, 15, 30

Common factors of 12 and 30   1, 2, 3, 6

Highest common factor of 12 and 30 is 6.

A

Copy and complete the second factor in each pair.

1. 16 → 2 and ☐
2. 35 → 7 and ☐
3. 44 → 11 and ☐
4. 27 → 3 and ☐
5. 40 → 5 and ☐
6. 24 → 8 and ☐
7. 90 → 9 and ☐
8. 48 → 6 and ☐
9. 28 → 4 and ☐
10. 72 → 12 and ☐
11. 100 → 2 and ☐
12. 5 → 5 and ☐

Find all the factors of the following numbers. The number of factors is shown in brackets.

13. 8 (4)
14. 25 (3)
15. 22 (4)
16. 18 (6)
17. 15 (4)
18. 32 (6)
19. 60 (12)
20. 36 (9)

B

Find all the factors of:

1. 98
2. 52
3. 66
4. 63
5. 48
6. 84
7. 102
8. 78
9. 90 (12)
10. 132 (12)
11. 140 (12)
12. 108 (12)
13. 127 (2)
14. 117 (6)
15. 124 (6)
16. 112. (10)

Find the common factors of each pair of numbers.

17. 6, 9
18. 8, 10
19. 12, 16
20. 18, 30
21. 20, 30
22. 40, 100
23. 24, 32
24. 12, 15
25. 15, 20
26. 14, 35
27. 8, 12
28. 6, 14
29. 24, 36
30. 12, 18
31. 20, 25
32. 27, 36

C

Find all the factors of:

1. 133 (4)
2. 138 (8)
3. 144 (15)
4. 162 (10)
5. 176 (10)
6. 182 (8)
7. 184 (8)
8. 250. (8)

Find the highest common factor of each group of numbers.

9. 6, 12, 16
10. 10, 25, 100
11. 16, 24, 40
12. 6, 12, 24
13. 20, 50, 100
14. 9, 12, 18
15. 8, 16, 20
16. 21, 28, 35
17. 50, 75, 100
18. 18, 36, 72
19. 30, 60, 75
20. 36, 48, 60

TARGET   To identify prime numbers and composite numbers.

A prime number is a number which is divisible by only two different numbers: by itself and by one.

The first four prime numbers are 2, 3, 5 and 7. Notice that 1 is *not* a prime number.
4, 6, 8, 9 and 10 are not prime numbers because they are divisible by at least one of the first four prime numbers.

To find out if a two-digit number is a prime number you need to work out if it is divisible by one of the first four prime numbers, 2, 3, 5 and 7. A whole number which is not a prime number is called a composite number.

Examples

29 is not divisible by 2, 3, 5 or 7.   29 is a prime number.
30 is divisible by 2, 3, and 5.   30 is a composite number.

A

Write down the prime number in each group.

1   4, 5, 6

2   9, 10, 11

3   27, 28, 29

4   37, 38, 39

5   43, 44, 45

6   51, 52, 53

7   61, 62, 63

8   77, 78, 79

9   Find the next prime number:

 a) after 20

 b) after 32.

10 Find all the prime numbers below 50. There are 15. Remember, 1 is not a prime number.

11 Explain why 730 is not a prime number.

B

Write down the two numbers in each group which are *not* prime numbers.

1   1   2   3   4

2   16   17   18   19

3   21   31   41   51

4   27   37   47   57

5   63   73   83   93

6   61   71   81   91

Write down the next prime number after:

7   8   11   62

8   24   12   80

9   38   13   90

10 53   14   74.

15 Find all the prime numbers below 100. There are 25.

16 Explain why these numbers are composite numbers.

 a) 1235   b) 9476

C

In the questions in this section you may need to work out if a number is divisible by prime numbers other than 2, 3, 5 and 7.

Example
121 is not a prime number because it is divisible by 11.

Decide whether each number is or is not a prime number.

1   105   6   143

2   113   7   149

3   119   8   152

4   131   9   163

5   137   10 201

Explain why the following numbers are composite numbers.

11 117   16 221

12 133   17 253

13 141   18 267

14 161   19 295

15 176   20 323

TARGET To know and use the vocabulary of prime numbers, prime factors and composite numbers.

Factors are numbers that divide exactly into another number.
A prime number is a number that is only divisible by itself and one.
A composite number is a number which is not a prime number.

PRIME FACTORS

A factor which is also a prime
number is a prime factor.
To find the prime factors of
a number we can use a
factor tree.

A factor tree for 70

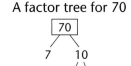

```
      70
     /  \
    7    10
        /  \
       5    2
```

70 = 7 × 2 × 5

A factor tree for 24

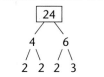

```
        24
       /   \
      4     6
     / \   / \
    2   2 2   3
```

24 = 2 × 2 × 2 × 3

A

Find all the factors of:

1 8
2 10
3 12
4 21
5 25
6 24
7 18
8 28.

Find all the prime numbers between:

9 10 and 20
10 20 and 30
11 30 and 40
12 40 and 50

Write down the next prime number after:

13 54
14 68
15 80
16 62
17 49
18 85
19 91
20 74.

Explain why these numbers are not prime numbers.

21 21
22 38
23 49
24 33

B

Use a factor tree to find all the prime factors of:

1 32
2 49
3 80
4 66
5 48
6 42
7 75
8 100.

Find a pair of prime numbers which give a total of:

9 12
10 14
11 21
12 28
13 36
14 48
15 54
16 61.

17 Find six pairs of prime numbers which give a total of 100.

Explain why these numbers are composite numbers.

18 91
19 57
20 85
21 121
22 178
23 119
24 717
25 143

C

Use a factor tree to find all the prime factors of:

1 45
2 68
3 72
4 99
5 120
6 104
7 168
8 216.

Break the second number down into prime factors to help work out:

9 46 × 15
10 38 × 24
11 62 × 35
12 57 × 32
13 84 × 36
14 75 × 56
15 48 × 45
16 71 × 64.

Explain why these numbers are composite numbers.

17 3447
18 203
19 253
20 3201
21 221
22 209
23 1857
24 323

25 Find all the prime numbers between 100 and 150.

TARGET   To multiply and divide numbers mentally.

A

| 3 | 5 | 6 | 8 |

Look at the above numbers.

1. Which of the numbers are factors of:
   a) 25   c) 40
   b) 30   d) 45?

2. What is the product of:
   a) the two largest numbers
   b) the three smallest numbers?

3. Make a square number using the above digits only.

Write Yes or No.

4. Is 90 a multiple of 5?

5. Is 56 a multiple of 2?

6. Is 63 a multiple of 6?

7. Is 46 a multiple of 3?

Complete these factor pairs of 80.

8. 20 and ☐

9. ☐ and 5

10. 10 and ☐

11. Find all eight factors of 70.

12. Find all seven factors of 64.

13. Find a number that is a multiple of both:
    a) 4 and 9
    b) 3 and 8.

B

| 4 | 6 | 7 | 9 |

Use the above digits.

1. Which numbers are factors of:
   a) 54   c) 126
   b) 84   d) 72?

2. Find the product of:
   a) the 3 largest numbers
   b) the 3 smallest numbers.

3. Make two 2-digit square numbers using the above digits only.

Break the second number down into factors to work out.

4. 24 × 15

5. 56 × 16

6. 1400 ÷ 35

7. 810 ÷ 18

8. Find two common multiples of:
   a) 3 and 7
   b) 6 and 11.

9. Find all the factors of:
   a) 78   b) 96.

10. What is the smallest number with exactly:
    a) 6 factors
    b) 5 factors?

11. What is the largest 2-digit number with:
    a) only 2 factors
    b) only 3 factors?

C

1. What is the smallest number that is a common multiple of:
   a) 2 and 7
   b) 6 and 9
   c) 10 and 4
   d) 6 and 8?

2. Find the highest factor shared by:
   a) 32 and 80
   b) 42 and 56
   c) 12 and 45
   d) 54 and 72.

3. Find the smallest two-digit number with exactly:
   a) 8 factors
   b) 9 factors
   c) 10 factors
   d) 12 factors.

4. What is the largest two-digit number with exactly:
   a) 7 factors
   b) 12 factors
   c) 9 factors
   d) 8 factors?

| 2 | 3 | 6 | 7 | 9 |

5. Use the above digits. Make as many two-digit numbers as you can that are multiples of:
   a) 6   b) 4   c) 3.

6. Find the largest 3-digit square number.

TARGET To apply known multiplication and division facts.

A

What is

1. 7×3
2. 11×2
3. 9×5
4. 7×8

5. $32 \div 4$
6. $100 \div 10$
7. $72 \div 6$
8. $77 \div 7$

9. 9×11
10. 12×9
11. 6×4
12. 10×0

13. $40 \div 5$
14. $72 \div 8$
15. $14 \div 2$
16. $66 \div 11$

17. 4×7
18. 8×10
19. 5×12
20. 7×6

21. $27 \div 3$
22. $45 \div 9$
23. $9 \div 1$
24. $96 \div 12$

B

Copy and complete.

1. $\square \times 9 = 81$
2. $\square \times 12 = 84$
3. $\square \div 6 = 12$
4. $\square \div 3 = 9$

5. $\square \times 7 = 42$
6. $\square \times 11 = 132$
7. $\square \div 9 = 8$
8. $\square \div 12 = 12$

9. $\square \times 8 = 56$
10. $\square \times 4 = 24$
11. $\square \div 11 = 11$
12. $\square \div 7 = 8$

Write the answer only.

13. 120×3
14. 80×8
15. 90×12
16. 60×5

25. $360 \div 6$
26. $480 \div 12$
27. $540 \div 9$
28. $1210 \div 11$

17. 120×11
18. 70×7
19. 90×6
20. 80×4

29. $400 \div 8$
30. $210 \div 3$
31. $1440 \div 12$
32. $630 \div 7$

21. 90×8
22. 50×11
23. 70×9
24. 110×12

33. $600 \div 5$
34. $480 \div 6$
35. $1080 \div 9$
36. $1320 \div 12$

C

Copy and complete.

1. $\square \times 11 = 1320$
2. $\square \times 3 = 180$
3. $\square \div 8 = 90$
4. $\square \div 6 = 80$

5. $\square \times 12 = 1440$
6. $\square \times 7 = 490$
7. $\square \div 5 = 70$
8. $\square \div 11 = 110$

9. $\square \times 9 = 540$
10. $\square \times 6 = 420$
11. $\square \div 7 = 120$
12. $\square \div 12 = 80$

Write the answer only.

13. 800×9
14. 1200×11
15. 600×7
16. 400×12

25. $2400 \div 6$
26. $4000 \div 8$
27. $8800 \div 11$
28. $4200 \div 7$

17. 900×4
18. 800×8
19. 800×3
20. 700×9

29. $4500 \div 5$
30. $7200 \div 12$
31. $5400 \div 6$
32. $2400 \div 4$

21. 600×6
22. 900×7
23. 1200×12
24. 700×11

33. $8100 \div 9$
34. $12\,100 \div 11$
35. $5600 \div 8$
36. $10\,800 \div 12$

TARGET To apply known multiplication and division facts.

A

What is

1. 9×11
2. 6×6
3. 8×5
4. 5×9

5. 4×7
6. 6×12
7. 50×8
8. 80×4

9. 80×9
10. 60×5
11. 40×6
12. 90×3

13. $560 \div 8$
14. $550 \div 11$
15. $630 \div 7$
16. $240 \div 4$

17. $540 \div 6$
18. $210 \div 3$
19. $540 \div 9$
20. $450 \div 5$

21. $840 \div 12$
22. $360 \div 4$
23. $120 \div 2$
24. $720 \div 8$

B

Copy and complete.

1. $\square \times 8 = 64$
2. $\square \times 7 = 42$
3. $\square \times 11 = 132$
4. $\square \times 12 = 480$
5. $\square \times 9 = 810$
6. $\square \times 3 = 270$

7. $\square \div 7 = 5$
8. $\square \div 11 = 11$
9. $\square \div 6 = 8$
10. $\square \div 8 = 40$
11. $\square \div 3 = 120$
12. $\square \div 9 = 3$

Write the answer only.

13. 90×6
14. 1100×12
15. 7000×7
16. 70×9

17. 800×3
18. 900×8
19. 7×70
20. 6×4000

21. 5×600
22. 12×110
23. 8×1200
24. 6×9000

25. $490 \div 7$
26. $3200 \div 8$
27. $16\,000 \div 2$
28. $360 \div 6$

29. $1800 \div 9$
30. $28\,000 \div 4$
31. $480 \div 8$
32. $2400 \div 6$

33. $300 \div 5$
34. $6300 \div 9$
35. $24\,000 \div 3$
36. $4200 \div 7$

C

Copy and complete.

1. $\square \times 9 = 540$
2. $\square \times 4 = 3600$
3. $\square \times 8 = 560$
4. $\square \times 12 = 96\,000$
5. $\square \times 3 = 1800$
6. $\square \times 7 = 490$

7. $\square \div 9 = 8000$
8. $\square \div 12 = 1100$
9. $\square \div 7 = 90$
10. $\square \div 6 = 7000$
11. $\square \div 12 = 120$
12. $\square \div 8 = 900$

Write the answer only.

13. 0.5×7
14. 0.3×6
15. 0.7×3
16. 0.3×8
17. 0.9×9
18. 0.7×12

19. $4.2 \div 7$
20. $2.7 \div 3$
21. $4.0 \div 8$
22. $12.1 \div 11$
23. $1.2 \div 2$
24. $7.2 \div 9$

25. 7×0.8
26. 6×0.4
27. 11×1.1
28. 9×0.12
29. 5×0.5
30. 6×0.6

31. $13.2 \div 11$
32. $3.2 \div 4$
33. $4.5 \div 9$
34. $6.0 \div 12$
35. $5.4 \div 6$
36. $5.6 \div 7$

TARGET   To apply known multiplication and division facts.

A

What is

1. 6×11
2. 5×7
3. 9×5
4. 6×8
5. 8×4
6. 4×9
7. 6×2
8. 9×7
9. 4×12
10. 3×8
11. 9×3
12. 7×6
13. $18 \div 2$
14. $28 \div 7$
15. $72 \div 12$
16. $45 \div 9$
17. $21 \div 3$
18. $54 \div 6$
19. $40 \div 5$
20. $42 \div 7$
21. $33 \div 11$
22. $72 \div 9$
23. $36 \div 4$
24. $32 \div 8$

B

Copy and complete.

1. $\square \times 7 = 56$
2. $\square \times 12 = 96$
3. $\square \times 6 = 30$
4. $\square \times 4 = 28$
5. $\square \times 8 = 48$
6. $\square \times 9 = 81$
7. $\square \div 11 = 5$
8. $\square \div 6 = 7$
9. $\square \div 7 = 9$
10. $\square \div 9 = 6$
11. $\square \div 5 = 7$
12. $\square \div 8 = 8$

Write the answer only.

13. 50×8
14. 700×12
15. 60×7
16. 90×9
17. 600×5
18. 800×6
19. 80×3
20. 700×7
21. 60×4
22. 900×8
23. 700×9
24. 1100×11
25. $180 \div 3$
26. $3600 \div 9$
27. $1080 \div 12$
28. $400 \div 8$
29. $5400 \div 6$
30. $490 \div 7$
31. $13\,200 \div 11$
32. $630 \div 9$
33. $360 \div 6$
34. $14\,400 \div 12$
35. $7200 \div 8$
36. $350 \div 7$

C

Copy and complete.

1. $\square \times 12 = 360$
2. $\square \times 6 = 5400$
3. $\square \times 8 = 5600$
4. $\square \times 11 = 1320$
5. $\square \times 3 = 2100$
6. $\square \times 9 = 720$
7. $\square \div 11 = 900$
8. $\square \div 7 = 50$
9. $\square \div 6 = 600$
10. $\square \div 12 = 70$
11. $\square \div 9 = 90$
12. $\square \div 8 = 700$

Write the answer only.

13. 0.9×12
14. 0.5×9
15. 0.8×7
16. 0.8×5
17. 0.9×8
18. 0.7×6
19. $3.2 \div 4$
20. $4.2 \div 7$
21. $2.7 \div 9$
22. $12.1 \div 11$
23. $6.0 \div 12$
24. $6.4 \div 8$
25. 9×0.4
26. 8×0.6
27. 12×0.12
28. 6×0.8
29. 8×0.9
30. 7×0.7
31. $13.2 \div 12$
32. $2.4 \div 8$
33. $2.7 \div 3$
34. $5.4 \div 9$
35. $2.4 \div 6$
36. $6.3 \div 7$

TARGET   To develop strategies to ×/÷ numbers mentally.

Examples

Using Factors	Partitioning	Multiplying Multiples of 10/100	Multiplying by 19/21
17×12	56×7	40×900	18×19
$17 \times 3 \times 4$	$(50 \times 7) + (6 \times 7)$	$(4 \times 9 = 36)$	$(18 \times 20) - (18 \times 1)$
51×4	$350 + 42$	$40 \times 900 = 36\,000$	$360 - 18$
204	392		342

Choose one strategy for each group of six problems.

A

Write the answer only.

1. 6×40
2. 5×20
3. 3×300
4. 8×50
5. 9×200
6. 7×400

7. 15×9
8. 13×9
9. 18×9
10. 12×11
11. 17×11
12. 14×11

13. 14×3
14. 17×3
15. 25×3
16. 13×4
17. 18×4
18. 24×4

19. 12×4
20. 15×8
21. 5×16
22. $96 \div 6$
23. $84 \div 4$
24. $64 \div 16$

B

Write the answer only.

1. 36×4
2. 29×5
3. 45×6
4. 28×7
5. 34×8
6. 47×9

7. 60×20
8. 80×400
9. 50×30
10. 80×200
11. 70×300
12. 40×50

13. 16×6
14. 13×8
15. 14×12
16. $168 \div 8$
17. $128 \div 16$
18. $180 \div 12$

19. 16×19
20. 23×19
21. 27×19
22. 14×21
23. 22×21
24. 26×21

C

Copy and complete.

1. $336 \div 7 = 48$
2. $444 \div 6 = 74$
3. $536 \div 8 = 67$
4. $765 \div 9 = 85$
5. $651 \div 7 = 93$
6. $576 \div 8 = 72$

7. $15 \times 16 = 240$
8. $13 \times 14 = 182$
9. $17 \times 18 = 306$
10. $192 \div 12 = 16$
11. $256 \div 16 = 16$
12. $198 \div 18 = 11$

13. $1606 \div 99 = 17$
14. $714 \div 51 = 14$
15. $1212 \div 101 = 12$
16. $539 \div 49 = 11$
17. $918 \div 51 = 18$
18. $1386 \div 99 = 14$

19. $30 \times 30 = 900$
20. $8 \times 200 = 1600$
21. $600 \times 50 = 30\,000$
22. $70 \times 400 = 28\,000$
23. $50 \times 70 = 3500$
24. $40 \times 600 = 24\,000$

TARGET To multiply and divide whole numbers by 10, 100 and 1000.

Multiplying – digits move to the left   Dividing – digits move to the right

Examples

×/÷ by 10 – digits move 1 place	$756 \times 10 = 7560$	$386\,100 \div 10 = 38\,610$
×/÷ by 100 – digits move 2 places	$819 \times 100 = 81\,900$	$9400 \div 100 = 94$
×/÷ by 1000 – digits move 3 places	$43 \times 1000 = 43\,000$	$152\,000 \div 1000 = 152$

A

Multiply by

(10)   (100)

1 58   7 70
2 631   8 3
3 720   9 26
4 896   10 48
5 47   11 93
6 145   12 100

Divide by

(10)   (100)

13 700   19 5100
14 2950   20 2000
15 4100   21 3700
16 60   22 800
17 8000   23 10 000
18 6340   24 4600

Copy and complete.

25 ☐ × 10 = 2560
26 ☐ ÷ 10 = 710
27 ☐ × 100 = 3900
28 ☐ ÷ 100 = 40

29 ☐ × 10 = 5700
30 ☐ ÷ 10 = 68
31 ☐ × 100 = 1000
32 ☐ ÷ 100 = 25

B

Write the answers only.

1 473 × 10
2 5900 ÷ 10
3 160 × 100
4 8200 ÷ 100

5 35 × 1000
6 90 000 ÷ 1000
7 64 000 × 10
8 27 000 ÷ 10

9 1810 × 100
10 43 000 ÷ 100
11 718 × 1000
12 520 000 ÷ 1000

Copy and complete.

13 ☐ × 10 = 89 500
14 ☐ ÷ 10 = 4200
15 ☐ × 100 = 73 000
16 ☐ ÷ 100 = 150
17 ☐ × 1000 = 900 000
18 ☐ ÷ 1000 = 60

19 How many £10 notes make one million pounds?

20 How many grams are there in 70 kilograms?

C

Copy and complete.

1 ☐ × 10 = 500 000
2 ☐ ÷ 10 = 21 000
3 ☐ × 100 = 3 840 000
4 ☐ ÷ 100 = 7600

5 ☐ × 1000 = 290 000
6 ☐ ÷ 1000 = 1483
7 17 100 × ☐ = 1 710 000
8 29 000 ÷ ☐ = 2900

9 840 × ☐ = 840 000
10 1 206 000 ÷ ☐ = 12 060
11 5 130 000 ÷ ☐ = 5130
12 15 360 × ☐ = 153 600

13 How many pounds is ten thousand pence?

14 What is 10 km in millimetres?

15 What is 25 kg in grams?

16 There are 50 pins in each packet. There are 40 packets in each box. How many pins are there in 2000 boxes?

17 How many pounds is four hundred 5p coins?

TARGET   To recognise and use square numbers.

When a number is multiplied by itself you get a square number.
They are called square numbers because they make square patterns.

   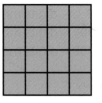

$1^2 = 1 \times 1 = 1$ $2^2 = 2 \times 2 = 4$ $3^2 = 3 \times 3 = 9$ $4^2 = 4 \times 4 = 16$

A

1 Complete this table up to 12^2.

$1^2 = 1 \times 1 = 1$

$2^2 = 2 \times 2 = 4$

$3^2 = 3 \times 3 = 9$

Work out the area of each square.

2 Sides 5 cm   **7** Sides 11 cm

3 Sides 9 cm   **8** Sides 7 cm

4 Sides 10 cm   **9** Sides 4 cm

5 Sides 6 cm   **10** Sides 12 cm

6 Sides 3 cm   **11** Sides 8 cm

B

Work out

1 $5^2 + 2^2$ **7** $10^2 + 6^2$

2 $11^2 + 4^2$ **8** $7^2 + 3^2$

3 $6^2 + 3^2$ **9** $12^2 + 1^2$

4 $7^2 - 4^2$ **10** $10^2 - 5^2$

5 $9^2 - 5^2$ **11** $11^2 - 9^2$

6 $8^2 - 2^2$ **12** $8^2 - 4^2$

Work out

13 10^2 **19** 70^2

14 20^2 **20** 50^2

15 60^2 **21** 40^2

16 80^2 **22** 90^2

17 30^2 **23** 120^2

18 110^2 **24** 100^2

Find a pair of square numbers which give a total of:

25 20   **31** 2000

26 85   **32** 6500

27 37   **33** 9000

28 89   **34** 14 900

29 153   **35** 6100

30 170   **36** 7200

C

Work out

1 100^2 **7** $100^2 - 70^2$

2 200^2 **8** $40^2 + 20^2$

3 500^2 **9** $70^2 - 30^2$

4 800^2 **10** $60^2 + 50^2$

5 600^2 **11** $90^2 - 30^2$

6 1000^2 **12** $80^2 + 40^2$

Lagrange's Theorem

Every whole number can be written as the sum of four or fewer square numbers.

Examples

$19 = 16 + 1 + 1 + 1$

$35 = 25 + 9 + 1$

Make the following numbers from four or fewer square numbers.

13 23   **19** 123

14 31   **20** 142

15 48   **21** 483

16 63   **22** 933

17 79   **23** 3485

18 96   **24** 8058

TARGET To use and understand square and cube numbers.

Examples

A square number is a number multiplied by itself. They make square patterns.

$3^2 = 3 \times 3 = 9$

3 squared = 9

A cube number is a number multiplied by itself and multiplied by itself again.

$2^3 = 2 \times 2 \times 2 = 8$

2 cubed = 8

A

Copy and complete.

1. $2^2 = \square$
2. $10^2 = \square$
3. $7^2 = \square$
4. $5^2 = \square$
5. $12^2 = \square$
6. $\square^2 = 81$
7. $\square^2 = 1$
8. $\square^2 = 36$
9. $\square^2 = 121$
10. $\square^2 = 64$

11. Copy and complete, continuing the pattern for the first six rows.

$1^2 = 1$
$2^2 = 1 + 3 = \square$
$3^2 = 1 + 3 + 5 = \square$
$4^2 = 1 + 3 + 5 + 7 = \square$

B

Copy and complete.

1. $\square^2 = 1600$
2. $\square^2 = 3600$
3. $\square^2 = 900$
4. $\square^2 = 400$
5. $\square^2 = 8100$
6. $\square^3 = 125$
7. $7^3 = \square$
8. $\square^3 = 27$
9. $12^3 = \square$
10. $\square^3 = 1000$

11. Copy and complete this table for all cube numbers to 12^3.

Cube		Calculation		Answer
1^3	=	$1 \times 1 \times 1$	=	1
2^3	=	$2 \times 2 \times 2$	=	8
3^3	=	$3 \times 3 \times 3$	=	27
$\vdots$		$\vdots$		$\vdots$

C

Copy and complete.

1. $\square^2 = 250\,000$
2. $\square^2 = 4900$
3. $\square^2 = 40\,000$
4. $\square^2 = 1\,000\,000$
5. $\square^2 = 12\,100$
6. $20^3 = \square$
7. $60^3 = \square$
8. $100^3 = \square$
9. $70^3 = \square$
10. $15^3 = \square$

11. Copy and complete this pattern for all square numbers to 20^2.

$0^2 = 0$
$1^2 = 0 + 1 = 1$
$2^2 = 1 + 3 = 4$
$3^2 = 4 + 5 = 9$
$4^2 = 9 + 7 = 16$

Add each successive odd number to the previous square number to find the next.

TARGET   To use a formal written method for short multiplication.

Examples

```
  348    8 × 6 = 48 (carry 4)              4 275
×   6    (4 × 6) + 4 = 28 (carry 2)      ×     9
────     (3 × 6) + 2 = 20                ──────
 2088                                     38 475
  2 4                                      2 6 4
```

A

Copy and complete.

1. 49 × 2

2. 36 × 6

3. 83 × 5

4. 67 × 4

5. 25 × 9

6. 58 × 3

7. 167 × 5

8. 472 × 7

9. 357 × 2

10. 839 × 4

11. 156 × 8

12. 674 × 3

13. Each bar of chocolate weighs 157 g. How much do six bars weigh?

14. Including the spare, cars need five tyres. How many tyres are needed for 294 new cars?

B

Copy and complete.

1. 295 × 6

2. 429 × 4

3. 873 × 9

4. 364 × 7

5. 748 × 8

6. 657 × 5

7. 1962 × 9

8. 4896 × 12

9. 1738 × 7

10. 2589 × 3

11. 3975 × 11

12. 5967 × 6

13. A theatre has 259 seats. All seven performances of a play are sold out. How many tickets have been sold?

14. A plane flies 1468 km. Its next flight is nine times longer. How far is that flight?

15. Each packet of paper has 436 sheets. How many sheets are there in eight packets?

C

Work out.

1. 31 654 × 9

2. 16 578 × 2

3. 46 839 × 8

4. 25 479 × 5

5. 30 864 × 6

6. 29 853 × 7

7. 18 647 × 3

8. 60 742 × 8

9. 41 728 × 6

10. 26 387 × 4

11. 24 796 × 9

12. 57 069 × 7

13. There are eight biscuits in each packet. How many biscuits are there in 12 937 packets?

14. To prevent flooding 40 582 sand bags are used. Each bag holds 9 kg of sand. How much sand is used altogether?

15. A clothing manufacturer makes £6 profit on every coat sold. How much profit is made if 29 156 coats are sold?

TARGET   To practise using a formal written method for short multiplication.

Examples

```
    826    6 × 12 = 72 (carry 7)              1 594
  ×  12    (2 × 12) + 7 = 31 (carry 3)      ×     7
  ─────                                     ──────
   9912    (8 × 12) + 3 = 99                11 158
    3 7                                       4 6 2
```

A

Copy and complete.

1   14   **5**   269
      × 5   ×   4

2   58   **6**   124
      × 3   ×   9

3   36   **7**   542
      × 6   ×   8

4   47   **8**   835
      × 2   ×   7

Work out

9 178 × 3

10 566 × 2

11 215 × 8

12 348 × 4

13 290 × 7

14 367 × 5

15 425 × 6

16 253 × 9

17 There are 275 staples in each box. How many are there in three boxes?

18 Each glass has a capacity of 235 ml. What is the capacity of eight glasses?

B

Work out

1 435 × 9   **9** 3057 × 8

2 687 × 12   **10** 1439 × 7

3 326 × 7   **11** 4876 × 3

4 479 × 6   **12** 1385 × 11

5 163 × 8   **13** 2984 × 9

6 729 × 9   **14** 7069 × 4

7 647 × 5   **15** 2578 × 7

8 964 × 6   **16** 3195 × 12

17 A factory canteen prepares 1358 meals every day. How many does it prepare in five days?

18 A holiday costs £739 per person. How much does it cost for seven people?

19 A cinema holds 478 people. All eight screenings of a film are sold out. How many people see the film?

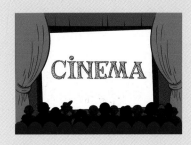

C

Work out

1 27 159 × 6

2 28 045 × 9

3 47 829 × 11

4 19 327 × 8

5 20 369 × 5

6 42 185 × 7

7 83 597 × 12

8 71 226 × 9

9 50 473 × 6

10 27 658 × 5

11 36 817 × 11

12 47 289 × 8

13 30 794 × 9

14 45 982 × 12

15 84 605 × 8

16 78 296 × 7

17 The runner up in a television talent show received 41 837 votes. Nine times as many people voted for the winner. How many votes did the winner receive?

18 Each packet of chewing gum has 6 sticks. How many sticks are there in 24 675 packets?

TARGET To use a formal written method for long multiplication.

Examples

```
        3 3
          6 7
    ×     3 5
        ───────
        3 3 5    (67 × 5)
      2 0₂1 0    (67 × 30)
      ─────────
      2 3 4 5    (Total)
```

```
          4 7
        1 5 9
    ×     2 8
      ─────────
      1 2 7 2    (159 × 8)
      3₁1₁8 0    (159 × 20)
      ─────────
      4 4 5 2    (Total)
        ───
        1 1
```

A

Copy and complete.

1
```
        1 6
    ×   1 5
              (16 × 5)
              (16 × 10)
    ───
```

2
```
        2 8
    ×   1 7
              (28 × 7)
              (28 × 10)
    ───
```

3
```
        2 5
    ×   2 4
              (25 × 4)
              (25 × 20)
    ───
```

4
```
        4 7
    ×   2 6
              (47 × 6)
              (47 × 20)
    ───
```

Work out

5 18 × 13 **9** 29 × 25

6 24 × 16 **10** 34 × 27

7 32 × 19 **11** 27 × 23

8 26 × 14 **12** 45 × 28

B

Copy and complete.

1
```
        6 8
    ×   4 5
              (68 × 5)
              (68 × 40)
    ───
```

2
```
      2 3 8
    ×   2 9
              (238 × 9)
              (238 × 20)
    ───
```

Work out

3 59 × 23   **11** 236 × 16
4 45 × 28   **12** 385 × 24
5 73 × 34   **13** 147 × 19
6 62 × 29   **14** 359 × 15
7 48 × 36   **15** 248 × 27
8 56 × 42   **16** 137 × 38
9 37 × 37   **17** 329 × 26
10 84 × 25 **18** 164 × 43

19
    6   7   8   9

Using each of the above numbers once only to make two 2-digit numbers, find:
a) the largest possible product
b) the smallest possible product.

C

Work out

1 1529 × 17
2 3648 × 23
3 2392 × 18
4 1728 × 39

5 1475 × 46
6 2936 × 54
7 1584 × 28
8 2768 × 32

9 237 × 185
10 384 × 247
11 176 × 135
12 249 × 164

13 465 × 408
14 308 × 152
15 257 × 217
16 579 × 249

17
    1   2   3   4   5   6

Using each of the above numbers once only to make two 3-digit numbers, find:
a) the largest possible product
b) the smallest possible product.

TARGET To practise using a formal written method for long multiplication.

Examples

```
        4 1
      8 7 3
  ×       4 6
  ─────────────
    5 2 3 8    (873 × 6)
  3 4₂9₁2 0    (873 × 40)
  4 0 1 5 8    (Total)
    1 1
```

```
        2 1
    1 9 6 2
  ×       2 3
  ─────────────
    5 8 8 6
  3₁9₁2 4 0
  4 5 1 2 6
    1  1  1
```

A

Copy and complete.

1
```
      36
  ×   16
  ─────
           (36 × 6)
  ─────
           (36 × 10)
  ─────
  ─────
```

2
```
      95
  ×   13
  ─────
           (95 × 3)
  ─────
           (95 × 10)
  ─────
```

3
```
      42
  ×   27
  ─────
           (42 × 7)
  ─────
           (42 × 20)
  ─────
  ─────
```

4
```
      53
  ×   39
  ─────
           (53 × 9)
  ─────
           (53 × 30)
  ─────
  ─────
```

Work out

5 83 × 13   **9** 49 × 32

6 24 × 15   **10** 62 × 25

7 78 × 24   **11** 74 × 43

8 37 × 26   **12** 45 × 37

B

Copy and complete.

1
```
      184
  ×    26
  ─────
            (184 × 6)
  ─────
            (184 × 20)
  ─────
```

2
```
     1563
  ×    48
  ─────
            (1563 × 8)
  ─────
            (1563 × 40)
  ─────
```

Work out

3 247 × 38   **11** 1376 × 39

4 529 × 14   **12** 1487 × 24

5 392 × 43   **13** 6532 × 51

6 638 × 19   **14** 3139 × 36

7 156 × 37   **15** 5814 × 17

8 415 × 42   **16** 4687 × 32

9 289 × 25   **17** 1926 × 45

10 748 × 23   **18** 7245 × 29

19 Each crate holds 48 bottles. How many bottles are there in 268 crates?

20 Moheen earns £16·75 per hour. He works 36 hours. How much does he earn?

C

Work out

1 12 319 × 17

2 27 493 × 35

3 74 806 × 23

4 36 028 × 42

5 80 572 × 26

6 41 735 × 34

7 32 054 × 59

8 26 490 × 61

9 218 × 197

10 675 × 145

11 394 × 372

12 564 × 286

13 943 × 257

14 639 × 427

15 483 × 159

16 726 × 368

17 The average number of words on the page of a book is 347. The book has 159 pages. How many words are there in the book?

TARGET To practise using a formal written method for short and long multiplication.

Examples

```
    3 5 4 8
  ×       8
  2 8 3 8 4
    4   3   6
```

```
      5 2 4
    1 8 3 7
  ×      2 6
  1 1 0 2 2   (1837 × 6)
  3₁6 7₁4 0   (1837 × 20)
  4 7 7 6 2   (Total)
```

A

Work out

1. 173 × 6
2. 529 × 8
3. 847 × 3
4. 365 × 5
5. 486 × 7
6. 709 × 2
7. 258 × 9
8. 637 × 4

Copy and complete.

9.
```
     25
  ×  18
          (25 × 8)
          (25 × 10)
          (Total)
```

10.
```
     46
  ×  23
          (46 × 3)
          (46 × 20)
          (Total)
```

Work out

11. 73 × 52
12. 58 × 47
13. 39 × 25
14. 24 × 19
15. 37 × 34
16. 42 × 26

B

Work out

1. 2579 × 11
2. 3248 × 6
3. 5824 × 4
4. 1763 × 8
5. 4607 × 9
6. 6952 × 3
7. 1638 × 7
8. 3480 × 12
9. 124 × 15
10. 367 × 27
11. 408 × 54
12. 539 × 29
13. 1276 × 32
14. 4690 × 16
15. 3285 × 43
16. 5347 × 28

17. £1 is worth 9 Norwegian krone. How many krone can you exchange for £1836?

18. There are 64 drawing pins in each box. How many are there in 1485 boxes?

C

Work out

1. 19 360 × 9
2. 84 219 × 5
3. 50 947 × 6
4. 28 175 × 8
5. 92 716 × 12
6. 64 073 × 7
7. 72 456 × 9
8. 36 128 × 11
9. 32 573 × 24
10. 56 489 × 38
11. 29 715 × 42
12. 14 308 × 65
13. 692 × 186
14. 785 × 253
15. 506 × 479
16. 924 × 537

17. Each bottle of flavouring holds 125 ml. How much flavouring is in 596 bottles in litres?

18. There are 28 tablets in every packet and 192 packets in each box. How many tablets are there in 36 boxes?

TARGET   To use a formal written method for division.

Examples

$$7)\overline{5\ 1^28}$$ 7 4

$$5)\overline{4\ 7^22}$$ 9 4 r 2 (94 remainder 2)

A

Work out

1. 33 ÷ 2
2. 87 ÷ 7
3. 55 ÷ 3
4. 84 ÷ 6
5. 138 ÷ 9
6. 87 ÷ 5
7. 96 ÷ 8
8. 79 ÷ 4
9. 164 ÷ 10
10. 111 ÷ 6
11. 80 ÷ 3
12. 109 ÷ 7
13. 136 ÷ 4
14. 119 ÷ 9
15. 215 ÷ 10
16. 100 ÷ 6
17. 94 ÷ 2
18. 114 ÷ 8
19. 129 ÷ 5
20. 134 ÷ 7

B

Work out

1. 237 ÷ 5
2. 216 ÷ 6
3. 339 ÷ 4
4. 232 ÷ 8
5. 410 ÷ 7
6. 242 ÷ 3
7. 423 ÷ 9
8. 613 ÷ 12
9. 299 ÷ 8
10. 277 ÷ 4
11. 322 ÷ 7
12. 772 ÷ 9
13. 471 ÷ 6
14. 518 ÷ 8
15. 533 ÷ 9
16. 804 ÷ 11

17. Five bottles hold 375 ml of perfume altogether. What is the capacity of one bottle?

18. T-shirts are sold in packs of three. How many packs are needed for 162 shirts?

19. Books of stamps have 6 stamps on each page. How many pages can be made from 516 stamps?

20. There are nine cereal bars in a packet. The total weight of the bars is 567 g. What does each bar weigh?

21. Jana is 750 months old. How old is this in years and months?

C

Work out

1. 2484 ÷ 9
2. 2982 ÷ 5
3. 4513 ÷ 8
4. 3812 ÷ 12
5. 1698 ÷ 6
6. 5431 ÷ 4
7. 3217 ÷ 7
8. 5813 ÷ 11
9. 1947 ÷ 3
10. 6344 ÷ 8
11. 3571 ÷ 2
12. 5085 ÷ 6
13. 4114 ÷ 11
14. 1882 ÷ 7
15. 6352 ÷ 12
16. 8588 ÷ 9

17. A cross-country race is four laps of a circuit. The race is 3740 m long. How long is the circuit?

18. There are seven pills in each strip. How many strips can be made from 1106 pills?

19. Eight friends rent a villa for a fortnight's holiday. The rental fee is £3896. How much should they each pay?

TARGET   To practise using a formal written method for division.

Examples
$$6\overline{)8^21^36}$$
$$1\ 3\ 6$$

$$9\overline{)1\ 3^42^65}$$
$$1\ 4\ 7\ r\ 2\ (147\ remainder\ 2)$$

A

Work out

1. 52 ÷ 4
2. 101 ÷ 8
3. 90 ÷ 6
4. 51 ÷ 3

5. 84 ÷ 7
6. 53 ÷ 2
7. 114 ÷ 8
8. 126 ÷ 9

9. 185 ÷ 10
10. 92 ÷ 5
11. 145 ÷ 6
12. 247 ÷ 8

13. 148 ÷ 4
14. 252 ÷ 7
15. 191 ÷ 10
16. 282 ÷ 3

17. 243 ÷ 9
18. 104 ÷ 2
19. 162 ÷ 6
20. 441 ÷ 8

B

Work out

1. 385 ÷ 11
2. 590 ÷ 6
3. 629 ÷ 8
4. 775 ÷ 5

5. 471 ÷ 3
6. 526 ÷ 7
7. 958 ÷ 9
8. 376 ÷ 4

9. 1758 ÷ 12
10. 1177 ÷ 7
11. 1279 ÷ 8
12. 1424 ÷ 6

13. 1933 ÷ 11
14. 1827 ÷ 8
15. 2076 ÷ 12
16. 1505 ÷ 9

17. How many weeks is 266 days?

18. Rena earns £1195 in five days. How much does she earn in one day?

19. Jethro walks at a pace of 4 km every hour. At this pace how many hours will it take him to walk the Thames Path, a distance of 294 km?

20. A set of 8 antique chairs costs £1560 altogether. How much does each chair cost?

C

Work out

1. 2637 ÷ 7
2. 3744 ÷ 4
3. 2919 ÷ 11
4. 5267 ÷ 8

5. 2740 ÷ 6
6. 4443 ÷ 9
7. 8808 ÷ 12
8. 2576 ÷ 3

9. 3176 ÷ 6
10. 5944 ÷ 7
11. 7623 ÷ 11
12. 2616 ÷ 8

13. 4239 ÷ 5
14. 7046 ÷ 9
15. 5837 ÷ 4
16. 11 621 ÷ 12

17. Elwyn earns £1380 each month. He saves one fifth of his salary. How much does he save each month?

18. Each coin weighs 12 g. How many coins can be made from 5·7 kg of metal?

19. Flowers are grown in trays of nine. How many trays are needed for 2556 seeds?

20. A pack of six cans of drink has a total capacity of 2·31 litres. How much drink does each can hold in millilitres?

21. Making the same journey each day, a coach travels 1799 km in 7 days. How far does it travel each day?

TARGET   To practise using a formal written method for division.

Examples

$$1\ 8\ 9$$
$$4\overline{)7^3 5^3 6}$$

$$1\ 7\ 6\ \text{r}\ 8\ (176\ \text{remainder}\ 8)$$
$$12\overline{)2\ 1^9 2^8 0}$$

A

Work out

1. 95 ÷ 5
2. 81 ÷ 6
3. 146 ÷ 10
4. 69 ÷ 4

5. 145 ÷ 8
6. 56 ÷ 2
7. 107 ÷ 6
8. 74 ÷ 3

9. 144 ÷ 9
10. 109 ÷ 7
11. 211 ÷ 8
12. 347 ÷ 6

13. 232 ÷ 4
14. 263 ÷ 3
15. 537 ÷ 10
16. 310 ÷ 9

17. 349 ÷ 7
18. 135 ÷ 2
19. 278 ÷ 6
20. 319 ÷ 8

B

Work out

1. 213 ÷ 7
2. 849 ÷ 12
3. 296 ÷ 5
4. 381 ÷ 6

5. 620 ÷ 8
6. 924 ÷ 11
7. 597 ÷ 4
8. 788 ÷ 9

9. 1211 ÷ 7
10. 1593 ÷ 6
11. 1344 ÷ 12
12. 1094 ÷ 8

13. 1109 ÷ 3
14. 1169 ÷ 6
15. 1313 ÷ 11
16. 1554 ÷ 9

17. Etta orders a new ring. She pays one sixth of the £882 price as a deposit. How much is the deposit?

18. Cakes are packed into boxes of four. How many boxes are needed for 1128 cakes?

19. How many £5 notes make £1840?

20. Nine bags hold an equal amount of compost each. The total capacity of the bags is 675 litres. How much compost is in each bag?

C

Work out

1. 3656 ÷ 8
2. 4429 ÷ 3
3. 10 406 ÷ 11
4. 4619 ÷ 6

5. 8050 ÷ 9
6. 6198 ÷ 4
7. 5103 ÷ 12
8. 6571 ÷ 7

9. 6793 ÷ 5
10. 10 157 ÷ 8
11. 19 609 ÷ 11
12. 8251 ÷ 6

13. 11 389 ÷ 7
14. 11 735 ÷ 2
15. 12 924 ÷ 9
16. 14 326 ÷ 12

17. Seven plane tickets cost £3703 altogether. What is the cost of one ticket?

18. Eight identical bottles have a total capacity of 7·4 litres. What is the capacity of each bottle?

19. Nails each weigh 3 g. How many can be made from 2·304 kg of metal?

20. It costs Cary £10 548 to rent his home for a year. How much rent does he pay each month?

21. There are 13 920 trees in a forest. One fifth are cut down. How many trees are cut down?

TARGET   To interpret remainders appropriately for the context.

Examples

How many complete years are there in
150 months?

150 ÷ 12 = 12 r 6 (Round down.)

Answer *12 complete years*

One nurse is needed for every 5 patients.
How many nurses are needed for 48 patients?

48 ÷ 5 = 9 r 3 (Round up.)

Answer *10 nurses are needed.*

A
Copy and complete.

1. 17 ÷ 3 = 5 r ☐
2. 15 ÷ 2 = 7 r ☐
3. 87 ÷ 10 = ☐ r ☐
4. 29 ÷ 5 = ☐ r ☐

5. What is the biggest remainder you can have when you divide a number by:
   a) 2
   b) 5?

6. Darts are sold in packets of three. How many packets can be made from 20 darts?

7. A class of 27 children are reading the same book. One book is shared by two children. How many books are needed?

8. Adam saves 10p coins. How many will he need to buy a toy for 75p?

9. How many complete weeks are there in 20 days?

B
Work out

1. 61 ÷ 4
2. 58 ÷ 6
3. 31 ÷ 7
4. 80 ÷ 11
5. 72 ÷ 5
6. 61 ÷ 9
7. 39 ÷ 12
8. 100 ÷ 8

9. What is the biggest remainder you can have when you divide a number by:
   a) 4   c) 12
   b) 7   d) 10?

10. Nine children can sit on each bench. There are 40 children. How many benches are needed?

11. A blacksmith has 50 horseshoes. How many horses can be given four new shoes?

12. A netball team has seven players. How many teams can be made from 24 players?

13. Six mushrooms fit into one bag. How many bags are needed for 32 mushrooms?

C
Work out

1. 136 ÷ 6
2. 143 ÷ 5
3. 100 ÷ 7
4. 130 ÷ 3
5. 650 ÷ 90
6. 430 ÷ 40
7. 400 ÷ 60
8. 700 ÷ 80

9. What is the biggest remainder you can have when you divide a number by 8? Give a reason for your answer.

10. Balloons are sold in packets of eight. How many packets can be made from 150 balloons?

11. Six people can sit at each table. How many tables are needed for 175 people?

12. Sweets cost 15p each. How many can be bought for one pound?

13. A ferry can carry 25 cars in one crossing of a river. There are 186 cars queuing to use the ferry. How many crossings will it take to clear the queue?

14. How many £20 notes are needed to pay £325?

TARGET   To interpret remainders appropriately for the context.

Examples

There are 6 children to each table.
There are 27 children in a class.
How many tables are needed?
27 ÷ 6 = 4 r 3 (Round up.)

Answer   *5 tables are needed.*

There are four cakes in each box.
30 cakes are baked.
How many boxes can be filled?
30 ÷ 4 = 7 r 2 (Round down.)

Answer   *7 boxes can be filled.*

A

1. There are 29 children in a class. How many pairs can be made?

2. Christmas cards are sold in packs of 10. Nina needs 32 cards. How many packs will she need?

3. Each car can carry 3 children. How many cars are needed to carry 16 children?

4. A garage has 26 tyres. How many cars can each be given 4 new tyres?

5. There are five sweets in each bag. How many bags can be made from 48 sweets?

6. A teacher hears six children read every day. How many days will it take her to hear the 28 children in her class?

B

1. How many 3 m lengths can be cut from 50 m of rope?

2. Four tennis balls can fit into one can. How many cans are needed for 42 balls?

3. Tommy has 100 matchsticks. How many hexagons can he make?

4. Each pack holds eight tomatoes. How many packs can be made from 46 tomatoes?

5. Verity saves 10p coins. How many will she need to collect before she has saved £1·25?

6. A baker makes 75 muffins. They are sold in boxes of twelve. How many boxes can be made up?

C

1. How many complete weeks are there in 125 days?

2. There are 110 guests at a wedding. They will sit at tables of eight. How many tables will be needed?

3. Theatre tickets cost £19 each. How many tickets can be bought with £100?

4. A ribbon is two metres long. How many 12 cm lengths can be cut from the ribbon?

5. Each crate holds 20 bottles. How many crates are needed for 450 bottles?

6. Glasses hold 150 ml. How many glasses will be needed to take four litres of juice?

TARGET   To interpret remainders appropriately for the context.

Examples

Each tray holds 9 plants.
How many trays are needed for 150 plants?
$150 \div 9 = 16 \text{ r } 6$ (Round up.)

Answer *17 trays are needed.*

Raffle tickets costs 20p each.
How many can be bought with £2·30?
$230 \div 20 = 11 \text{ r } 10$ (Round down.)

Answer *11 tickets can be bought.*

A

1. There are three cakes on each plate. How many plates are needed for 44 cakes?

2. Egg boxes hold six eggs. How many boxes can be made up from 40 eggs?

3. Each can of paint holds 4 litres. How many cans can be filled from 30 litres?

4. Shane can carry 20 bricks in each barrow load. How many journeys will he need to make to carry 250 bricks?

5. Betsy has £50 notes only. How many will she need to pay £280?

6. Footballs cost £8 each. How many can a school buy with £70?

7. Each box holds 12 pencils. How many boxes are needed for the 30 children in a class to have a pencil each?

B

1. How many complete weeks are there in 60 days?

2. Bottles are put into crates of twelve. How many crates are needed for 100 bottles?

3. One bag of dog food lasts Rex for six days. How many bags will he need for 75 days?

4. Cards are sold in packets of eight. How many packets can be made from 150 cards?

5. Bags of sand hold 25 kg. Robin needs 340 kg. How many bags does he need to buy?

6. Apples are sold in bags of nine. How many bags can be filled from 140 apples?

7. There are four tennis balls in each can. How many cans are needed for 75 balls?

C

1. Patio tiles are 60 cm long. How many are needed to make a row 10 m long?

2. Pencil crayons cost 29p each. How many can Sadiq buy for £5.

3. There are 220 people attending a conference. They will sit at tables of six. How many tables will be needed?

4. A bus journey takes 45 minutes. How many complete journeys can the bus make in 16 hours?

5. A bag of fertilizer holds 75 litres. How many bags can be filled from 1000 litres?

6. A hotel has 500 g of salt. Saltpots hold 30 g. How many saltpots will be needed to take all the salt?

TARGET   To express a remainder as a fraction and as a decimal.

Examples

REMAINDERS AS FRACTIONS
$57 \div 4 = 14\frac{1}{4}$
$138 \div 5 = 27\frac{3}{5}$

REMAINDERS AS DECIMALS
$57 \div 4 = 14.25$
$138 \div 5 = 27.6$

MONEY
$£57 \div 4 = £14.25$
$£138 \div 5 = £27.60$

A

Give the remainder as a fraction.

1. $35 \div 2$
2. $38 \div 5$
3. $54 \div 4$
4. $34 \div 6$
5. $49 \div 3$
6. $127 \div 10$
7. $27 \div 4$
8. $72 \div 5$
9. $31 \div 2$
10. $65 \div 6$

Give the remainder as a decimal.

11. $£15 \div 2$
12. $£24 \div 5$
13. $£36 \div 10$
14. $£15 \div 4$
15. $£41 \div 5$
16. $£74 \div 10$
17. $£35 \div 4$
18. $£39 \div 2$
19. $£28 \div 5$
20. $£37 \div 4$

21. Ten bus tickets cost £18. What does one ticket cost?

22. A piece of wood is 27 cm long. It is cut in half. How long is each piece?

23. Five full buckets of water make 22 litres. How much does one bucket hold?

24. Angus buys four shirts for £31. How much does one shirt cost?

B

Give the remainder as a fraction.

1. $93 \div 4$
2. $42 \div 8$
3. $67 \div 3$
4. $58 \div 9$
5. $50 \div 6$
6. $133 \div 5$
7. $32 \div 7$
8. $168 \div 10$
9. $65 \div 8$
10. $535 \div 100$

Give the remainder as a decimal.

11. $75 \div 2$
12. $452 \div 10$
13. $111 \div 4$
14. $164 \div 5$
15. $39 \div 6$
16. $£127 \div 4$
17. $£137 \div 5$
18. $£92 \div 8$
19. $£83 \div 2$
20. $£375 \div 12$

21. Ten identical boxes weigh 94 kg. What does one box weigh?

22. Travis earns £75 for working six hours. How much does he earn each hour?

C

Copy and complete.

1. $\square \div 9 = 11\frac{2}{9}$
2. $\square \div 6 = 24\frac{5}{6}$
3. $\square \div 8 = 7\frac{6}{8}$
4. $\square \div 7 = 19\frac{3}{7}$
5. $\square \div 10 = 13\frac{4}{10}$
6. $\square \div 9 = 8\frac{5}{9}$
7. $\square \div 100 = 2\frac{73}{100}$
8. $\square \div 7 = 14\frac{5}{7}$

Give the answer as a decimal. Round to one decimal place where necessary.

9. $119 \div 4$
10. $91 \div 5$
11. $172 \div 6$
12. $116 \div 8$
13. $112 \div 3$
14. $142 \div 9$
15. $93 \div 7$
16. $105 \div 6$

17. Eight identical jars of jam hold 3 litres altogether. How much does each jar hold?

18. Katie earns £278. One fifth is taken off in tax. How much is she paid after the tax is taken off?

19. Kelvin buys 250 g of nuts. They cost £6 per kilogram. How much does he pay?

TARGET To practise using a formal written method for short multiplication and division.

Examples

```
   2 837
 ×     9
  25 533
    7  3 6
```

```
      1 4 7  r 3 (147 remainder 3)
7) 1 0³3⁵2
```

A

Work out

1. 142 × 8
2. 483 × 4
3. 267 × 9
4. 758 × 2
5. 149 × 7
6. 825 × 5
7. 614 × 3
8. 390 × 8
9. 574 × 6
10. 208 × 9
11. 177 ÷ 6
12. 202 ÷ 3
13. 230 ÷ 9
14. 463 ÷ 10
15. 312 ÷ 8
16. 142 ÷ 5
17. 224 ÷ 4
18. 305 ÷ 7
19. 224 ÷ 6
20. 157 ÷ 2

B

Work out

1. 3916 × 5
2. 2830 × 6
3. 9278 × 3
4. 5096 × 8
5. 4385 × 7
6. 2569 × 4
7. 6097 × 12
8. 1954 × 9
9. 1120 ÷ 6
10. 1725 ÷ 11
11. 1176 ÷ 7
12. 1315 ÷ 2
13. 1899 ÷ 5
14. 1731 ÷ 8
15. 1644 ÷ 12
16. 1240 ÷ 9

17. Hamish earns £3467 every month. How much does he earn in six months?

18. A square field has a perimeter of 1128 m. How long is one side of the field?

19. Each toffee weighs 8 g. How many sweets can be made from 1312 g of toffee mixture?

20. A trawler nets 1795 fish. On its next trip it nets five times as many fish. How many fish are caught on the second trip?

C

Work out

1. 36 857 × 3
2. 14 873 × 5
3. 52 946 × 11
4. 95 627 × 6
5. 17 489 × 8
6. 32 684 × 9
7. 27 065 × 7
8. 13 857 × 12
9. 3662 ÷ 8
10. 2881 ÷ 5
11. 14 832 ÷ 9
12. 15 578 ÷ 4
13. 4176 ÷ 11
14. 11 910 ÷ 6
15. 5575 ÷ 7
16. 10 384 ÷ 12

17. A plastics company produces 46 358 bags each holding 8 balloons. How many balloons are in the bags?

18. A syndicate of 11 people win a lottery prize of £16 907. How much should they each receive?

19. Tickets for an open air concert cost £9 each. 25 937 tickets are sold. How much is made from ticket sales?

TARGET To solve number and multi-step word problems involving all four operations using mental methods.

A

Copy and complete.

1. ☐ − 2·7 = 6
2. ☐ + 7 = 9·7
3. ☐ × 5 = 90
4. ☐ ÷ 4 = 40

5. 1·8 + ☐ = 3·1
6. 7 − ☐ = 4·5
7. 200 ÷ ☐ = 50
8. 3 × ☐ = 99

9. Twenty-six balls are being used in the PE lesson. There are 18 more balls in a box. How many balls are there altogether?

10. There are forty sheep in a flock. One fifth have been sheared. How many have not been sheared?

11. A caravan park has two rows of 12 vans and four rows of 8 vans. How many vans are there altogether?

12. A bottle of medicine holds 120 ml. Brett takes six 5 ml doses. How much medicine is left?

B

Copy and complete.

1. 0·6 × ☐ = 4·2
2. £10·00 − ☐ = £3·19
3. 268 + ☐ = 400
4. 6·3 ÷ ☐ = 0·63

5. ☐ − 1·6 = 5·4
6. ☐ ÷ 7 = 1·4
7. ☐ + 0·33 = 0·8
8. ☐ × 12 = 144

9. In a box of 40 chocolates, there are four more chocolates with a soft centre than with a hard centre. How many chocolates are there with a hard centre and how many with a soft centre?

10. A farmer has 120 eggs. He makes up four boxes of 12 eggs and the rest he puts into boxes of 6. How many boxes of 6 does he fill?

11. Megan is travelling 238 miles. She drives 74 miles. How much further does she have to go to reach half way?

12. Five 50 g weights are put in the left pan of a balance. Six 20 g weights are put in the right pan. How much weight needs to be added to which pan to balance the scale?

C

Copy and complete.

1. 0·272 + ☐ = 0·3
2. 4·8 ÷ ☐ = 0·06
3. 1·4 − ☐ = 0·55
4. 5 × ☐ = 14

5. ☐ ÷ 11 = 1·1
6. ☐ + 1·65 = 5
7. ☐ × 50 = 24
8. ☐ − 1·48 = 3·8

9. A football team plays 42 matches. They lose one third of their games. They win three quarters of the rest. How many do they draw?

10. In one day 72 guests arrive at an hotel and 27 leave. There are now 219 people staying there. How many people were staying at the hotel at the start of the day?

11. One shampoo sachet holds 30 ml. How many sachets can be made from the shampoo in four containers each holding 1·5 litres?

12. Serena buys three sandwiches for £2·25 each and three drinks for 85p each. She pays with a £20 note. How much change does she receive?

TARGET To solve 1- and 2-step word problems involving all four operations.

Example

In one hour 1258 vehicles are counted travelling west and half as many travelling east. How many vehicles are counted altogether?

$1258 \div 2 = 629$
$1258 + 629 = 1887$
Answer *1887 vehicles*

A

1. There are 54 books in Cora's bookcase and 37 on her shelf. How many books does she have altogether?

2. There are 85 children in Year 5. 39 are girls. How many are boys?

3. There are six fish fillets in each pack. How many packs can be made from 48 fillets?

4. Lorna collects three boxes of pills from the chemist. There are 40 pills in each box. Each pill weighs 2 g. What is the total weight of the pills in the three boxes?

5. Carly has 84 smarties. She eats 18 and shares the rest with a friend. How many smarties does Carly's friend have?

6. Sweets cost 9p. Luke buys five. How much change does he get if he pays one pound?

B

1. There are 48 stamps on each sheet. How many stamps are there on 12 sheets?

2. The afternoon performance of a play is watched by 217 people. 146 more people watch the evening performance. How many people watch the two performances altogether?

3. Floyd buys a sofa and an armchair for £918 altogether. The sofa costs £669. What does the armchair cost?

4. Two parcels have a combined weight of 4·6 kg. The larger parcel weighs 0·8 kg more than the smaller one. What is the weight of each parcel?

5. Isabel buys five apples and one pear. Apples cost 25p. She pays £2 and receives 45p change. What does the pear cost?

C

1. School Concert programmes cost 25p. 147 are sold. How much money has been raised by programme sales?

2. One can of beans holds 400 g. How many can be filled from 60 kg?

3. There is 750 ml of juice in each bottle of orange. There are 24 bottles in each crate. How much juice is there in eight full crates?

4. A motor bike costs £4999. In a sale its price is reduced by one tenth. What is the new price?

5. In an election the winning candidate received 12 369 votes. The only other candidate received 3517 fewer votes. How many people voted?

6. A school orders 240 new pencils. Two fifths are given out. How many are left in stock?

TARGET To solve 2-step word problems involving all four operations.

Example

An athlete buys a stopwatch for £29·50 and a pair of running shoes. He pays £100 and receives £4·51 change. How much do the shoes cost?

£100 − £4·51 = £95·49
£95·49 − £29·50 = £65·99

Answer *The shoes cost £65·99.*

A

1. There are 83 children on a playground. 46 go in for lunch. 29 come out from lessons. How many children are on the playground now?

2. A quarter of the 24 chocolates in a box have been eaten. The rest are shared equally by three friends. How many do they have each?

3. There are eight more people on the upper deck of a boat than on the lower deck. There are 27 people on the lower deck. How many people are on the boat altogether?

4. How many seconds are there in five hours?

5. Daniel's book has 110 pages. He reads half the book. He then reads another 18 pages. How many pages has he read?

B

1. Amber's washing machine costs £450. She pays one fifth as a deposit. How much does she have left to pay?

2. A farm shop sells four boxes of 12 eggs and nine boxes of 6 eggs. How many eggs are sold altogether?

3. A total of 1872 people live in a village. 539 are men. 617 are women. How many children live in the village?

4. Cheese costs £6·00 per kilogram. Victor buys 300 g. How much does he pay?

5. On Friday 108 people attend the Casualty Department of a hospital. On Saturday the number of patients increases by one third. How many people attend the Casualty Department on both days altogether?

C

1. There are 84 children in Year 5. One twelfth are absent. 28 are on a school trip. How many Year 5 children are in school?

2. Each carton of juice holds 750 ml. There are 24 cartons in each box. How much juice is there in five boxes?

3. Warren buys a bike. He pays one quarter of the price as a deposit. He still has £78 to pay. How much does the bike cost?

4. A cable is 180 m long. 45 m is used. Seven ninths of the remaining cable is used. How much cable is left?

5. Mervin and Jonah both earn £640. Mervin saves £150. Jonah saves three eighths of his earnings. How much more does Jonah save?

TARGET   To solve number problems involving all four operations.

Example

Find two consecutive numbers:

① with a total of 151   Answer *75 and 76*

② with a product of 380.   Answer *19 and 20*

A

Find the pair of numbers.

① a sum of 36
a difference of 2

② a sum of 80
a difference of 10

③ a sum of 17
a product of 60

④ a sum of 22
a product of 96

Find three consecutive
numbers with a total of:

⑤ 18   ⑦ 51

⑥ 30   ⑧ 87.

Find two consecutive
numbers with a product of:

⑨ 20   ⑪ 90

⑩ 42   ⑫ 132.

⑬ I think of a number.
I add 25.
I take 7.
The answer is 43.
What is my number?

⑭ I think of a number.
I multiply by 4.
I add 18.
The answer is 66.
What is my number?

B

Find the number.

① a square number
the product of its digits
is 24

② a 2-digit number
a prime number
the sum of its digits is 14

③ a 2-digit number
a prime number
the product of its digits
is 12

④ a 2-digit number
a square number
the sum of its digits is 13

⑤ a 2-digit number
a prime number
a factor of 152

⑥ a 3-digit number
a multiple of 8
the sum of its digits is 4

Copy and complete.

⑦ ☐ $- 46 \times 6 = 24$

⑧ $26 +$ ☐ $\div 5 = 8$

⑨ ☐ $\times 10 + 30 = 100$

⑩ $36 \div$ ☐ $- 9 = 3$

⑪ ☐ $\div 2 + 14 = 38$

⑫ $8 \times$ ☐ $- 25 = 47$

C

Find a pair of square
numbers with:

① a sum of 193

② a product of 900

③ a difference of 27

④ a product of 6400.

Find a pair of prime
numbers with:

⑤ a sum of 12

⑥ a product of 143

⑦ a sum of 31

⑧ a product of 62.

Find two consecutive
numbers with a product
of:

⑨ 210   ⑪ 702

⑩ 342   ⑫ 930.

Find three consecutive
numbers with a product
of:

⑬ 60   ⑮ 720

⑭ 210   ⑯ 2730.

⑰ Find the first five
3-digit prime
numbers.

TARGET To identify, name and write equivalent fractions of a given fraction.

Examples

You can change a fraction into an equivalent fraction by multiplying or dividing (cancelling).

 $\dfrac{1 \,(\times 3)}{4 \,(\times 3)} = \dfrac{3}{12}$

 $\dfrac{8 \,(\div 2)}{10 \,(\div 2)} = \dfrac{4}{5}$

A

Write the equivalent fractions shown in each pair of diagrams.

1

2

3

4

5

6

7

8

B

Copy and complete.

1 $\dfrac{1}{2} = \dfrac{\square}{6}$ 9 $\dfrac{2}{6} = \dfrac{4}{\square}$

2 $\dfrac{3}{4} = \dfrac{\square}{12}$ 10 $\dfrac{1}{3} = \dfrac{2}{\square}$

3 $\dfrac{1}{3} = \dfrac{\square}{9}$ 11 $\dfrac{1}{2} = \dfrac{50}{\square}$

4 $\dfrac{3}{10} = \dfrac{\square}{100}$ 12 $\dfrac{3}{4} = \dfrac{6}{\square}$

5 $\dfrac{3}{6} = \dfrac{\square}{12}$ 13 $\dfrac{4}{5} = \dfrac{8}{\square}$

6 $\dfrac{1}{4} = \dfrac{\square}{8}$ 14 $\dfrac{2}{3} = \dfrac{6}{\square}$

7 $\dfrac{1}{5} = \dfrac{\square}{10}$ 15 $\dfrac{1}{4} = \dfrac{3}{\square}$

8 $\dfrac{2}{3} = \dfrac{\square}{12}$ 16 $\dfrac{5}{6} = \dfrac{10}{\square}$

Write the odd one out in each set of fractions.

17 $\dfrac{4}{12}$ $\dfrac{3}{8}$ $\dfrac{2}{6}$ $\dfrac{3}{9}$

18 $\dfrac{5}{10}$ $\dfrac{6}{12}$ $\dfrac{2}{5}$ $\dfrac{3}{6}$

19 $\dfrac{8}{12}$ $\dfrac{75}{100}$ $\dfrac{9}{12}$ $\dfrac{6}{8}$

20 $\dfrac{9}{12}$ $\dfrac{8}{12}$ $\dfrac{4}{6}$ $\dfrac{6}{9}$

C

Copy and complete.

1 $\dfrac{5}{8} = \dfrac{\square}{16}$ 9 $\dfrac{25}{100} = \dfrac{\square}{4}$

2 $\dfrac{3}{4} = \dfrac{\square}{20}$ 10 $\dfrac{10}{15} = \dfrac{\square}{3}$

3 $\dfrac{2}{7} = \dfrac{\square}{14}$ 11 $\dfrac{12}{20} = \dfrac{\square}{5}$

4 $\dfrac{7}{10} = \dfrac{\square}{100}$ 12 $\dfrac{8}{16} = \dfrac{\square}{2}$

5 $\dfrac{4}{9} = \dfrac{8}{\square}$ 13 $\dfrac{55}{100} = \dfrac{11}{\square}$

6 $\dfrac{3}{5} = \dfrac{30}{\square}$ 14 $\dfrac{5}{25} = \dfrac{1}{\square}$

7 $\dfrac{5}{8} = \dfrac{10}{\square}$ 15 $\dfrac{14}{18} = \dfrac{7}{\square}$

8 $\dfrac{4}{5} = \dfrac{80}{\square}$ 16 $\dfrac{45}{50} = \dfrac{9}{\square}$

Write the odd one out in each set of fractions.

17 $\dfrac{5}{20}$ $\dfrac{4}{10}$ $\dfrac{2}{8}$ $\dfrac{25}{100}$

18 $\dfrac{80}{100}$ $\dfrac{20}{24}$ $\dfrac{12}{15}$ $\dfrac{16}{20}$

19 $\dfrac{6}{60}$ $\dfrac{3}{18}$ $\dfrac{2}{12}$ $\dfrac{5}{30}$

20 $\dfrac{12}{16}$ $\dfrac{15}{20}$ $\dfrac{8}{12}$ $\dfrac{75}{100}$

TARGET   To compare fractions with different denominators.

To compare two fractions with different denominators convert one or both so that they have the same denominator.

Examples   Which is larger, $\frac{1}{2}$ or $\frac{3}{8}$?   Which is larger, $\frac{1}{2}$ or $\frac{3}{5}$?

$\frac{1}{2} = \frac{4}{8}$ $\frac{1}{2} = \frac{5}{10}$ $\frac{3}{5} = \frac{6}{10}$

$\frac{1}{2}$ is larger than $\frac{3}{8}$. $\frac{3}{5}$ is larger than $\frac{1}{2}$.

A

1
$$\frac{1}{3} \quad \frac{5}{8} \quad \frac{3}{6} \quad \frac{2}{5} \quad \frac{7}{10}$$
$$\frac{2}{4} \quad \frac{2}{6} \quad \frac{3}{5} \quad \frac{3}{10} \quad \frac{4}{8}$$

Which of the fractions in the box are:
a) equal to one half
b) less than one half
c) greater than one half?

Which fraction is larger?

2 $\frac{1}{3}$ or $\frac{1}{4}$

3 $\frac{1}{8}$ or $\frac{1}{2}$

4 $\frac{3}{10}$ or $\frac{4}{10}$

5 $\frac{1}{6}$ or $\frac{1}{7}$

6 $\frac{6}{11}$ or $\frac{4}{11}$

7 $\frac{2}{9}$ or $\frac{2}{3}$

8 $\frac{3}{4}$ or $\frac{3}{5}$

Write each group of fractions in order of size, smallest first.

9 $\frac{1}{5}$ $\frac{1}{8}$ $\frac{1}{3}$

10 $\frac{4}{5}$ $\frac{4}{11}$ $\frac{4}{7}$

11 $\frac{1}{6}$ $\frac{1}{4}$ $\frac{1}{10}$

12 $\frac{7}{10}$ $\frac{7}{12}$ $\frac{7}{8}$

B

For each of the following pairs of numbers:
a) list the first 12 multiples of each number
b) write down the common multiples
c) write down the lowest common multiple.

1   2 and 5

2   3 and 4

3   5 and 3

4   4 and 7

Copy and complete to find the larger fraction.

5 $\frac{1}{2}$ or $\frac{3}{8} \rightarrow \frac{\boxed{4}}{8}$ or $\frac{3}{8}$
$\boxed{}$ is larger.

6 $\frac{3}{5}$ or $\frac{7}{10} \rightarrow \frac{\boxed{}}{10}$ or $\frac{7}{10}$
$\boxed{}$ is larger.

7 $\frac{5}{6}$ or $\frac{2}{3} \rightarrow \frac{5}{6}$ or $\frac{\boxed{}}{6}$
$\boxed{}$ is larger.

8 $\frac{7}{12}$ or $\frac{3}{4} \rightarrow \frac{7}{12}$ or $\frac{\boxed{}}{12}$
$\boxed{}$ is larger.

9 $\frac{2}{3}$ or $\frac{3}{4} \rightarrow \frac{\boxed{}}{12}$ or $\frac{\boxed{}}{12}$
$\boxed{}$ is larger.

C

Copy and complete to find the larger fraction.

1 $\frac{9}{10}$ or $\frac{89}{100} \rightarrow \frac{\boxed{}}{100}$ or $\frac{89}{100}$
$\boxed{}$ is larger.

2 $\frac{3}{4}$ or $\frac{5}{6} \rightarrow \frac{\boxed{}}{12}$ or $\frac{\boxed{}}{12}$
$\boxed{}$ is larger.

3 $\frac{4}{10}$ or $\frac{5}{12} \rightarrow \frac{\boxed{}}{60}$ or $\frac{\boxed{}}{60}$
$\boxed{}$ is larger.

4 $\frac{5}{8}$ or $\frac{7}{12} \rightarrow \frac{\boxed{}}{48}$ or $\frac{\boxed{}}{48}$
$\boxed{}$ is larger.

5 $\frac{3}{5}$ or $\frac{4}{6} \rightarrow \frac{\boxed{}}{\boxed{}}$ or $\frac{\boxed{}}{\boxed{}}$

6 $\frac{1}{4}$ or $\frac{2}{7} \rightarrow \frac{\boxed{}}{\boxed{}}$ or $\frac{\boxed{}}{\boxed{}}$

7 $\frac{1}{3}$ or $\frac{2}{5} \rightarrow \frac{\boxed{}}{\boxed{}}$ or $\frac{\boxed{}}{\boxed{}}$

8 $\frac{2}{6}$ or $\frac{3}{8} \rightarrow \frac{\boxed{}}{\boxed{}}$ or $\frac{\boxed{}}{\boxed{}}$

9 $\frac{2}{3}$ or $\frac{7}{10} \rightarrow \frac{\boxed{}}{\boxed{}}$ or $\frac{\boxed{}}{\boxed{}}$

10 $\frac{2}{5}$ or $\frac{3}{8} \rightarrow \frac{\boxed{}}{\boxed{}}$ or $\frac{\boxed{}}{\boxed{}}$

TARGET To compare and order fractions with different denominators.

To order fractions with different denominators convert one or more so that they have the same denominator.

Example

Write in order smallest first, $\frac{1}{2}, \frac{3}{10}, \frac{2}{5}$. $\frac{1}{2} = \frac{5}{10}$ $\frac{2}{5} = \frac{4}{10}$ Answer $\frac{3}{10}, \frac{2}{5}, \frac{1}{2}$

A

Which fraction is larger?

1. $\frac{3}{5}$ or $\frac{4}{5}$ 5. $\frac{4}{9}$ or $\frac{4}{6}$

2. $\frac{2}{3}$ or $\frac{2}{7}$ 6. $\frac{3}{8}$ or $\frac{3}{11}$

3. $\frac{8}{10}$ or $\frac{7}{10}$ 7. $\frac{5}{7}$ or $\frac{6}{7}$

4. $\frac{5}{12}$ or $\frac{5}{9}$ 8. $\frac{6}{11}$ or $\frac{6}{12}$

Copy and complete to find the larger fraction.

9. $\frac{1}{2}$ or $\frac{5}{12} \rightarrow \frac{\square}{12}$ or $\frac{5}{12}$
   $\square$ is larger.

10. $\frac{4}{5}$ or $\frac{9}{10} \rightarrow \frac{\square}{10}$ or $\frac{9}{10}$
    $\square$ is larger.

11. $\frac{3}{4}$ or $\frac{5}{8} \rightarrow \frac{\square}{8}$ or $\frac{5}{8}$
    $\square$ is larger.

12. $\frac{1}{2}$ or $\frac{4}{10} \rightarrow \frac{\square}{10}$ or $\frac{4}{10}$
    $\square$ is larger.

13. $\frac{1}{3}$ or $\frac{1}{6} \rightarrow \frac{\square}{6}$ or $\frac{1}{6}$
    $\square$ is larger.

14. $\frac{2}{3}$ or $\frac{7}{9} \rightarrow \frac{\square}{9}$ or $\frac{7}{9}$
    $\square$ is larger.

B

To find the larger fraction convert one of each pair so that they share a common denominator.

1. $\frac{5}{6}$ or $\frac{11}{12}$ 4. $\frac{2}{5}$ or $\frac{3}{10}$

2. $\frac{1}{3}$ or $\frac{3}{12}$ 5. $\frac{1}{2}$ or $\frac{5}{8}$

3. $\frac{5}{10}$ or $\frac{51}{100}$ 6. $\frac{3}{4}$ or $\frac{8}{12}$

To find the larger fraction convert both fractions so that they share a common denominator.

7. $\frac{2}{3}$ or $\frac{4}{5}$ 10. $\frac{4}{6}$ or $\frac{5}{9}$

8. $\frac{1}{4}$ or $\frac{2}{6}$ 11. $\frac{1}{2}$ or $\frac{4}{7}$

9. $\frac{3}{5}$ or $\frac{7}{12}$ 12. $\frac{3}{8}$ or $\frac{5}{12}$

Write these fractions in order, smallest first.

13. $\frac{1}{2}, \frac{3}{8}, \frac{1}{4}, \frac{1}{8}$

14. $\frac{2}{3}, \frac{1}{6}, \frac{1}{3}, \frac{1}{2}$

15. $\frac{2}{5}, \frac{3}{5}, \frac{1}{2}, \frac{3}{10}$

16. $\frac{3}{4}, \frac{3}{8}, \frac{7}{12}, \frac{1}{2}$

17. $\frac{5}{6}, \frac{1}{2}, \frac{2}{3}, \frac{5}{12}$

18. $\frac{3}{4}, \frac{4}{5}, \frac{1}{2}, \frac{6}{10}$

C

Write the larger fraction.

1. $\frac{5}{6}, \frac{7}{10}$ 5. $\frac{3}{4}, \frac{4}{5}$

2. $\frac{4}{5}, \frac{9}{11}$ 6. $\frac{4}{9}, \frac{5}{12}$

3. $\frac{1}{4}, \frac{2}{9}$ 7. $\frac{2}{3}, \frac{5}{8}$

4. $\frac{4}{7}, \frac{7}{12}$ 8. $\frac{5}{7}, \frac{7}{9}$

Write in ascending order.

9. $\frac{5}{6}, \frac{2}{3}, \frac{7}{9}, \frac{7}{12}$

10. $\frac{3}{5}, \frac{1}{2}, \frac{7}{10}, \frac{55}{100}$

11. $\frac{1}{2}, \frac{5}{8}, \frac{7}{16}, \frac{3}{4}$

12. $\frac{3}{4}, \frac{8}{12}, \frac{5}{6}, \frac{4}{5}$

Find the fraction which is halfway between each pair of numbers.

13. $\frac{1}{2}$ and $\frac{3}{4}$

14. $\frac{1}{5}$ and $\frac{2}{5}$

15. $\frac{1}{6}$ and $\frac{1}{3}$

16. $\frac{5}{8}$ and $\frac{3}{4}$

17. $\frac{7}{12}$ and $\frac{2}{3}$

18. $\frac{1}{2}$ and $\frac{5}{8}$

19. $\frac{4}{5}$ and $\frac{9}{10}$

20. $\frac{1}{3}$ and $\frac{1}{2}$

TARGET   To recognise an improper fraction and write as a mixed number.

Examples

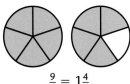

$$\frac{9}{5} = 1\frac{4}{5}$$

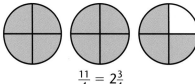

$$\frac{11}{4} = 2\frac{3}{4}$$

21 tenths = $2\frac{1}{10}$

$$\frac{21}{10} = 2\frac{1}{10}$$

A

Use the diagram to help complete the fraction.

1 $1 = \dfrac{\square}{5}$

2 $1 = \dfrac{\square}{\square}$

3 $1 = \dfrac{\square}{\square}$

4 $1 = \dfrac{\square}{\square}$

Copy and complete.

5 $1 = \square$ thirds

6 $1 = \square$ eighths

7 $1 = \square$ quarters

8 $1 = \square$ ninths

Write the next four terms in each sequence using mixed numbers.

9 $0, \frac{1}{4}, \frac{2}{4}, \frac{3}{4}, 1, 1\frac{1}{4}$

10 $0, \frac{1}{2}, 1, 1\frac{1}{2}, 2, 2\frac{1}{2}$

11 $0, \frac{1}{3}, \frac{2}{3}, 1, 1\frac{1}{3}, 1\frac{2}{3}$

12 $0, \frac{1}{8}, \frac{2}{8}, \frac{3}{8}, \frac{4}{8}, \frac{5}{8}$

B

Write the shaded area as:
a) an improper fraction
b) a mixed number.

1 ◓◓◔

2 ◕◕

3 ◓◓◓◓◔

4 ⊕⊕⊕⊕

5 ✳✳

6 ◓◓◓◔

7 ✳✳✳

8 ✳✳✳✳✳

Write as an improper fraction and complete the mixed number.

9 7 quarters = $1\square$

10 5 halves = $\square\frac{1}{2}$

11 17 tenths = $1\square$

12 8 fifths = $\square\frac{3}{5}$

13 7 thirds = $\square$

14 15 eighths = $\square$

15 10 sixths = $\square$

16 9 quarters = $\square$

C

Change to mixed numbers.

1 $\frac{7}{2}$ **5** $\frac{29}{4}$

2 $\frac{21}{5}$ **6** $\frac{55}{6}$

3 $\frac{29}{10}$ **7** $\frac{346}{100}$

4 $\frac{13}{8}$ **8** $\frac{53}{12}$

Copy and complete.

9 $3\frac{3}{4} = \square$ quarters

10 $5\frac{7}{10} = \square$ tenths

11 $6\frac{3}{5} = \square$ fifths

12 $2\frac{19}{100} = \square$ hundredths

13 $4\frac{5}{6} = \square$ sixths

14 $3\frac{4}{9} = \square$ ninths

15 $7\frac{3}{8} = \square$ eighths

16 $6\frac{4}{7} = \square$ sevenths

Write the next four terms in each sequence using mixed numbers.

17 $\frac{1}{7}, \frac{3}{7}, \frac{5}{7}, 1$

18 $\frac{1}{6}, \frac{2}{6}, \frac{3}{6}, \frac{4}{6}$

19 $\frac{1}{10}, \frac{3}{10}, \frac{5}{10}, \frac{7}{10}$

20 $\frac{1}{9}, \frac{3}{9}, \frac{5}{9}, \frac{7}{9}$

TARGET To change an improper fraction to a mixed number and vice versa.

Examples

Change $\frac{20}{3}$ to a mixed number.

$\frac{20}{3} = 20 \div 3$

$= 6$ remainder 2

$= 6\frac{2}{3}$

Change $3\frac{2}{5}$ to an improper fraction.

$3\frac{2}{5} = 3 + \frac{2}{5}$

$= \frac{15}{5} + \frac{2}{5}$

$= \frac{17}{5}$

A

Write the next five pairs of numbers in each number line.

1 0 $\frac{1}{2}$ $\frac{2}{2}$ $\frac{3}{2}$ $\frac{4}{2}$ $\frac{5}{2}$

0 $\frac{1}{2}$ 1 $1\frac{1}{2}$ 2 $2\frac{1}{2}$

2 0 $\frac{1}{3}$ $\frac{2}{3}$ $\frac{3}{3}$ $\frac{4}{3}$ $\frac{5}{3}$

0 $\frac{1}{3}$ $\frac{2}{3}$ 1 $1\frac{1}{3}$ $1\frac{2}{3}$

3 0 $\frac{1}{4}$ $\frac{2}{4}$ $\frac{3}{4}$ $\frac{4}{4}$ $\frac{5}{4}$

0 $\frac{1}{4}$ $\frac{2}{4}$ $\frac{3}{4}$ 1 $1\frac{1}{4}$

4 0 $\frac{1}{5}$ $\frac{2}{5}$ $\frac{3}{5}$ $\frac{4}{5}$ $\frac{5}{5}$

0 $\frac{1}{5}$ $\frac{2}{5}$ $\frac{3}{5}$ $\frac{4}{5}$ 1

Use your number lines to write these improper fractions as mixed numbers.

5 $\frac{7}{2}$ **9** $\frac{9}{2}$

6 $\frac{5}{3}$ **10** $\frac{7}{3}$

7 $\frac{11}{4}$ **11** $\frac{5}{4}$

8 $\frac{8}{5}$ **12** $\frac{11}{5}$

Use your number lines to write these mixed numbers as improper fractions.

13 $2\frac{1}{2}$ **17** $5\frac{1}{2}$

14 $3\frac{1}{3}$ **18** $2\frac{2}{3}$

15 $1\frac{3}{4}$ **19** $2\frac{1}{4}$

16 $1\frac{4}{5}$ **20** $1\frac{1}{5}$

B

Copy and complete.

1 $\frac{7}{5} = 1\,\square$

2 $\frac{13}{4} = \square\,\frac{1}{4}$

3 $7\frac{1}{2} = \square$

4 $3\frac{2}{3} = \square$

Change to mixed numbers.

5 $\frac{17}{2}$ **9** $\frac{23}{5}$

6 $\frac{17}{6}$ **10** $\frac{11}{8}$

7 $\frac{21}{4}$ **11** $\frac{16}{3}$

8 $\frac{22}{9}$ **12** $\frac{27}{10}$

Change to improper fractions.

13 $4\frac{3}{4}$ $\frac{19}{4}$ **17** $1\frac{2}{9}$ $\frac{11}{9}$

14 $2\frac{5}{7}$ $\frac{19}{7}$ **18** $2\frac{4}{5}$ $\frac{14}{5}$

15 $6\frac{2}{3}$ $\frac{20}{3}$ **19** $3\frac{3}{10}$ $\frac{33}{10}$

16 $4\frac{1}{6}$ $\frac{25}{6}$ **20** $2\frac{7}{8}$ $\frac{23}{8}$

Write as both mixed numbers and improper fractions.

21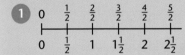

22

23

24

25

C

Change to mixed numbers.

1 $\frac{24}{5}$ **9** $\frac{89}{20}$

2 $\frac{25}{3}$ **10** $\frac{648}{100}$

3 $\frac{49}{10}$ **11** $\frac{43}{12}$

4 $\frac{27}{8}$ **12** $\frac{37}{16}$

5 $\frac{29}{4}$ **13** $\frac{114}{25}$

6 $\frac{41}{7}$ **14** $\frac{105}{40}$

7 $\frac{37}{6}$ **15** $\frac{96}{15}$

8 $\frac{41}{9}$ **16** $\frac{167}{50}$

Change to improper fractions.

17 $6\frac{3}{4}$ **25** $9\frac{1}{11}$

18 $8\frac{1}{10}$ **26** $5\frac{6}{100}$

19 $3\frac{7}{9}$ **27** $3\frac{18}{30}$

20 $7\frac{3}{5}$ **28** $3\frac{7}{18}$

21 $5\frac{7}{8}$ **29** $2\frac{7}{24}$

22 $8\frac{5}{6}$ **30** $5\frac{39}{50}$

23 $9\frac{2}{3}$ **31** $4\frac{2}{13}$

24 $4\frac{4}{7}$ **32** $5\frac{5}{21}$

TARGET To add and subtract fractions with the same denominator and multiples of the same number.

SAME DENOMINATOR
Add or subtract the numerators.
Put the answer over the same denominator.

Examples

$\frac{5}{12} + \frac{2}{12} = \frac{7}{12}$

$\frac{7}{9} - \frac{4}{9} = \frac{3}{9}$

DIFFERENT DENOMINATORS
Convert one of the fractions to an equivalent fraction with the same denominator as the other fraction.

Examples

$\frac{5}{8} + \frac{1}{4} = \frac{5}{8} + \frac{2}{8} = \frac{7}{8}$

$\frac{11}{12} - \frac{1}{3} = \frac{11}{12} - \frac{4}{12} = \frac{7}{12}$

A

Work out

1. $\frac{3}{6} + \frac{1}{6}$
2. $\frac{2}{5} + \frac{2}{5}$
3. $\frac{2}{4} + \frac{1}{4}$
4. $\frac{4}{7} + \frac{2}{7}$
5. $\frac{2}{12} + \frac{9}{12}$
6. $\frac{3}{8} + \frac{4}{8}$
7. $\frac{4}{10} + \frac{4}{10}$
8. $\frac{1}{5} + \frac{3}{5}$
9. $\frac{5}{9} + \frac{2}{9}$
10. $\frac{3}{11} + \frac{6}{11}$
11. $\frac{1}{8} + \frac{5}{8}$
12. $\frac{5}{12} + \frac{4}{12}$
13. $\frac{7}{10} - \frac{3}{10}$
14. $\frac{4}{6} - \frac{2}{6}$
15. $\frac{6}{8} - \frac{1}{8}$
16. $\frac{5}{5} - \frac{2}{5}$
17. $\frac{3}{4} - \frac{1}{4}$
18. $\frac{8}{9} - \frac{5}{9}$
19. $\frac{10}{12} - \frac{3}{12}$
20. $\frac{2}{3} - \frac{1}{3}$
21. $\frac{5}{7} - \frac{3}{7}$
22. $\frac{9}{10} - \frac{4}{10}$
23. $\frac{8}{12} - \frac{6}{12}$
24. $\frac{5}{6} - \frac{4}{6}$

B

Copy and complete.

1. $\frac{2}{3} + \frac{1}{9} = \frac{\square}{9} + \frac{1}{9} = \frac{\square}{9}$
2. $\frac{1}{2} + \frac{2}{6} = \frac{\square}{6} + \frac{2}{6} = \frac{\square}{6}$
3. $\frac{3}{8} + \frac{1}{4} = \frac{3}{8} + \frac{\square}{\square} = \frac{\square}{\square}$
4. $\frac{7}{12} + \frac{1}{6} = \frac{7}{12} + \frac{\square}{\square} = \frac{\square}{\square}$
5. $\frac{2}{5} - \frac{1}{10} = \frac{\square}{10} - \frac{1}{10} = \frac{\square}{10}$
6. $\frac{5}{8} - \frac{1}{2} = \frac{5}{8} - \frac{\square}{8} = \frac{\square}{8}$
7. $\frac{4}{6} - \frac{3}{12} = \frac{\square}{\square} - \frac{3}{12} = \frac{\square}{\square}$
8. $\frac{11}{12} - \frac{2}{3} = \frac{11}{12} - \frac{\square}{\square} = \frac{\square}{\square}$

Work out

9. $\frac{1}{10} + \frac{3}{5}$
10. $\frac{1}{2} + \frac{4}{10}$
11. $\frac{1}{6} + \frac{1}{3}$
12. $\frac{3}{4} + \frac{1}{12}$
13. $\frac{3}{4} - \frac{5}{8}$
14. $\frac{1}{2} - \frac{1}{12}$
15. $\frac{1}{3} - \frac{2}{9}$
16. $\frac{8}{10} - \frac{3}{5}$

C

Copy and complete.

1. $\frac{1}{2} + \frac{1}{3} = \frac{\square}{6} + \frac{\square}{6} = \frac{\square}{6}$
2. $\frac{3}{5} + \frac{1}{6} = \frac{\square}{30} + \frac{\square}{30} = \frac{\square}{30}$
3. $\frac{2}{3} + \frac{1}{5} = \frac{\square}{15} + \frac{\square}{15} = \frac{\square}{15}$
4. $\frac{2}{6} + \frac{1}{4} = \frac{\square}{12} + \frac{\square}{12} = \frac{\square}{12}$
5. $\frac{3}{4} - \frac{1}{3} = \frac{\square}{12} - \frac{\square}{12} = \frac{\square}{12}$
6. $\frac{1}{2} - \frac{2}{5} = \frac{\square}{10} - \frac{\square}{10} = \frac{\square}{10}$
7. $\frac{2}{3} - \frac{3}{10} = \frac{\square}{30} - \frac{\square}{30} = \frac{\square}{30}$
8. $\frac{4}{5} - \frac{5}{8} = \frac{\square}{40} - \frac{\square}{40} = \frac{\square}{40}$

Work out

9. $\frac{3}{4} + \frac{1}{6}$
10. $\frac{1}{2} + \frac{1}{10}$
11. $\frac{3}{5} + \frac{1}{2}$
12. $\frac{2}{3} + \frac{1}{4}$
13. $\frac{5}{6} - \frac{3}{5}$
14. $\frac{7}{10} - \frac{1}{4}$
15. $\frac{2}{3} - \frac{5}{8}$
16. $\frac{2}{5} - \frac{2}{12}$

TARGET   To add and subtract fractions involving mixed numbers.

Examples

SAME DENOMINATORS

$\frac{5}{8} + \frac{7}{8} = \frac{12}{8} = 1\frac{4}{8}$

$1\frac{3}{10} - \frac{6}{10} = \frac{13}{10} - \frac{6}{10} = \frac{7}{10}$

DIFFERENT DENOMINATORS

$\frac{3}{4} + \frac{7}{12} = \frac{9}{12} + \frac{7}{12} = \frac{16}{12} = 1\frac{4}{12}$

$1\frac{4}{9} - \frac{2}{3} = \frac{13}{9} - \frac{6}{9} = \frac{7}{9}$

A

Work out

1. $\frac{5}{12} + \frac{1}{12}$
2. $\frac{2}{6} + \frac{3}{6}$
3. $\frac{1}{5} + \frac{3}{5}$
4. $\frac{8}{12} + \frac{2}{12}$
5. $\frac{1}{4} + \frac{2}{4}$
6. $\frac{1}{6} + \frac{2}{6}$
7. $\frac{2}{5} + \frac{2}{5}$
8. $\frac{4}{12} + \frac{4}{12}$
9. $\frac{5}{6} - \frac{4}{6}$
10. $\frac{7}{12} - \frac{2}{12}$
11. $\frac{4}{5} - \frac{3}{5}$
12. $\frac{3}{4} - \frac{2}{4}$
13. $\frac{3}{3} - \frac{1}{3}$
14. $\frac{11}{12} - \frac{6}{12}$
15. $\frac{4}{6} - \frac{2}{6}$
16. $\frac{5}{5} - \frac{1}{5}$

17. Four twelfths of the people on a bus are boys. Five twelfths are girls. What fraction are adults?

18. Four fifths of the chocolates in a box are left. A further two fifths are eaten. What fraction of the chocolates is left?

B

Work out

1. $\frac{1}{2} + \frac{3}{10}$
2. $\frac{2}{6} + \frac{3}{12}$
3. $\frac{1}{4} + \frac{5}{12}$
4. $\frac{4}{5} + \frac{3}{5}$
5. $\frac{2}{3} + \frac{2}{3}$
6. $\frac{7}{10} + \frac{9}{10}$
7. $\frac{4}{5} + \frac{3}{10}$
8. $\frac{2}{3} + \frac{4}{9}$
9. $\frac{1}{2} + \frac{11}{12}$
10. $\frac{1}{2} + \frac{3}{4}$
11. $\frac{3}{4} + \frac{5}{8}$
12. $\frac{5}{6} + \frac{7}{12}$
13. $\frac{5}{8} - \frac{1}{2}$
14. $\frac{7}{10} - \frac{3}{5}$
15. $\frac{2}{3} - \frac{1}{6}$
16. $\frac{13}{12} - \frac{3}{4}$
17. $\frac{3}{2} - \frac{7}{10}$
18. $\frac{8}{6} - \frac{7}{12}$
19. $1\frac{1}{6} - \frac{4}{6}$
20. $1\frac{3}{10} - \frac{5}{10}$
21. $1\frac{2}{7} - \frac{6}{7}$
22. $1\frac{1}{4} - \frac{3}{8}$
23. $1\frac{2}{5} - \frac{7}{10}$
24. $1\frac{1}{12} - \frac{2}{3}$

25. Victor has one and a half packets of flour. He uses five eighths of a packet. What fraction of a complete packet is left?

C

Work out

1. $\frac{1}{3} + \frac{1}{2}$
2. $\frac{2}{5} + \frac{1}{4}$
3. $\frac{1}{2} + \frac{3}{7}$
4. $\frac{2}{3} + \frac{4}{5}$
5. $\frac{5}{6} + \frac{3}{4}$
6. $\frac{3}{5} + \frac{1}{2}$
7. $\frac{3}{4} + \frac{2}{3}$
8. $\frac{5}{6} + \frac{2}{5}$
9. $\frac{2}{3} - \frac{1}{5}$
10. $\frac{3}{4} - \frac{1}{6}$
11. $\frac{1}{2} - \frac{2}{5}$
12. $\frac{7}{5} - \frac{3}{4}$
13. $1\frac{1}{2} - \frac{2}{3}$
14. $1\frac{3}{5} - \frac{5}{6}$
15. $1\frac{1}{4} - \frac{1}{3}$
16. $1\frac{3}{10} - \frac{2}{3}$

17. A football team wins two fifths of their matches and draws one third. What fraction of their matches are lost?

18. A quarter of a cake is eaten and the next day one third is eaten. What fraction of the cake is left?

TARGET To practise the addition and subtraction of fractions involving mixed numbers.

SAME DENOMINATORS

$\frac{9}{11} + \frac{5}{11} = \frac{14}{11} = 1\frac{3}{11}$

$1\frac{5}{8} - \frac{7}{8} = \frac{13}{8} - \frac{7}{8} = \frac{6}{8}$

DIFFERENT DENOMINATORS

$\frac{3}{5} + \frac{7}{10} = \frac{6}{10} + \frac{7}{10} = \frac{13}{10} = 1\frac{3}{10}$

$1\frac{1}{2} - \frac{5}{8} = \frac{3}{2} - \frac{5}{8} = \frac{12}{8} - \frac{5}{8} = \frac{7}{8}$

A
Work out

1. $\frac{3}{12} + \frac{5}{12}$
2. $\frac{1}{6} + \frac{4}{6}$
3. $\frac{2}{5} + \frac{1}{5}$
4. $\frac{1}{8} + \frac{5}{8}$
5. $\frac{11}{12} + \frac{7}{12}$
6. $\frac{5}{6} + \frac{2}{6}$
7. $\frac{3}{5} + \frac{4}{5}$
8. $\frac{6}{12} + \frac{9}{12}$
9. $\frac{5}{6} - \frac{2}{6}$
10. $\frac{9}{12} - \frac{4}{12}$
11. $\frac{3}{3} - \frac{2}{3}$
12. $\frac{6}{7} - \frac{3}{7}$
13. $\frac{5}{4} - \frac{2}{4}$
14. $\frac{7}{5} - \frac{4}{5}$
15. $\frac{14}{12} - \frac{7}{12}$
16. $\frac{9}{6} - \frac{5}{6}$

17. A can of paint is seven eighths full. A further three eighths is used. What fraction of the paint is left?

18. Three tenths of the children in Year 5 go to school by bus, four tenths walk. What fraction of the children go to school in other ways?

B
Work out

1. $\frac{1}{2} + \frac{1}{6}$
2. $\frac{1}{3} + \frac{5}{12}$
3. $\frac{4}{5} + \frac{3}{10}$
4. $\frac{3}{4} + \frac{7}{12}$
5. $\frac{1}{2} + \frac{7}{8}$
6. $\frac{5}{6} + \frac{1}{3}$
7. $\frac{9}{10} + \frac{3}{5}$
8. $\frac{11}{12} + \frac{1}{6}$
9. $\frac{2}{3} - \frac{4}{9}$
10. $\frac{7}{10} - \frac{2}{5}$
11. $\frac{7}{4} - \frac{11}{12}$
12. $\frac{9}{6} - \frac{2}{3}$
13. $1\frac{3}{10} - \frac{1}{2}$
14. $1\frac{1}{4} - \frac{7}{8}$
15. $1\frac{2}{5} - \frac{6}{10}$
16. $1\frac{7}{12} - \frac{2}{3}$

17. A postman has delivered half his letters. He delivers a further two fifths. What fraction of his letters has he delivered?

18. Ashra has one and a third jugs of drink. She pours out five sixths of the full jug. What fraction of a full jug of drink does she have left?

C
Work out

1. $1\frac{1}{2} + \frac{7}{12}$
2. $1\frac{9}{10} + \frac{4}{5}$
3. $1\frac{2}{3} + 1\frac{5}{6}$
4. $1\frac{5}{12} + \frac{3}{4}$
5. $\frac{1}{2} + \frac{4}{5}$
6. $\frac{2}{3} + \frac{3}{4}$
7. $\frac{1}{5} + \frac{7}{8}$
8. $\frac{3}{4} + \frac{5}{6}$
9. $1\frac{7}{10} - \frac{1}{2}$
10. $1\frac{1}{3} - \frac{5}{9}$
11. $2\frac{1}{4} - \frac{7}{8}$
12. $4\frac{1}{12} - \frac{1}{6}$
13. $1\frac{3}{4} - \frac{4}{5}$
14. $2\frac{1}{3} - \frac{1}{2}$
15. $1\frac{7}{10} - \frac{3}{4}$
16. $1\frac{1}{5} - \frac{2}{3}$

17. Luigi makes two identical pizzas. Three fifths of one is eaten and three quarters of the other pizza is eaten. What fraction of a whole pizza is left?

18. One and a half packets of biscuits are put out on plates. When everyone has finished eating, two thirds of a packet are left. What fraction of a packet has been eaten?

TARGET To find fractions of numbers, writing remainders as fractions.

Examples

$\frac{1}{3}$ of 17 = 17 ÷ 3   or $\frac{1}{3}$ of 17 = $\frac{17}{3}$ $\frac{2}{3}$ of 17 = $\frac{17 \times 2}{3}$

$= 5\frac{2}{3}$ $= 5\frac{2}{3}$ $= \frac{34}{3}$

$= 11\frac{1}{3}$

A

Work out

1. $\frac{1}{2}$ of 16
2. $\frac{1}{5}$ of 30
3. $\frac{1}{4}$ of 28
4. $\frac{1}{10}$ of 50

5. $\frac{1}{3}$ of 24
6. $\frac{1}{8}$ of 48
7. $\frac{1}{6}$ of 18
8. $\frac{1}{9}$ of 36

9. $\frac{1}{7}$ of 63
10. $\frac{1}{5}$ of 45
11. $\frac{1}{4}$ of 20
12. $\frac{1}{12}$ of 96

13. $\frac{1}{8}$ of 16
14. $\frac{1}{11}$ of 77
15. $\frac{1}{3}$ of 36
16. $\frac{1}{9}$ of 81

17. $\frac{1}{6}$ of 66
18. $\frac{1}{2}$ of 60
19. $\frac{1}{7}$ of 35
20. $\frac{1}{10}$ of 100

B

Find $\frac{1}{10}$ of:

1. 21
2. 87
3. 119
4. 43.

Find $\frac{1}{5}$ of:

5. 38
6. 21
7. 27
8. 49.

Find $\frac{1}{8}$ of:

9. 41
10. 29
11. 59
12. 71.

Find $\frac{1}{9}$ of:

13. 57
14. 95
15. 21
16. 70.

Work out

17. $\frac{1}{6}$ of 25
18. $\frac{1}{3}$ of 17
19. $\frac{1}{7}$ of 26
20. $\frac{1}{12}$ of 67
21. $\frac{1}{2}$ of 13
22. $\frac{1}{4}$ of 51
23. $\frac{1}{11}$ of 30
24. $\frac{1}{6}$ of 47
25. $\frac{1}{3}$ of 28
26. $\frac{1}{12}$ of 52
27. $\frac{1}{2}$ of 23
28. $\frac{1}{4}$ of 33
29. $\frac{1}{8}$ of 75
30. $\frac{1}{3}$ of 35
31. $\frac{1}{7}$ of 60
32. $\frac{1}{12}$ of 89
33. $\frac{1}{6}$ of 55
34. $\frac{1}{10}$ of 67
35. $\frac{1}{9}$ of 51
36. $\frac{1}{11}$ of 124

C

Copy and complete.

1. $\frac{1}{4}$ of ☐ = $6\frac{1}{4}$
2. $\frac{1}{3}$ of ☐ = $7\frac{2}{3}$
3. $\frac{1}{10}$ of ☐ = $9\frac{3}{10}$
4. $\frac{1}{5}$ of ☐ = $3\frac{2}{5}$

5. $\frac{1}{12}$ of ☐ = $2\frac{11}{12}$
6. $\frac{1}{8}$ of ☐ = $12\frac{5}{8}$
7. $\frac{1}{9}$ of ☐ = $3\frac{4}{9}$
8. $\frac{1}{6}$ of ☐ = $5\frac{5}{6}$

Work out

9. $\frac{5}{6}$ of 7
10. $\frac{3}{5}$ of 14
11. $\frac{2}{3}$ of 11
12. $\frac{7}{10}$ of 3
13. $\frac{3}{8}$ of 15
14. $\frac{4}{7}$ of 8
15. $\frac{3}{4}$ of 17
16. $\frac{11}{12}$ of 9
17. $\frac{8}{11}$ of 10
18. $\frac{5}{9}$ of 12
19. $\frac{2}{5}$ of 23
20. $\frac{3}{10}$ of 57

21. $\frac{2}{7}$ of 31
22. $\frac{6}{11}$ of 16
23. $\frac{4}{5}$ of 19
24. $\frac{3}{4}$ of 21
25. $\frac{5}{12}$ of 29
26. $\frac{3}{8}$ of 33
27. $\frac{2}{3}$ of 14
28. $\frac{9}{10}$ of 25
29. $\frac{4}{9}$ of 20
30. $\frac{3}{11}$ of 35
31. $\frac{5}{7}$ of 17
32. $\frac{99}{100}$ of 3

TARGET To solve word problems involving finding fractions of numbers and quantities.

Example

The Hadrian's Wall Path is 84 miles long. Esme has walked five twelfths of its length. How much further does she have to walk to complete the whole Path?

$84 \div 12 = 7$
$7 \times 5 = 35$
$84 - 35 = 49$
Answer *49 miles*

A

1. There are 24 footballs. One third need pumping up. How many are ready to use?

2. A television programme lasts for one hour. One fifth of the time is adverts. How long is the programme itself?

3. There are 120 tissues in a box. One sixth are used. How many are left?

4. There are 36 cars in a car park. A quarter of the cars are white. How many are not white?

5. A bicycle costs £70. In a sale the price is cut by one tenth. What is the new price?

6. A piece of wood is 60 cm long. One third is cut off. How long are the two pieces?

B

1. Red and yellow paint is mixed to make one litre of orange paint. Four fifths of the paint is yellow. How much is red?

2. There are sixty pupils in Year 4. Three tenths live more than one mile from school. How many live nearer to the school?

3. A packet of muesli weighs 350 g. Four sevenths of the mixture is oat flakes. What is the weight of the other ingredients?

4. There are 72 stalls at a market. Three eighths sell food. How many do not sell food?

5. There are 27 children in a class. Seven ninths belong to sports clubs. How many do not belong to a sports club?

6. A cake weighs 300 g. Three quarters is eaten. How much is left?

C

1. A shop sells 144 bottles of milk. Four ninths are full fat milk. How many are skimmed or semi-skimmed?

2. Chloe has 161 books. Three sevenths of the books are on her top shelf. How many does she keep on her other shelf?

3. There are 240 tea bags in a packet. Nine twentieths are used. How many are left?

4. A holiday costs £2000. Duncan has saved five eighths of the money. How much more does he need?

5. A roll of wrapping paper is six metres long. Seven twelfths has been used. How much is left?

6. What is one fifth of one quarter of one kilogram?

TARGET   To multiply fractions and mixed numbers by whole numbers.

Examples

To multiply a fraction by a whole number multiply the numerator by the whole number and change to a mixed number.

$$\frac{3}{4} \times 5 = \frac{15}{4} = 3\frac{3}{4}$$

To multiply a mixed number change it to an improper fraction and put the whole number over 1 before multiplying.

$$2\frac{1}{4} \times 5 = \frac{9}{4} \times \frac{5}{1} = \frac{45}{4} = 11\frac{1}{4}$$

Simplify by cancelling either number with either denominator.

$$2\frac{1}{4} \times 6 = \frac{9}{\cancel{4}_2} \times \frac{\cancel{6}^3}{1} = \frac{27}{2} = 13\frac{1}{2}$$

A

Copy and complete.

1. $\frac{1}{2} \times 9 = \frac{9}{2} = \square$

2. $\frac{3}{5} \times 4 = \frac{12}{5} = \square$

3. $\frac{7}{12} \times 3 = \frac{\square}{12} = \square$

4. $\frac{5}{6} \times 7 = \frac{\square}{6} = \square$

Work out

5. $\frac{2}{9} \times 5$ 9. $\frac{2}{3} \times 10$

6. $\frac{3}{4} \times 11$ 10. $\frac{6}{11} \times 4$

7. $\frac{9}{10} \times 6$ 11. $\frac{4}{7} \times 3$

8. $\frac{5}{8} \times 2$ 12. $\frac{2}{5} \times 8$

B

Copy and complete.

1. $2\frac{3}{4} \times 3 = \frac{11}{4} \times \frac{3}{1} = \frac{\square}{4} = \square$

2. $5\frac{1}{6} \times 9 = \frac{31}{\cancel{6}_2} \times \frac{\cancel{9}^3}{1} = \frac{93}{2} = \square$ $46\frac{1}{2}$

3. $4\frac{7}{10} \times 2 = \frac{\square}{\cancel{10}^5} \times \frac{\cancel{2}^1}{1} = \frac{\square}{\square} = \square$

4. $1\frac{4}{5} \times 6 = \frac{\square}{5} \times \frac{6}{1} = \square = \square$

Work out

5. $1\frac{3}{8} \times 4$ 9. $1\frac{1}{2} \times 8$ 13. $2\frac{5}{6} \times 12$

6. $2\frac{2}{3} \times 12$ 10. $2\frac{11}{12} \times 3$ 14. $3\frac{1}{4} \times 6$

7. $1\frac{2}{7} \times 8$ 11. $1\frac{4}{9} \times 6$ 15. $1\frac{4}{11} \times 2$

8. $2\frac{3}{5} \times 2$ 12. $2\frac{1}{10} \times 4$ 16. $5\frac{1}{3} \times 9$

C

Work out

1. $3\frac{3}{4} \times 12$ 5. $7\frac{1}{2} \times 12$ 9. $3\frac{2}{3} \times 7$ 13. $8\frac{5}{12} \times 4$

2. $2\frac{1}{6} \times 8$ 6. $9\frac{7}{8} \times 4$ 10. $4\frac{3}{10} \times 8$ 14. $7\frac{1}{4} \times 8$

3. $7\frac{9}{10} \times 5$ 7. $4\frac{4}{7} \times 2$ 11. $2\frac{4}{5} \times 6$ 15. $3\frac{5}{6} \times 5$

4. $4\frac{2}{5} \times 3$ 8. $5\frac{2}{9} \times 6$ 12. $5\frac{1}{8} \times 12$ 16. $6\frac{4}{5} \times 9$

TARGET To connect multiplication by a fraction to finding fractions of whole numbers.

Examples

$\frac{3}{5}$ of 30 = (30 ÷ 5) × 3   or $\frac{3}{5} \times 30 = \frac{90}{5}$

$\quad\quad\quad = 6 \times 3$ $\quad\quad\quad\quad\quad\quad\quad\quad = 18$

$\quad\quad\quad = 18$

What number is $1\frac{3}{5}$ times larger than 30?

$1\frac{3}{5} = \frac{8}{5}$ $\quad$ $\frac{8}{5} \times 30 = \frac{240}{5} = 48$

$\quad\quad\quad$ or

$\frac{8}{5}$ of 30 = (30 ÷ 5) × 8

$\quad\quad\quad = 6 \times 8$

$\quad\quad\quad = 48$

A

Find

1. $\frac{1}{5}$ of 30

2. $\frac{1}{4}$ of 28

3. $\frac{1}{8}$ of 40

4. $\frac{1}{3}$ of 27

5. $\frac{1}{10}$ of 50

6. $\frac{1}{6}$ of 24

7. $\frac{1}{9}$ of 18

8. $\frac{1}{7}$ of 70

9. $\frac{1}{12}$ of 36

10. $\frac{1}{10}$ of 110

11. $\frac{1}{4}$ of 20

12. $\frac{3}{4}$ of 20

13. $\frac{1}{5}$ of 40

14. $\frac{2}{5}$ of 40

15. $\frac{1}{10}$ of 60

16. $\frac{9}{10}$ of 60

17. $\frac{1}{6}$ of 42

18. $\frac{5}{6}$ of 42

B

Work out

1. $\frac{2}{3}$ of 18

2. $\frac{3}{4}$ of 32

3. $\frac{2}{5}$ of 45

4. $\frac{5}{6}$ of 60

5. $\frac{4}{7}$ of 28

6. $\frac{3}{8}$ of 56

7. $\frac{7}{9}$ of 81

8. $\frac{9}{10}$ of 20

9. $\frac{6}{11} \times 55$

10. $\frac{5}{12} \times 96$

11. $\frac{2}{100} \times 400$

12. $\frac{3}{5} \times 60$

13. $\frac{3}{10} \times 200$

14. $\frac{7}{8} \times 24$

15. $\frac{4}{9} \times 45$

16. $\frac{2}{7} \times 42$

Find the number which is:

17. $1\frac{1}{2}$ times greater than 50

18. $1\frac{2}{3}$ times greater than 24

19. $2\frac{1}{4}$ times greater than 48

20. $2\frac{2}{5}$ times greater than 20

21. $3\frac{1}{6}$ times greater than 18

22. $1\frac{7}{10}$ times greater than 100

23. $2\frac{5}{8}$ times greater than 48

24. $4\frac{3}{4}$ times greater than 20

25. $1\frac{4}{5}$ times greater than 40

26. $2\frac{1}{3}$ times greater than 36.

C

Work out

1. $\frac{3}{5}$ of 35

2. $\frac{6}{7}$ of 8·4

3. $\frac{7}{12}$ of 1440

4. $\frac{9}{10}$ of 210

5. $\frac{3}{4}$ of 200

6. $\frac{2}{9}$ of 5·4

7. $\frac{5}{6}$ of 480

8. $\frac{3}{8}$ of 3200

9. $\frac{21}{100} \times 50$

10. $\frac{2}{3} \times 270$

11. $\frac{8}{11} \times 9·9$

12. $\frac{5}{7} \times 2100$

13. $\frac{7}{10} \times 4$

14. $\frac{5}{9} \times 360$

15. $\frac{11}{12} \times 6000$

16. $\frac{3}{100} \times 16$

Find the number which is:

17. $1\frac{5}{6}$ times larger than 540

18. $4\frac{1}{2}$ times larger than 14

19. $2\frac{1}{3}$ times larger than 150

20. $6\frac{2}{5}$ times larger than 25

21. $1\frac{4}{11}$ times larger than 3300

22. $1\frac{5}{8}$ times larger than 96

23. $3\frac{2}{10}$ times larger than 250

24. $2\frac{1}{4}$ times larger than 60

25. $1\frac{7}{9}$ times larger than 72

26. $4\frac{3}{7}$ times larger than 49.

TARGET To read and write decimal numbers as fractions and vice versa.

$\frac{3}{10} + \frac{2}{100} + \frac{6}{1000} = \frac{326}{1000}$

$0 \cdot 3 + 0 \cdot 02 + 0 \cdot 006 = 0 \cdot 326$

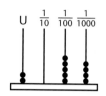

$2\frac{54}{1000} = 2 \cdot 054$

A

Write as a decimal.

1. $2\frac{64}{100}$ 7. $4\frac{71}{100}$
2. $\frac{32}{100}$ 8. $\frac{26}{100}$
3. $5\frac{17}{100}$ 9. $7\frac{48}{100}$
4. $9\frac{5}{100}$ 10. $3\frac{45}{100}$
5. $\frac{23}{100}$ 11. $\frac{99}{100}$
6. $6\frac{18}{100}$ 12. $15\frac{1}{100}$

Write as a fraction.

13. $3 \cdot 5$ 19. $2 \cdot 34$
14. $0 \cdot 92$ 20. $0 \cdot 82$
15. $1 \cdot 38$ 21. $6 \cdot 7$
16. $5 \cdot 1$ 22. $9 \cdot 56$
17. $4 \cdot 67$ 23. $0 \cdot 9$
18. $0 \cdot 4$ 24. $7 \cdot 15$

Partition using fractions.

25. $1 \cdot 28$ 31. $10 \cdot 59$
26. $0 \cdot 75$ 32. $4 \cdot 93$
27. $3 \cdot 61$ 33. $0 \cdot 16$
28. $8 \cdot 14$ 34. $6 \cdot 07$
29. $2 \cdot 42$ 35. $0 \cdot 39$
30. $0 \cdot 86$ 36. $24 \cdot 25$

B

Write as a decimal.

1. $1\frac{42}{100}$ 7. $3\frac{185}{1000}$
2. $\frac{4}{1000}$ 8. $\frac{291}{1000}$
3. $8\frac{579}{1000}$ 9. $1\frac{58}{1000}$
4. $\frac{26}{100}$ 10. $4\frac{13}{100}$
5. $\frac{413}{1000}$ 11. $5\frac{306}{1000}$
6. $2\frac{7}{100}$ 12. $\frac{87}{1000}$

Write as mixed numbers.

13. $12 \cdot 7$ 19. $8 \cdot 005$
14. $6 \cdot 524$ 20. $23 \cdot 618$
15. $0 \cdot 046$ 21. $5 \cdot 083$
16. $47 \cdot 19$ 22. $4 \cdot 237$
17. $0 \cdot 361$ 23. $2 \cdot 202$
18. $1 \cdot 9$ 24. $19 \cdot 059$

Partition using fractions.

25. $4 \cdot 138$ 31. $3 \cdot 621$
26. $1 \cdot 906$ 32. $7 \cdot 854$
27. $6 \cdot 28$ 33. $0 \cdot 069$
28. $2 \cdot 417$ 34. $6 \cdot 375$
29. $0 \cdot 592$ 35. $2 \cdot 702$
30. $5 \cdot 043$ 36. $4 \cdot 518$

C

Copy and complete.

1. $0 \cdot 279 = \frac{2}{10} + \square + \frac{9}{1000}$
2. $0 \cdot 543 = \square + \frac{4}{100} + \frac{3}{1000}$
3. $0 \cdot 316 = \square + \frac{6}{1000}$
4. $0 \cdot 985 = \frac{9}{10} + \square$
5. $2 \cdot 104 = 2 + \square + \frac{4}{1000}$
6. $1 \cdot 821 = 1 + \square + \frac{1}{1000}$
7. $6 \cdot 457 = 6 + \frac{4}{10} + \square$
8. $3 \cdot 692 = 3 + \frac{9}{100} + \square$

Increase the following numbers by:

$\frac{17}{100}$ $\frac{99}{1000}$

9. $0 \cdot 295$ 13. $0 \cdot 134$
10. $0 \cdot 038$ 14. $0 \cdot 95$
11. $1 \cdot 903$ 15. $2 \cdot 082$
12. $0 \cdot 861$ 16. $0 \cdot 201$

Give the answer as a decimal.

17. $\frac{3}{4} + 0 \cdot 64$
18. $\frac{1}{2} - 0 \cdot 333$
19. $0 \cdot 481 + \frac{1}{4}$
20. $0 \cdot 2 - \frac{175}{1000}$

TARGET
To recognise and use thousandths and relate them to tenths, hundredths and decimal equivalents.

Examples

$$\frac{64}{100} = 0.64$$

$$\frac{427}{1000} = 0.427$$

$$0.427 = \frac{4}{10} + \frac{2}{100} + \frac{7}{1000}$$

$$0.427 = 0.4 + 0.02 + 0.007$$

The value of a digit depends upon its position in a number.

Each digit in a number is 10 times greater than the digit to the right. This applies to decimal fractions as well as to whole numbers.

	T	U	·	$\frac{1}{10}$	$\frac{1}{100}$	$\frac{1}{1000}$
30 =	3	0	·	0		
3 =		3	·	0		
$\frac{3}{10}$ =		0	·	3		
$\frac{3}{100}$ =		0	·	0	3	
$\frac{3}{1000}$ =		0	·	0	0	3

A

Express the shaded part of each shape as a fraction and as a decimal fraction.

1 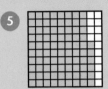   5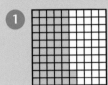

2 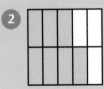   6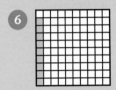

3 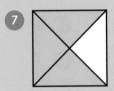   7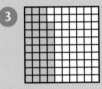

4 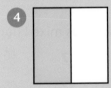   8

Give the value of the underlined figure in each of these numbers.

9   3.4<u>2</u>   13   <u>2</u>2.16   17   60.6<u>5</u>

10   15.3<u>1</u>   14   48.<u>7</u>   18   57.8<u>9</u>

11   31.<u>9</u>7   15   4.5<u>3</u>   19   <u>8</u>.01

12   6.0<u>5</u>   16   1<u>9</u>.24   20   32.4<u>7</u>

Write each number shown by the arrows as a decimal fraction.

21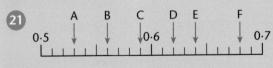

22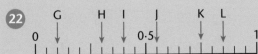

B

Write the decimal fraction shown on each abacus.

1 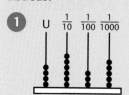 U $\frac{1}{10}$ $\frac{1}{100}$ $\frac{1}{1000}$

5 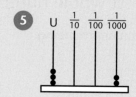 U $\frac{1}{10}$ $\frac{1}{100}$ $\frac{1}{1000}$

2 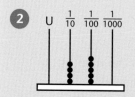 U $\frac{1}{10}$ $\frac{1}{100}$ $\frac{1}{1000}$

6 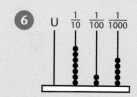 U $\frac{1}{10}$ $\frac{1}{100}$ $\frac{1}{1000}$

3 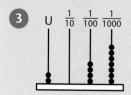 U $\frac{1}{10}$ $\frac{1}{100}$ $\frac{1}{1000}$

7 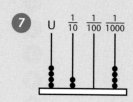 U $\frac{1}{10}$ $\frac{1}{100}$ $\frac{1}{1000}$

4 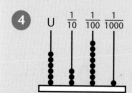 U $\frac{1}{10}$ $\frac{1}{100}$ $\frac{1}{1000}$

8 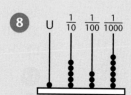 U $\frac{1}{10}$ $\frac{1}{100}$ $\frac{1}{1000}$

Give the value of the underlined figure in each of these numbers.

9 8.8<u>6</u> **13** 2.40<u>7</u> **17** <u>3</u>0.71

10 4.<u>3</u>91 **14** 67.<u>6</u> **18** 9.28<u>4</u>

11 0.24<u>9</u> **15** 0.1<u>5</u> **19** 1.6<u>3</u>

12 13.<u>5</u>7 **16** 5.<u>9</u>28 **20** 7.05<u>6</u>

Write each number shown by the arrows as a decimal fraction.

21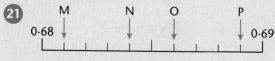

22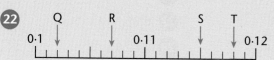

C

Write each number shown by the arrows as a decimal fraction.

1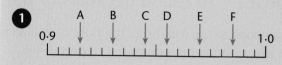

2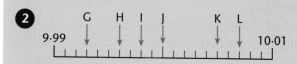

Increase the following numbers by:

$\frac{1}{10}$ $\frac{1}{100}$ $\frac{1}{1000}$

3 1.98   **7** 4.2   **11** 3

4 5   **8** 0.39   **12** 2.46

5 2.436   **9** 8   **13** 9.999

6 7.9   **10** 6.095   **14** 1.7

Copy and complete.

15 $2 + \frac{3}{10} + \frac{7}{100} + \frac{5}{1000} = \boxed{}$

16 $4 + \boxed{} + \frac{1}{1000} = 4.801$

17 $\frac{4}{10} + \frac{2}{100} + \boxed{} = 0.429$

18 $1 + \boxed{} + \frac{3}{1000} = 1.063$

Copy and complete.

19 $4.618 + 0.5 = \boxed{}$

20 $1.723 - 0.004 = \boxed{}$

21 $0.925 + 0.08 = \boxed{}$

22 $2.284 - 0.6 = \boxed{}$

23 $5.994 + 0.009 = \boxed{}$

24 $1.456 + \boxed{} = 1.461$

25 $2.381 - \boxed{} = 1.681$

26 $0.792 + \boxed{} = 0.8$

27 $3.033 - \boxed{} = 2.933$

28 $6.005 + \boxed{} = 6.275$

TARGET To round decimals to the nearest whole number or tenth.

Always look at the column to the right of that to which you are rounding.
5 or more, round up. Less than 5, round down.

Examples
Round to the nearest whole number. 5·18 → 5 7·53 → 8
Round to the nearest tenth. 5·18 → 5·2 7·53 → 7·5

A

Round to the nearest whole number.

1 0·6
2 3·28
3 6·5
4 12·7
5 1·05
6 18·4
7 15·84
8 2·9
9 16·3
10 0·52
11 10·17
12 21·63

Round to the nearest pound.

13 £4·25
14 £11·73
15 £5·48
16 £9·52
17 £16·90
18 £3·17
19 £2·62
20 £8·07
21 £10·83
22 £7·28
23 £1·54
24 £15·39

Approximate by rounding to the nearest pound.

25 £15·81 + £7·38
26 £32·47 + £6·72
27 £10·53 + £4·94
28 £8·26 + £2·06
29 £21·64 − £5·80
30 £16·18 − £3·93
31 £43·45 − £9·29
32 £39·09 − £1·51

B

Round to the nearest:
a) whole number
b) tenth.

1 2·39
2 7·138
3 1·85
4 16·074
5 9·52
6 3·263
7 8·947
8 15·63
9 4·453
10 0·78

Round to the nearest:
a) pound
b) 10p.

11 £3·93
12 £5·28
13 £9·46
14 £14·73
15 £0·61
16 £2·09
17 £6·54
18 £3·37
19 £8·82
20 £11·15

Approximate by rounding to the nearest whole number.

21 57·53 + 18·35
22 32·92 + 24·74
23 75·29 − 16·08
24 51·16 − 9·81
25 14·62 × 8
26 6·49 × 12
27 44·7 ÷ 5
28 68·51 ÷ 3

C

Round to the nearest:
a) hundredth
b) tenth.

1 0·263
2 3·745
3 1·452
4 0·179
5 7·824
6 2·397
7 0·036
8 4·981
9 8·505
10 5·658

Round to the nearest:
a) 10 grams
b) 100 grams.

11 6·738 kg
12 2·351 kg
13 0·915 kg
14 5·287 kg
15 1·594 kg
16 0·472 kg
17 3·066 kg
18 7·643 kg
19 0·959 kg
20 4·125 kg

Approximate by rounding to the nearest tenth.

21 6·548 + 3·97
22 4·39 + 2·751
23 9·605 − 1·82
24 7·48 − 3·236
25 8·06 × 7
26 4·71 × 9
27 6·35 ÷ 4
28 7·825 ÷ 6

TARGET To compare numbers with up to three decimal places.

Compare the highest value digits first
and then the next highest, and so on.

Example

Which number is larger, $0.6 = 0.6$
0.613 or 0.631? $0.01 < 0.03$

Answer *0.631 is larger.*

Add zeros to give each number the
same number of decimal places.

Example

Which number is larger,   0.270
0.27 or 0.072?   0.072

Answer *0.27 is larger.*

A

Copy and complete by writing < or > in the box.

1 3.5 ☐ 3.7
2 4.26 ☐ 4.6
3 6.6 ☐ 6.11
4 9.88 ☐ 8.99
5 3.45 ☐ 4.53

6 7.8 ☐ 7.18
7 9.42 ☐ 9.24
8 1.13 ☐ 1.3
9 5.66 ☐ 6.05
10 2.75 ☐ 2.8

What number lies halfway between:

11 0.35 and 0.39
12 1.6 and 1.7
13 4.2 and 5
14 1 and 1.5
15 8.72 and 8.92

16 3 and 3.3
17 1.8 and 2.2
18 6.34 and 6.44
19 0.96 and 1
20 2.5 and 2.8?

B

Write < or > in each box.

1 0.144 ☐ 0.411
2 0.5 ☐ 0.49
3 0.993 ☐ 0.939
4 0.417 ☐ 0.47
5 2.55 ☐ 0.258

6 0.061 ☐ 0.16
7 0.734 ☐ 0.674
8 0.376 ☐ 1.38
9 0.88 ☐ 0.808
10 0.626 ☐ 0.662

What number lies halfway between:

11 0.388 and 0.39
12 5.13 and 5.18
13 0.294 and 0.3
14 0.52 and 0.55

15 0.844 and 0.848
16 0.62 and 0.63
17 1.991 and 1.999
18 0.11 and 0.18?

Write these numbers in order, smallest first.

19 0.636, 0.366, 0.633, 0.363
20 0.404, 0.004, 0.444, 0.044
21 1.89, 1.99, 1.88, 1.98
22 0.275, 0.277, 0.257, 0.255

C

What number lies halfway between:

1 1.394 and 1.4
2 5.46 and 5.51
3 1.678 and 1.69
4 0.132 and 0.552

5 2.8 and 2.83
6 3 and 3.25
7 1.72 and 1.73
8 0.67 and 0.8?

Arrange these numbers in ascending order.

9 92.2, 9.25, 0.99, 9.225, 0.952
10 3.47, 4.73, 3.417, 4.137, 3.174
11 6.118, 1.186, 1.6, 6.18, 1.81
12 0.13, 1.023, 0.113, 1.03, 0.123

Give the next five numbers in each sequence.

13 0.01   0.03   0.05   0.07   0.09
14 0.16   0.15   0.14   0.13   0.12
15 0.9   0.92   0.94   0.96   0.98
16 1.2   1.18   1.16   1.14   1.12
17 0.005   0.01   0.015   0.02   0.025
18 1.75   1.65   1.55   1.45   1.35

TARGET   To order numbers with up to three decimal places.

Example

Arrange these numbers in ascending order.	Write in columns	Put in zeros	Arrange in order
2·32, 2, 2·232, 2·3	2·32	2·320	2, 2·232, 2·3, 2·32
	2	2·000	
	2·232	2·232	
	2·3	2·300	

A

Give the next five numbers in each sequence.

1. 0·01, 0·02, 0·03, 0·04, 0·05
2. 0·93, 0·94, 0·95, 0·96, 0·97
3. 0·02, 0·04, 0·06, 0·08, 0·1
4. 0·05, 0·1, 0·15, 0·2, 0·25
5. 1·12, 1·1, 1·08, 1·06, 1·04

Arrange these decimals in order, smallest first.

6. 1·53, 3·15, 1·33, 1·35
7. 5·61, 6·51, 15·6, 5·16
8. 2·78, 0·78, 2·07, 0·87
9. 7·23, 7·33, 7·22, 7·32
10. 6·49, 4·96, 6·94, 4·69

B

Arrange these decimals in ascending order.

1. 3·85, 3·58, 0·853, 5·38
2. 4·29, 4·229, 2·94, 2·492
3. 1·667, 6·17, 1·676, 1·67
4. 3·46, 3·446, 4·343, 4·334

Give the next five terms in each sequence.

5. 0·993, 0·994, 0·995, 0·996, 0·997
6. 0·8, 0·75, 0·7, 0·65, 0·6
7. 1·111, 1·113, 1·115, 1·117, 1·119
8. 0·465, 0·47, 0·475, 0·48, 0·485
9. Copy the line and locate the numbers.

0·95	0·975	0·935
0·985	0·92	0·96

0·9 _____ 1·0

C

Arrange these decimals in ascending order.

1. 3·37, 3·77, 3·337, 3·377, 3·737
2. 6·446, 6·66, 6·44, 6·664, 6·4
3. 2·55, 2·225, 2·522, 2·25, 2·525
4. 9·989, 9·898, 9·888, 9·99, 9·89

Give the next five terms in each sequence.

5. 0·986, 0·988, 0·99, 0·992, 0·994
6. 0·407, 0·406, 0·405, 0·404, 0·403
7. 1·965, 1·97, 1·975, 1·98, 1·985
8. 3·019, 3·016, 3·013, 3·01, 3·007
9. Copy the line and locate the numbers.

2·005	1·996	2·008
1·993	2·001	1·999

1·99 _____ 2·01

TARGET To practise adding and subtracting decimals mentally.

It can help to imagine missing zeros.

Examples

1 − 0·39   1·00 − 0·39   8·5 − 1·46   8·50 − 1·46
           Answer 0·61   Answer 7·04

A
Copy and complete.

1 0·1 + ☐ = 1
2 0·7 + ☐ = 1
3 0·5 + ☐ = 1
4 1 − ☐ = 0·2
5 1 − ☐ = 0·4
6 1 − ☐ = 0·9
7 0·35 + ☐ = 1
8 0·75 + ☐ = 1
9 0·15 + ☐ = 1
10 1 − ☐ = 0·45
11 1 − ☐ = 0·95
12 1 − ☐ = 0·65
13 0·6 + ☐ = 0·8
14 1·2 + ☐ = 1·6
15 0·3 + ☐ = 0·9
16 ☐ + 0·4 = 2·75
17 ☐ + 1·43 = 1·5
18 ☐ + 0·3 = 3·82
19 0·9 − 0·2 = ☐
20 2·6 − 0·37 = ☐
21 1·8 − ☐ = 1·4
22 3·51 − ☐ = 3·3
23 ☐ − 0·5 = 0·2
24 ☐ − 0·49 = 1·6

B
Make 1.

1 0·26 + ☐
2 0·83 + ☐
3 0·45 + ☐
4 ☐ + 0·79
5 ☐ + 0·12
6 ☐ + 0·64
7 0·37 + ☐
8 0·91 + ☐
9 0·08 + ☐
10 ☐ + 0·53
11 ☐ + 0·72
12 ☐ + 0·29
13 0·32 + ☐
14 0·87 + ☐
15 0·41 + ☐
16 ☐ + 0·69
17 ☐ + 0·16
18 ☐ + 0·73
19 0·98 + ☐
20 0·24 + ☐
21 0·57 + ☐
22 ☐ + 0·05
23 ☐ + 0·86
24 ☐ + 0·31

Work out

25 1·4 + 0·83
26 3·716 + 0·3
27 6·5 + 0·95
28 3·58 − 0·9
29 1·325 − 0·52
30 5·4 − 0·14
31 2·6 + 0·57
32 4·9 + 0·436
33 5·18 + 0·721
34 4·7 − 0·08
35 9·22 − 0·7
36 8·093 − 4
37 2·4 + 0·65
38 1·735 + 0·9
39 5·31 + 0·282
40 6·489 − 2·05
41 7 − 0·36
42 1·6 − 0·75
43 3 + 0·819
44 8·92 + 1·2
45 4·7 + 0·637
46 2·39 − 0·9
47 7·1 − 0·025
48 4·24 − 0·111

C
Copy and complete.

1 0·625 + ☐ = 1
2 0·185 + ☐ = 1
3 0·935 + ☐ = 1
4 1 − ☐ = 0·815
5 1 − ☐ = 0·095
6 1 − ☐ = 0·275
7 0·755 + ☐ = 1
8 0·565 + ☐ = 1
9 0·345 + ☐ = 1
10 1 − ☐ = 0·435
11 1 − ☐ = 0·905
12 1 − ☐ = 0·155
13 3·15 = 2·108 + ☐
14 4·3 = ☐ + 0·81
15 7·527 = 6·9 + ☐
16 5·84 = ☐ + 0·404
17 8 = 7·725 + ☐
18 2·409 = ☐ + 0·6
19 5 − ☐ = 4·299
20 ☐ − 0·7 = 6·58
21 9·46 − ☐ = 8·9
22 ☐ − 0·92 = 1·845
23 8·135 − ☐ = 7·53
24 ☐ − 0·625 = 3

TARGET To count using fractions.

Examples

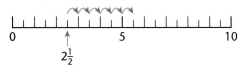

$2\frac{1}{2}$

Count on six steps of one half from $2\frac{1}{2}$.

Answer $2\frac{1}{2}$, 3, $3\frac{1}{2}$, 4, $4\frac{1}{2}$, 5, $5\frac{1}{2}$

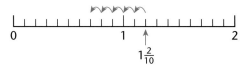

$1\frac{2}{10}$

Count back five steps of one tenth from $1\frac{2}{10}$.

Answer $1\frac{2}{10}$, $1\frac{1}{10}$, 1, $\frac{9}{10}$, $\frac{8}{10}$, $\frac{7}{10}$

A

Give the first six numbers.

1 Count on in tenths from 0.

2 Count on in twelfths from $\frac{4}{12}$.

3 Count on in halves from $5\frac{1}{2}$.

4 Count on in eighths from $\frac{2}{8}$.

5 Count on in quarters from $2\frac{1}{4}$.

6 Count on in sixths from 0.

Count back to 0:

7 in thirds from 2

8 in fifths from 1

9 in halves from 4

10 in tenths from $\frac{7}{10}$

11 in sevenths from 1

12 in quarters from $1\frac{1}{2}$.

B

Give the first six numbers.

1 Count on in steps of $\frac{1}{6}$ from $\frac{3}{6}$.

2 Count on in steps of $\frac{1}{10}$ from $\frac{5}{10}$.

3 Count on in steps of $\frac{1}{12}$ from $\frac{8}{12}$.

4 Count on in steps of $\frac{2}{9}$ from 0.

5 Count on in steps of $\frac{2}{5}$ from 0.

6 Count on in steps of $\frac{3}{4}$ from 0.

Count back six steps:

7 of one eighth from $1\frac{4}{8}$

8 of two thirds from 4

9 of one fifth from 2

10 of one half from $3\frac{3}{4}$

11 of two tenths from $1\frac{6}{10}$

12 of three twelfths from $1\frac{9}{12}$.

C

Copy and complete each sequence.

1 $1\frac{2}{5}$ $1\frac{4}{5}$ ☐ ☐ 3 ☐

2 ☐ $1\frac{6}{8}$ ☐ 1 ☐ $\frac{2}{8}$

3 $\frac{5}{7}$ ☐ $1\frac{2}{7}$ ☐ ☐ $2\frac{1}{7}$

4 $5\frac{1}{4}$ ☐ $6\frac{3}{4}$ $7\frac{1}{2}$ ☐ ☐

5 ☐ ☐ $2\frac{2}{3}$ 4 $5\frac{1}{3}$ ☐

6 ☐ $1\frac{4}{9}$ ☐ 1 ☐ $\frac{5}{9}$

Copy and complete.

7 $\frac{1}{3} \times 8 = $ ☐

8 $\frac{2}{5} \times 6 = $ ☐

9 $\frac{4}{10} \times $ ☐ $ = 2\frac{8}{10}$

10 $\frac{3}{8} \times $ ☐ $ = 1\frac{7}{8}$

11 ☐ $ \times 4 = 3$

12 ☐ $ \times 7 = 2\frac{11}{12}$

13 $\frac{1}{7} \times 12 = $ ☐

14 $\frac{3}{11} \times 4 = $ ☐

15 $\frac{2}{3} \times $ ☐ $ = 3\frac{1}{3}$

16 $\frac{5}{8} \times $ ☐ $ = 5$

17 ☐ $ \times 7 = 1\frac{5}{9}$

18 ☐ $ \times 6 = 3\frac{3}{5}$

TARGET   To count on and back in decimal steps.

Examples

Start at 0.
Count on four steps of 0·8

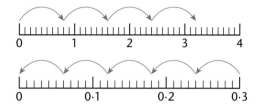

Answer *3·2*

Count back in steps
of 0·06 from 0·3

Answer *5 steps*

A

Write out each sequence.
Start at 0 each time.

1 Count on 4 steps of 0·2.

2 Count on 5 steps of 0·3.

3 Count on 6 steps of 0·5.

4 Count on 4 steps of 0·8.

5 Count on 7 steps of 0·4.

Write out each sequence.

6 Count back in steps of 0·2 from 1·6.

7 Count back in steps of 0·3 from 2·1.

8 Count back in steps of 0·5 from 3·5.

9 Count back in steps of 0·7 from 2·1.

10 Count back in steps of 0·9 from 1·8.

11 Count back in steps of 0·6 from 2·4.

B

Complete each sequence.

1 2·4 3·2 ☐ ☐ ☐ 6·4

2 5·4 ☐ ☐ ☐ 3·0 2·4

3 0·05 0·1 0·15 ☐ ☐ ☐

4 0·18 0·16 0·14 ☐ ☐ ☐

5 0·22 ☐ 0·3 ☐ 0·38 ☐

Write out each sequence.

6 Count on seven steps of 0·6 from 0.

7 Count back six steps of 0·8 from 7·2.

8 Count on five steps of 0·9 from 0.

9 Count back eight steps of 0·5 from 6·0.

10 Count on nine steps of 0·3 from 0.

C

Complete each sequence.

1 ☐ 0·5 ☐ 1·0 ☐ 1·5

2 ☐ 0·95 ☐ 0·81 ☐ 0·67

3 ☐ 0·01 ☐ 0·02 ☐ 0·03

4 ☐ 1·5 ☐ 3·0 ☐ 4·5

5 ☐ 0·05 ☐ 0·1 ☐ 0·15

Copy and complete.

6 0·02 × ☐ = 0·18

7 0·06 × ☐ = 0·48

8 0·07 × ☐ = 0·49

9 0·005 × ☐ = 0·03

10 0·008 × ☐ = 0·32

Copy and complete.

11 0·21 ÷ ☐ = 0·03

12 0·72 ÷ ☐ = 0·09

13 0·4 ÷ ☐ = 0·05

14 0·063 ÷ ☐ = 0·007

15 0·04 ÷ ☐ = 0·008

TARGET   To count through zero using decimals and fractions.

Examples

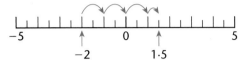

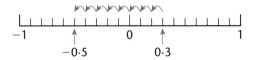

Count on 3·5 from −2.
Answer *1·5*

Count back 0·8 from 0·3.
Answer *−0·5*

A

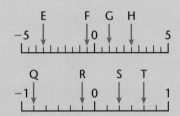

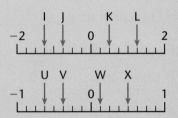

1 Give the value of each of the letters A–L in decimals.

2 Give the value of each of the letters M–X in mixed numbers and fractions.

B

Look at the number lines in Section A.

1 Count on 0·6 from B.

2 Count on $\frac{5}{6}$ from R.

3 Count on 0·75 from J.

4 Count back 1 from O.

5 Count back 1·5 from G.

6 Count back $\frac{6}{8}$ from W.

7 Count on $1\frac{1}{3}$ from N.

8 Count on 2·5 from F.

9 Count on 1 from V.

10 Count back 0·8 from C.

11 Count back $\frac{5}{6}$ from S.

12 Count back 1·5 from K.

C

Look at the number lines in Section A.

1 Count on 2 from M.

2 Count on 5 from E.

3 Count on $1\frac{3}{8}$ from U.

4 Count back 1·4 from D.

5 Count back $1\frac{1}{6}$ from T.

6 Count back 2·5 from L.

7 Count on 0·9 from A.

8 Count on $1\frac{4}{6}$ from Q.

9 Count on 2·75 from I.

10 Count back $1\frac{2}{3}$ from P.

11 Count back 4 from H.

12 Count back $1\frac{3}{8}$ from X.

TARGET To solve number puzzles involving decimals.

A

In an addition pyramid, pairs of numbers are added together to make the number above them. (See page 109.)

Copy and complete the addition pyramids.

1

2·5 ☐

0·8   1·7   1·6

2
☐

☐   ☐

1·4   0·7   0·9

3
☐

1·7   ☐

☐   1·2   0·6

4
8·3

4   ☐

1·5   ☐   ☐

5
15

☐   8·6

2·9   ☐   ☐

B

In an arithmagon the pair of numbers at the end of each side are added together to give the number between them. (See page 22.)

Find the missing numbers.

1
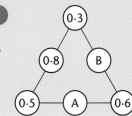

0·3 / 0·8 / B / 0·5 / A / 0·6

2
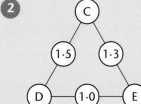

C / 1·5 / 1·3 / D / 1·0 / E

3

F / 2·1 / 2·4 / G / 1·9 / H

4
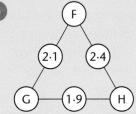

I / 3·3 / 2·9 / J / 3·8 / K

C

In a magic square the sum of each row, column and diagonal is the same. (See page 23.)

Copy and complete the magic squares.

1

0·6		
	0·9	
	0·7	1·2

2

	1·8	1·5
	1·4	
	1	

3

1·7	2·2	1·5
2·1		

4

1·8		2·6
	2·3	
2		

TARGET   To add decimals with the same number of decimal places.

Line up the decimal points and add.

Examples

$3 \cdot 592 + 1 \cdot 487$

```
  3·592
+ 1·487
───────
  5·079
  ₁ ₁
```

$29 \cdot 46 + 7 \cdot 56$

```
  29·46
+  7·56
───────
  37·02
  ₁ ₁ ₁
```

A

Copy and complete.

1
```
   57·3
+ 26·8
```

2
```
  5·92
+ 2·54
```

3
```
  8·48
+ 3·67
```

4
```
  16·63
+  4·66
```

5
```
  29·59
+  7·83
```

6
```
  18·36
+  6·95
```

7
```
  38·58
+ 15·62
```

8
```
  53·27
+ 34·84
```

9
```
  49·45
+ 26·91
```

10
```
  25·77
+ 17·33
```

11 A plant is 24·8 cm tall. In the following week it grows a further 17·5 cm. How tall is the plant at the end of the week?

12 Algy holds his breath for 36·49 seconds. Audrey holds it 8·27 seconds longer. How long does Audrey hold her breath?

B

Copy and complete.

1
```
  9·581
+ 3·942
```

2
```
  13·96
+  7·45
```

3
```
  6·493
+ 2·574
```

4
```
  5·257
+ 3·956
```

5
```
  28·87
+ 14·67
```

6
```
  37·85
+  4·35
```

7
```
  82·39
+ 26·73
```

8
```
  4·768
+ 3·999
```

9
```
  9·645
+ 6·076
```

10
```
  6·569
+ 1·472
```

11 Jason caught 7·419 kg of fish. Ray caught 4·863 kg more. How much fish did Ray catch?

12 Jodie walks 8·275 km in the morning and 6·185 km in the afternoon. How far has she walked altogether?

13 There is 77·28 litres of water in a puddle. After a short shower there is a further 9·36 litres. How much water is in the puddle after the shower?

C

Set out as in the examples.

1 $13 \cdot 28 + 8 \cdot 625$

2 $8 \cdot 956 + 36 \cdot 8$

3 $145 \cdot 7 + 9 \cdot 83$

4 $7 \cdot 573 + 58 \cdot 75$

5 $44 \cdot 69 + 7 \cdot 894$

6 $249 \cdot 3 + 15 \cdot 86$

7 $6 \cdot 847 + 23 \cdot 48$

8 $118 \cdot 5 + 9 \cdot 805$

9 $17 \cdot 93 + 2 \cdot 751$

10 $365 \cdot 68 + 2 \cdot 382$

11 $4 \cdot 976 + 19 \cdot 254$

12 $28 \cdot 57 + 3 \cdot 839$

13 A racing car drives 8·675 km during warm up laps and 324·5 km in the race. How far does the car travel altogether?

14 A horse trough holds 35·66 litres of water. 7·925 litres is added. How much water is in the trough?

15 A motorbike weighs 529·88 kg. Its rider weighs 78·134 kg. What is the combined weight of bike and rider?

TARGET   To add decimals with different numbers of decimal places.

Line up the decimal points when setting out.

Example
Add 18·75 and 6·925.

```
   18·75
+   6·925
   25·675
    1 1
```

A
Copy and complete.

1
```
    546·1
+    23·6
```

7
```
    56·77
+   23·46
```

2
```
    192·7
+    56·8
```

8
```
    71·83
+   27·18
```

3
```
    432·9
+   126·3
```

9
```
    3·947
+   1·759
```

4
```
    764·8
+   219·2
```

10
```
    6·574
+   4·957
```

5
```
    35·63
+   34·39
```

11
```
    8·946
+   1·645
```

6
```
    28·56
+   15·48
```

12
```
    4·758
+   3·369
```

13 Fiona buys a dress for £86·49 and shoes for £27·75. How much does she spend altogether?

14 Mary's car has a mileage of 926·5 miles at the start of May. During the month she drives 487·6 miles. What is the car's mileage at the end of May?

B
Set out as in the examples.

1 35·9 + 8·314

2 4·275 + 146·8

3 23·76 + 4·645

4 658·7 + 61·59

5 19·943 + 26·37

6 159·6 + 97·82

7 6·744 + 783·9

8 579·63 + 8·157

9 498·5 + 92·91

10 96·475 + 43·86

11 79·359 + 555·7

12 134·794 + 25·78

13 In an endurance event competitors cycle 52·38 km and run 18·675 km. What is the total length of the course?

14 A mineshaft is 638·7 m deep. The miners drill down a further 47·55 m. How deep is the shaft now?

C
Set out correctly and work out.

1
```
    297·56
     17·9
+   28·643
```

6
```
    8·764
   41·97
+ 157·8
```

2
```
    14·238
   268·6
+    5·948
```

7
```
   129·75
    0·385
+  36·59
```

3
```
    17·57
   125·8
+   2·944
```

8
```
   186·3
    54·842
+ 348·47
```

4
```
   148·66
    26·9
+   9·783
```

9
```
   231·36
    89·677
+   4·599
```

5
```
    24·638
     3·247
+  616·57
```

10
```
    27·745
     6·558
+  318·96
```

11 Grant buys 3·428 kg of potatoes, 1·29 kg of carrots and 0·375 kg of onions. What is the total weight of his shopping?

12 A dairy produces 87·5 litres of milk on Monday, 117·225 litres on Tuesday and 93·75 litres on Wednesday. How much milk is produced in the three days altogether?

TARGET   To subtract decimals with the same number of decimal places.

Line up the decimal points and subtract.

Examples

$3·62 - 1·78$

$$\begin{array}{r} {}^{2}\,{}^{15}{}^{1} \\ \cancel{3}·\cancel{6}2 \\ -1·78 \\ \hline 1·84 \end{array}$$

$9·318 - 0·425$

$$\begin{array}{r} {}^{8}\,{}^{12}{}^{1} \\ \cancel{9}·\cancel{3}18 \\ -0·425 \\ \hline 8·893 \end{array}$$

A

Copy and complete.

1. $\begin{array}{r} 45·6 \\ -13·9 \\ \hline \end{array}$
6. $\begin{array}{r} 6·63 \\ -2·28 \\ \hline \end{array}$

2. $\begin{array}{r} 38·4 \\ -22·5 \\ \hline \end{array}$
7. $\begin{array}{r} 2·49 \\ -0·83 \\ \hline \end{array}$

3. $\begin{array}{r} 73·7 \\ -56·3 \\ \hline \end{array}$
8. $\begin{array}{r} 4·75 \\ -3·16 \\ \hline \end{array}$

4. $\begin{array}{r} 9·92 \\ -4·74 \\ \hline \end{array}$
9. $\begin{array}{r} 7·08 \\ -2·62 \\ \hline \end{array}$

5. $\begin{array}{r} 8·15 \\ -3·48 \\ \hline \end{array}$
10. $\begin{array}{r} 8·52 \\ -5·45 \\ \hline \end{array}$

11. Yalda has £9·27. She spends £4·58. How much does she have left?

12. A rope is 31·5 m long. 17·4 m is cut off. How much rope is left?

13. Keith has 5·91 litres of paint. He uses 2·62 litres. How much is left?

14. A large bag of flour weighs 4·25 kg. A smaller bag weighs 1·75 kg less. What is the weight of the smaller bag?

B

Copy and complete.

1. $\begin{array}{r} 29·35 \\ -16·72 \\ \hline \end{array}$
6. $\begin{array}{r} 8·251 \\ -5·434 \\ \hline \end{array}$

2. $\begin{array}{r} 7·573 \\ -3·748 \\ \hline \end{array}$
7. $\begin{array}{r} 4·718 \\ -1·657 \\ \hline \end{array}$

3. $\begin{array}{r} 92·82 \\ -19·36 \\ \hline \end{array}$
8. $\begin{array}{r} 6·464 \\ -5·372 \\ \hline \end{array}$

4. $\begin{array}{r} 5·066 \\ -3·954 \\ \hline \end{array}$
9. $\begin{array}{r} 1·923 \\ -0·831 \\ \hline \end{array}$

5. $\begin{array}{r} 34·17 \\ -27·97 \\ \hline \end{array}$
10. $\begin{array}{r} 4·055 \\ -3·396 \\ \hline \end{array}$

11. It takes Kabir 82·1 seconds to solve a puzzle. Melody takes 14·19 fewer seconds. How long does Melody take to solve the puzzle?

12. A greengrocer has 87·46 kg of pears. 58·65 kg are sold. How much is left?

13. The 18 hole golf course is 6·307 km long. The 9 hole course is 2·955 km long. How much longer is the 18 hole course?

C

Set out as in the examples.

1. $14·36 - 6·54$
2. $9·82 - 4·763$
3. $25·47 - 1·95$
4. $7·61 - 5·834$
5. $60·2 - 0·81$
6. $8·749 - 2·86$
7. $31·2 - 5·75$
8. $6·53 - 2·146$
9. $92·07 - 65·22$
10. $13·91 - 7·588$
11. $4·538 - 2·59$
12. $71·33 - 9·336$

13. An oxygen tank holds 12·125 litres of liquid oxygen. 7·58 litres is used. How much oxygen is left?

14. A farm has an area of 34·2 square kilometres. 18·47 km² is grazing land. How much of the farm is not grazing land?

15. A bag of compost holds 73·5 kg. 8·825 kg is used. How much is left?

TARGET   To subtract decimals with different numbers of decimal places.

When setting out line up the decimal points and put in the missing zeros.

Example

Subtract 0·625 from 27·45.

$$\begin{array}{r} {\scriptstyle 6\ \ 1\ 4\ 1} \\ 2\cancel{7}\cdot4\cancel{5}0 \\ -\ \ \ 0\cdot625 \\ \hline 26\cdot825 \end{array}$$

A

Work out

1   4·73
    − 2·36

2   61·8
    − 35·2

3   7·54
    − 6·35

4   80·9
    − 47·4

5   5·62
    − 1·47

6   95·9
    − 38·7

7   67·1
    − 55·7

8   83·8
    − 29·6

9   76·0
    − 41·3

10   52·5
    − 39·2

11   91·7
    − 74·2

12   48·3
    − 35·7

13 The upper playground is 52·3 m long. The lower playground is 38·6 m long. How much longer is the upper playground?

14 Ross has £82·26. He spends £43·89. How much does he have left?

15 A sack of potatoes weighs 32·7 kg. 14·6 kg is used. How much is left?

B

Work out

1   56·2
    − 24·63

2   3·374
    − 1·56

3   17·81
    − 3·649

4   92·8
    − 53·25

5   4·736
    − 3·19

6   80·9
    − 23·78

7   5·17
    − 3·852

8   54·636
    − 25·7

9   7·92
    − 6·595

10   91·44
    − 25·461

11   76·4
    − 18·35

12   6·245
    − 4·75

13 A bath uses 92·6 litres of water. A shower uses 45·35 litres. How much less water is used by the shower?

14 A footpath is 417·28 km long. In two days Rhoda walks 53·7 km. How much further does she have to go to complete the walk?

15 An ice cream tub holds 1·535 litres. 0·865 litres is used: How much is left?

C

Set out as in the examples.

1 6·512 − 0·837

2 5·635 − 2·52

3 72·1 − 19·41

4 4·706 − 2·77

5 85·27 − 9·684

6 16·4 − 2·935

7 9·619 − 5·73

8 11·03 − 6·472

9 4·925 − 1·96

10 12·58 − 5·734

11 3·348 − 1·476

12 50·26 − 3·822

13 The summit of Ben Nevis is 1·344 km above sea level. The highest mountain in England, Scafell Pike, has a height of 0·977 km. How much higher is the Scottish mountain?

14 A large parcel weighs 2·51 kg. A smaller one is 0·716 kg lighter. What is the weight of the smaller parcel?

TARGET **To write fractions and decimals as percentages.**

Per cent means out of 100.
Percentages are fractions with a denominator of 100.
The symbol for per cent is %.

Example

$$\frac{37}{100} = 0{\cdot}37 = 37\%$$

To express fractions as percentages, change them to equivalent fractions with denominators of 100.

Examples

$$\frac{9}{10} = \frac{90}{100} = 90\% \qquad \frac{1}{4} = \frac{25}{100} = 25\%$$

To express decimals as percentages, multiply by 100.

Examples
$$0{\cdot}6 = (0{\cdot}6 \times 100)\% = 60\%$$
$$0{\cdot}42 = (0{\cdot}42 \times 100)\% = 42\%$$

It is useful to know that:
$$\frac{1}{100} = 0{\cdot}01 = 1\%, \ \frac{2}{100} = 0{\cdot}02 = 2\%, \text{ etc.}$$

$$\frac{1}{10} = 0{\cdot}1 = 10\%, \ \frac{2}{10} = 0{\cdot}2 = 20\%, \text{ etc.}$$

$$\frac{1}{4} = 25\%, \ \frac{1}{2} = 50\%, \ \frac{3}{4} = 75\%.$$

A

Use 10 × 10 grids of small squares.
Shade in:

1 10 squares   **3** 40 squares

2 3 squares   **4** 8 squares

Express each shaded area as:

a) a fraction
b) a decimal
c) a percentage.

5 Copy and complete the table.

Fraction	Decimal	Percentage
$\frac{1}{10}$		
$\frac{1}{2}$		
$\frac{1}{100}$		
$\frac{3}{10}$		
1		
	0·25	
	0·6	
	0·17	
	0·9	
	0·75	

Copy the sentences changing each fraction to a percentage.

6 Vicki and Jay each had half of the sweets.

7 When the bus stopped one quarter of the passengers got off.

8 Seven hundredths of the apples were rotten.

9 The postman had completed three quarters of his round.

10 Seven tenths of the children at the party were 10 years old.

B

Express each shaded area as:
a) a fraction
b) a decimal
c) a percentage.

1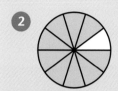

2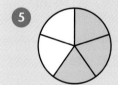

3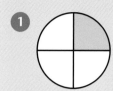

4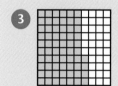

5

6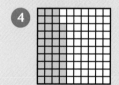

7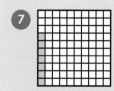

8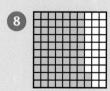

9

10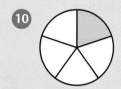

11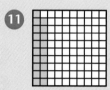

12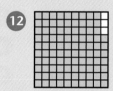

13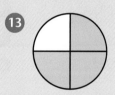

14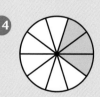

15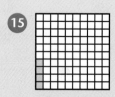

16

C

Write each fraction as
a) a decimal
b) a percentage.

1 $\frac{3}{10}$ **5** $\frac{8}{10}$ **9** $\frac{1}{20}$

2 $\frac{79}{100}$ **6** $\frac{3}{4}$ **10** $\frac{4}{5}$

3 $\frac{1}{2}$ **7** $\frac{1}{5}$ **11** $\frac{39}{50}$

4 $\frac{7}{10}$ **8** $\frac{1}{4}$ **12** $\frac{21}{25}$

Write each percentage as:
a) a fraction in its simplest form
b) a decimal.

13 10%   **17** 47%   **21** 60%

14 1%   **18** 90%   **22** 50%

15 40%   **19** 25%   **23** 4%

16 75%   **20** 3%   **24** 15%

25 17% of the pupils at a school came by bus. What percentage did not come by bus?

26 Hats were worn by 85% of the ladies at a wedding. What percentage did not wear hats?

27 Two fifths of the milk sold in a shop was skimmed milk and 32% was semi skimmed. What percentage was full fat milk?

28 One quarter of the audience at a film were women. 19% were men. What percentage were children?

29 Copy and complete the table.

Item	Total made	Sold	%age sold	%age unsold
Loaves	100	83		
Rolls	200	154		
Pies	25	14		
Pasties	20	13		
Cakes	50	46		

TARGET To make connections between fractions, decimals and percentages.

Examples

$\frac{1}{10} = 0.1 = 10\%$ $\frac{1}{100} = 0.01 = 1\%$ $\frac{1}{4} = 0.25 = 25\%$

$\frac{2}{10} = 0.2 = 20\%$ $\frac{2}{100} = 0.02 = 2\%$ $\frac{1}{2} = 0.5 = 50\%$

$\frac{3}{10} = 0.3 = 30\%$ $\frac{3}{100} = 0.03 = 3\%$ $\frac{3}{4} = 0.75 = 75\%$

and so on   and so on

A

Write True or False.

1. $\frac{3}{10} = 0.3$
2. $\frac{1}{2} = 0.2$
3. $\frac{1}{4} = 25\%$
4. $\frac{7}{10} = 70\%$
5. $0.4 = \frac{1}{4}$
6. $0.75 = \frac{3}{4}$
7. $0.1 = 10\%$
8. $0.8 = 8\%$
9. $6\% = \frac{6}{100}$
10. $50\% = \frac{1}{2}$
11. $9\% = \frac{9}{10}$
12. $25\% = \frac{2}{5}$

13. Match each fraction with either a decimal or a percentage.

$\frac{6}{10}$	75%
$\frac{34}{100}$	0.12
$\frac{1}{2}$	6%
$\frac{12}{100}$	0.34
$\frac{6}{100}$	50%
$\frac{3}{4}$	0.6

B

Write as fractions.

1. 0.32
2. 0.5
3. 0.7
4. 0.65
5. 25%
6. 8%
7. 20%
8. 47%

Write as decimals.

9. $\frac{75}{100}$
10. $\frac{71}{100}$
11. $\frac{4}{10}$
12. $\frac{9}{100}$
13. 54%
14. 50%
15. 86%
16. 90%

Write as percentages.

17. $\frac{15}{100}$
18. $\frac{3}{10}$
19. $\frac{1}{4}$
20. $\frac{68}{100}$
21. 0.02
22. 0.1
23. 0.75
24. 0.99

Give the answer as a decimal.

25. $\frac{37}{100} + 0.2$
26. $0.95 - \frac{1}{2}$
27. $\frac{4}{10} + 0.33$
28. $\frac{1}{4} - 0.06$

Give the answer as a percentage.

29. $\frac{3}{4} + 10\%$
30. $66\% - \frac{38}{100}$
31. $\frac{1}{4} + 9\%$
32. $92\% - \frac{4}{10}$

C

Write in ascending order.

1. $\frac{66}{100}$ 0.16 61%
2. 0.5 15% $\frac{1}{5}$
3. 61% $\frac{6}{10}$ 0.166
4. $\frac{3}{4}$ 0.43 40%
5. 0.8 38% $\frac{3}{8}$
6. 21% $\frac{2}{10}$ 0.201
7. $\frac{1}{4}$ 0.14 41%
8. 0.19 9% $\frac{1}{9}$

Give the answer as a percentage.

9. $0.4 + \frac{3}{10}$
10. $\frac{3}{4} - 0.19$
11. $0.49 + \frac{1}{2}$
12. $\frac{58}{100} - 0.38$

Give the answer as a decimal.

13. $\frac{6}{10} + 15\%$
14. $55\% - \frac{1}{4}$
15. $\frac{2}{5} + 2\%$
16. $10\% - \frac{3}{100}$

TARGET To find percentages of amounts and quantities.

Examples

10% of 40	30% of 40	25% of 40	5% of 40
$\frac{1}{10}$ of 40	(10% of 40) × 3	$\frac{1}{4}$ of 40	(10% of 40) ÷ 2
40 ÷ 10	4 × 3	40 ÷ 4	4 ÷ 2
4	12	10	2

A

Find 10% of:

1. 20
2. 70
3. 500
4. 140
5. 800
6. 300
7. 240
8. 900
9. 650
10. 410

Find 10% of:

11. 80p
12. 30p
13. £2·00
14. £7·50
15. £4·90
16. £1·70
17. £17·00
18. £0·20
19. £5·60
20. £8·10.

Find 10% of:

21. 60 mm
22. 90 kg
23. 400 ml
24. 110 cm
25. 830 m
26. 700 g
27. 350 ml
28. 280 km
29. 490 m
30. 120 kg.

31. A bag of flour weighs 850 g. 10% is used. How much flour is left?

B

Find
a) 10% of: b) 20% of:

1. 300
2. 90
3. £4·80
4. 620 m

Find
a) 10% of: b) 30% of:

5. 140
6. 2100
7. 700 ml
8. £12·50

Find
a) 25% of: b) 75% of:

9. 32
10. 600
11. £4·80
12. 10 m

Find

13. 20% of 160
14. 30% of 30
15. 50% of 2800
16. 25% of 64
17. 1% of 200
18. 40% of 450 g
19. 90% of £4·00
20. 75% of 36p
21. 60% of 1200 ml
22. 5% of £10·00

C

Find the new price if the price shown is reduced by:
a) 10% b) 5% c) 15%.

1. £25·00
2. £3·20
3. £70·00
4. £9·80

How much interest is paid into a savings account for each amount if the interest rate is:
a) 10% b) 1% c) 3%.

5. £540
6. £1900
7. £10 000
8. £216

Find

9. 1% of 5800
10. 5% of 4
11. 99% of 7000
12. 15% of 12
13. 2% of £79
14. 11% of £35
15. 95% of 600 g
16. 7% of 1 litre
17. 9% of 500 ml
18. 3% of 2 kg
19. 45% of 240 m
20. 21% of £30 000

TARGET To convert metric units of measure.

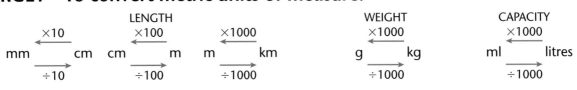

Examples

47 mm = 4·7 cm   138 cm = 1·38 m   790 m = 0·79 km   80 g = 0·08 kg   2650 ml = 2·65 ℓ

A

Copy and complete.

1. 8 mm = ☐ cm
2. 13 mm = ☐ cm
3. 7·5 cm = ☐ mm
4. 0·2 cm = ☐ mm

5. 30 cm = ☐ m
6. 200 cm = ☐ m
7. 0·6 m = ☐ cm
8. 1·7 m = ☐ cm

9. 400 m = ☐ km
10. 5900 m = ☐ km
11. 0·8 km = ☐ m
12. 6·5 km = ☐ m

13. 9000 g = ☐ kg
14. 4100 g = ☐ kg
15. 0·7 kg = ☐ g
16. 8·2 kg = ☐ g

17. 1300 ml = ☐ litres
18. 600 ml = ☐ litres
19. 3 litres = ☐ ml
20. 7·6 litres = ☐ ml

B

Copy and complete.

1. 24 mm = ☐ cm
2. 601 mm = ☐ cm
3. 5·9 cm = ☐ mm
4. 18·6 cm = ☐ mm

5. 472 cm = ☐ m
6. 95 cm = ☐ m
7. 3·13 m = ☐ cm
8. 0·08 m = ☐ cm

9. 1160 m = ☐ km
10. 30 m = ☐ km
11. 0·84 km = ☐ m
12. 3·02 km = ☐ m

13. 650 g = ☐ kg
14. 9280 g = ☐ kg
15. 0·01 kg = ☐ g
16. 0·96 kg = ☐ g

17. 70 ml = ☐ litres
18. 4130 ml = ☐ litres
19. 0·79 litres = ☐ ml
20. 8·54 litres = ☐ ml

C

Copy and complete.

1. 983 mm = ☐ m
2. 5841 mm = ☐ m
3. 0·027 m = ☐ mm
4. 0·306 m = ☐ mm

5. 1 cm = ☐ m
6. 3420 cm = ☐ m
7. 70 m = ☐ cm
8. 65·18 m = ☐ cm

9. 54 m = ☐ km
10. 2106 m = ☐ km
11. 0·673 km = ☐ m
12. 0·009 km = ☐ m

13. 1297 g = ☐ kg
14. 32 g = ☐ kg
15. 0·005 kg = ☐ g
16. 4·068 kg = ☐ g

17. 983 ml = ☐ litres
18. 5841 ml = ☐ litres
19. 0·027 litres = ☐ ml
20. 0·306 litres = ☐ ml

TARGET To convert between different units of metric measures.

Give the measurement indicated by each arrow in both required units.

A

Write as cm and mm.

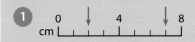

Write as litres and ml.

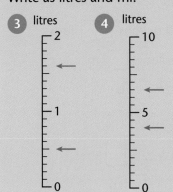

Write as kg and g.

Write as m and cm.

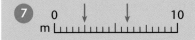

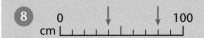

B

Write as cm and mm.

Write as litres and ml.

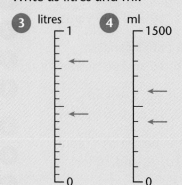

Write as kg and g.

Write as m and km.

C

Write as m and cm.

Write as litres and ml.

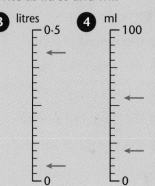

Write as kg and g.

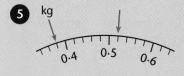

Write as km and m.

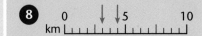

TARGET To understand and use common imperial measures and their metric equivalents.

These are the most commonly used imperial units and their metric equivalents.
The sign ≈ means 'is approximately equal to'.

Examples

LENGTH		WEIGHT	CAPACITY
1 inch ≈ 2·5 cm	1 mile ≈ 1·6 km	1 oz (ounce) ≈ 30 g	1 pint ≈ 0·6 litres
1 foot ≈ 30 cm	8 km ≈ 5 miles	1 kg ≈ 2·2 lb (pounds)	1 gallon ≈ 4·5 litres
1 yard ≈ 90 cm			

A

Which imperial unit would you use to measure:

1. a field's length
2. the weight of a cup
3. the width of a sea
4. a sink's capacity
5. the height of a fence
6. the weight of a dog
7. a bottle's capacity
8. the length of a pencil.

Copy and complete.

9. 10 inches ≈ ☐ cm
10. 2 pints ≈ ☐ litres
11. 3 miles ≈ ☐ km
12. 4·4 pounds ≈ ☐ kg
13. 6 feet ≈ ☐ cm
14. 2 gallons ≈ ☐ litres
15. 8 ounces ≈ ☐ g
16. 2 yards ≈ ☐ m
17. 4 inches ≈ ☐ cm
18. 10 pints ≈ ☐ litres
19. ☐ pounds ≈ 3 kg
20. 5 miles ≈ ☐ km

B

Choose the best estimate.

1. a golfer's drive
   2, 20 and 200 yards
2. a bath's capacity
   6, 16 and 60 gallons
3. an egg's weight
   2, 12 and 20 ounces
4. the height of a room
   10, 20 and 30 feet

Copy and complete.

5. 11 lb ≈ ☐ kg
6. 20 yards ≈ ☐ m
7. 15 pints ≈ ☐ litres
8. 8 inches ≈ ☐ cm
9. 100 miles ≈ ☐ km
10. 10 oz ≈ ☐ g
11. 3 gallons ≈ ☐ litres
12. 12 feet ≈ ☐ m
13. ☐ pounds ≈ 100 kg
14. 11 inches ≈ ☐ cm
15. 0·5 pints ≈ ☐ ml
16. ☐ miles ≈ 4 km

C

Copy and complete.

1. 12 inches ≈ ☐ cm
2. 5000 gallons ≈ ☐ litres
3. 55 miles ≈ ☐ km
4. 16 oz ≈ ☐ g
5. 75 feet ≈ ☐ m
6. 2·5 pints ≈ ☐ litres
7. 5·5 lb ≈ ☐ kg
8. 60 yards ≈ ☐ m
9. 90 gallons ≈ ☐ litres
10. 200 miles ≈ ☐ km
11. 0·25 oz ≈ ☐ g
12. 9 inches ≈ ☐ cm

13. To the nearest tenth of a litre, how many litres are there in:
    a) 7 gallons   c) 4 pints
    b) 50 gallons   d) 21 pints?

14. To the nearest tenth of a kilometre, how many kilometres are there in:
    a) 84 miles   c) 3000 yards
    b) 19 miles   d) 15 000 feet?

TARGET To practise using common imperial measures and their metric equivalents.

These are the most commonly used imperial units and their metric equivalents.
The sign ≈ means 'is approximately equal to'.

Examples

LENGTH
1 inch ≈ 2·5 cm   1 mile ≈ 1·6 km
1 foot ≈ 30 cm   8 km ≈ 5 miles
1 yard ≈ 90 cm

WEIGHT
1 oz (ounce) ≈ 30 g
1 kg ≈ 2·2 lb (pounds)

CAPACITY
1 pint ≈ 0·6 litres
1 gallon ≈ 4·5 litres

A

Which imperial unit would you use to measure:

1. the length of a worm
2. the capacity of a bowl
3. a wardrobe's height
4. a suitcase's weight
5. the distance between two cities
6. a lake's capacity
7. a corridor's length
8. a sparrow's weight

Copy and complete.

9. 2 miles ≈ ☐ km
10. 22 pounds ≈ ☐ kg
11. 7 pints ≈ ☐ litres
12. 3 inches ≈ ☐ cm
13. 5 yards ≈ ☐ m
14. 4 ounces ≈ ☐ g
15. 10 gallons ≈ ☐ litres
16. 10 feet ≈ ☐ m
17. ☐ pounds ≈ 5 kg
18. 10 miles ≈ ☐ km
19. 5 pints ≈ ☐ litres
20. 2 inches ≈ ☐ cm

B

Choose the best estimate.

1. Great Britain's length 60, 600 or 6000 miles
2. a cat's weight 11, 55 or 110 pounds
3. a ruler's length 2, 12 or 20 inches
4. a washing up bowl's capacity 1, 5 or 10 pints

Copy and complete.

5. 20 inches ≈ ☐ cm
6. 12 pints ≈ ☐ litres
7. 15 miles ≈ ☐ km
8. 6·6 lb ≈ ☐ kg
9. 7 feet ≈ ☐ m
10. 8 gallons ≈ ☐ litres
11. 12 oz ≈ ☐ g
12. 100 yards ≈ ☐ m
13. ☐ pounds ≈ 20 kg
14. 11 inches ≈ ☐ cm
15. ☐ pints ≈ 2·4 litres
16. ☐ miles ≈ 80 km

C

Copy and complete by putting > or < in the box.

1. 7 inches ☐ 18 cm
2. 1·5 gallons ☐ 6·5 litres
3. 240 miles ☐ 400 km
4. 7·5 oz ☐ 220 g
5. 28 000 feet ☐ 8 km
6. 3 pints ☐ 2 litres
7. 143 lb ☐ 66 kg
8. 25 yards ☐ 22 m
9. 4 gallons ☐ 20 litres
10. 35 miles ☐ 55 km
11. 9 oz ☐ 275 g
12. 25 inches ☐ 60 cm
13. 50 feet ☐ 15 m
14. 9 lb ☐ 4 kg
15. 40 yards ☐ 37 m
16. 50 pints ☐ 32 litres
17. Rewrite Questions 1 to 4 in Section B, changing each measurement to the metric equivalent.

TARGET To solve word problems involving conversion of units of length.

Example

The first steeplechase was 3·8 km long.
The next race was 630 m longer.
How long was the second race?

3·8 km = 3800 m
3800 + 630 = 4430
4430 m = 4·43 km
Answer: *4·43 km*

A

1. A running track is 400 m long. Carrie runs eight laps. How far is this in kilometres?

2. Last year Lee's foot was 14·5 cm long. This year it is 8 mm longer. How long is Lee's foot now?

3. A pipe is three metres long. Three 60 cm lengths are cut off. How long is the pipe which is left in metres?

4. Mark walks between home and school four times each day. He works out that he walks 2·8 km daily. How far is it from Mark's home to his school in metres?

5. A 10p coin is 2·4 cm wide. A 5p coin is 7 mm shorter. How wide is a 5p coin?

6. Carl is 1·25 m tall. His father is 40 cm taller. How tall is Carl's father?

B

1. A one pound coin is 3 mm thick. How tall is a stack of twelve £1 coins in centimetres?

2. The end of a garden is 12·4 m wide. There is a gate 80 cm wide exactly in the centre of the garden wall. How long is the wall either side of the gate?

3. Rolls of cable are 200 m long. 4·8 km of cable is needed. How many rolls are required?

4. A shadow is 14·2 cm long. Thirty minutes later it is 27 mm shorter. How long is the shadow now?

5. A rope is 5·3 m long. Four equal lengths are cut off. 3·7 m is left. How long are the four lengths in centimetres?

6. The course of a cross-country race is 2 laps of 1·4 km and 3 laps of 750 m. How long is the race?

C

1. A stamp is 26 mm long and 17 mm wide. What is the perimeter of the stamp in centimetres?

2. Wind turbines are spaced 150 m apart. There are 25 in a row. How long is the row in kilometres?

3. A pile of 25 books is 20 cm tall. How thick is each book in millimetres?

4. Square carpet tiles are 40 cm long. How many are needed to cover the floor of a room 6 m long and 4·8 m wide?

5. There are eighteen candles in a packet. Each candle is 12 cm long. What is the total length of the candles?

6. A rectangular field has a perimeter of 2·09 km. It is 480 m wide. How long is the field?

TARGET To solve word problems involving conversion of units of weight.

Example

Each salmon fillet weighs 200 g. There are 6 fillets in each pack. What is the weight of 50 packs in kilograms?

$200 \text{ g} \times 6 = 1200 \text{ g}$
$1200 \text{ g} \times 50 = 60\,000 \text{ g}$
$60\,000 \text{ g} = 60 \text{ kg}$
Answer: *60 kg*

A

1. When he was born Frank weighed 4·2 kg. This was 500 g more than Sally. What did Sally weigh at birth?

2. A bird feeder holds 200 g of seeds. How many times can it be filled from 1 kg of seed?

3. A cereal bar weighs 100 g. There are 24 in a box. What is the total weight of the bars in kilograms?

4. Three 500 g weights are put on a balance. Four 200 g weights are added. How much weight is on the balance altogether, in kilograms?

5. A small box of cornflakes weighs 750 g. A large box weighs 500 g more. What does the large box weigh in kilograms?

6. Bradley buys 0·6 kg of mince. One quarter is used. How much is left in grams?

B

1. A bag of chips weighs 2·35 kg. 700 g is eaten. How much is left?

2. A can of fish weighs 165 g. What do ten cans weigh in kilograms?

3. Sugar cubes weigh 10 g. How many cubes are there in a 1·2 kg box?

4. A chef is preparing a meal for 120 people. Each meal needs 200 g of potatoes. How many 6 kg bags of potatoes are needed?

5. A box containing thirty packets of biscuits weighs 4·1 kg. Each packet of biscuits weighs 130 g. What does the box itself weigh?

6. Laurel's suitcase and luggage weigh 20·4 kg. She takes out boots weighing 900 g and puts in sandals weighing 450 g. What is the weight of the suitcase and luggage now?

C

1. Scott cooks 0·8 kg of pasta. This provides five servings. How much pasta is in each serving in grams?

2. A laptop weighs 2·47 kg. Its case weighs 725 g. What is the combined weight of laptop and case?

3. A bar of soap weighs 85 g. What is the weight of forty bars in kilograms?

4. A 2 kg bag provides enough flour for 25 rolls. How much flour is needed for eight rolls in grams?

5. Jamie orders three 24 kg bags of coal. During November, December and January he uses 600 g daily. How much coal is left at the end of January?

6. Marina buys 0·6 kg of cheese. She uses two fifths. She uses a further 175 g. How much cheese is left?

TARGET To solve word problems involving conversion of units of capacity.

Example

A saucepan holds 2·3 litres of boiling water. 25 ml evaporates every minute. How much water is left if it boils for 30 minutes?

25 ml × 30 = 750 ml
750 ml = 0·75 litres
2·3 − 0·75 = 1·55
Answer: *1·55 litres*

A

1. Thirteen people order soup in a restaurant. Each bowl holds 300 ml. How much soup is served in litres?

2. A watering can holds 3 litres. 600 ml is used. How much water is left in the can?

3. April has 800 ml of paint left. She buys a 2·5 litre can. How much paint does she have now?

4. At a party there are three jugs each holding 1·5 litres of drink, and two bottles, each holding 700 ml. How much drink is there altogether at the party?

5. A tub holds two litres of ice cream. A quarter is used. The rest is divided into ten equal servings. How much ice cream is in each serving?

B

1. Each lolly is made using 50 ml of juice. How many lollies can be made from 4·8 litres of juice?

2. A bowl is filled with 1·9 litres of hot water and 850 ml of cold water. How much water is in the bowl?

3. A kettle holds 1·6 litres of water. Three mugs of tea are made each using 250 ml of water. How much water is left in the kettle?

4. A milk bottle holds two litres. One fifth is used at breakfast. A further 220 ml is used at lunchtime. How much milk is left?

5. A hose uses 300 ml of water every second. How much water is used in one and half minutes in litres?

C

1. A small tube of paint holds 24 ml. How many tubes can be made from 1·2 litres?

2. Each bottle of lemon juice holds 120 ml. There are 36 bottles in a box. How much lemon juice is in the box?

3. A drink is made with 1·8 litres of water and 450 ml of juice. It is poured equally into nine glasses. How much drink is in each glass?

4. At a steady speed a car uses 80 ml of petrol every minute. How much will it use in 1 hour and 45 minutes?

5. At a wedding the 64 guests are each served with a 150 ml glass of champagne. How many 1·2 litre bottles are needed?

TARGET   To calculate the area and perimeter of squares and rectangles.

The area of a shape is the amount of surface it covers.
The perimeter of a shape is the distance around its edges.

Example

Perimeter = (length + width) × 2
= 18 cm × 2
= 36 cm

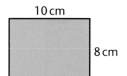

10 cm

8 cm

Area = length × width
= (10 × 8) cm²
= 80 cm²

A

Use 1 cm² paper. Copy the shapes.
Give the area and perimeter of each shape.

1 3 cm 2 cm

3 4 cm 2 cm

2 4 cm 3 cm

4 3 cm 3 cm

For each of these shapes work out:
a) the area   **b)** the perimeter

5 rectangle
    sides 5 cm 3 cm

6 square
    sides 4 cm

7 rectangle
    sides 7 cm 2 cm

8 square
    sides 5 cm

9 rectangle
    sides 10 cm 2 cm

10 rectangle
    sides 6 cm 4 cm

B

Give the area and perimeter of each shape.

1 8 cm 3 cm

3 7 m 7 m

2 6 cm 9 cm

4 20 m 15 m

For each shape work out:
a) the area   **b)** the perimeter

5 rectangle
    sides 8 cm 6 cm

7 square
    sides 12 cm

6 rectangle
    sides 5 m 17 m

8 rectangle
    sides 15 m 3 m

9 A rectangular field is 80 m long and 50 m
    wide. Find its area and perimeter.

C

1 Copy and complete the table.

Length (cm)	Width (cm)	Perimeter (cm)	Area (cm²)
8	5		
	4	34	
12			84
9		36	
	5		100

For each of the following shapes find:
a) the perimeter (cm)   **b)** the area (cm²).

2

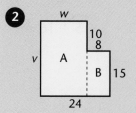

w
v   A
10
8
B   15
24

3

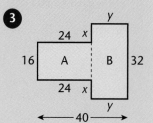

y
24   x
16   A   B   32
24   x
y
← 40 →

TARGET To calculate the area and perimeter of squares, rectangles and related irregular shapes.

To understand the difference between area and perimeter think of a field. The perimeter is the length of the fence around the field. The area is the field itself.

Examples

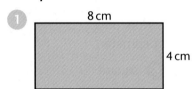

Area = length × width
= (8 × 4) cm²
= 32 cm²

Perimeter = 2 × (length + width)
= 2 × (8 + 4) cm
= 2 × 12 cm
= 24 cm

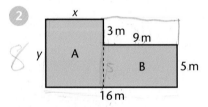

$x = 7\,\text{m}\ (16\,\text{m} - 9\,\text{m})$
$y = 8\,\text{m}\ (5\,\text{m} + 3\,\text{m})$

Area of A = (8 × 7) m²
= 56 m²
Area of B = (9 × 5) m²
= 45 m²
Total area = (56 + 45) m²
= 101 m²

Perimeter = (8 + 7 + 3 + 9 + 5 + 16) m
= 48 m

A

Measure each rectangle and work out:

a) the perimeter   b) the area.

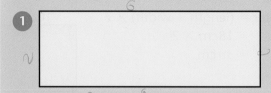
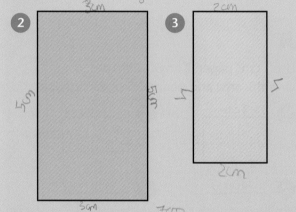

For each of the following shapes work out:

a) the perimeter   b) the area

5 square
sides 3 cm

7 square
sides 5 cm

6 rectangle
sides 2 cm 8 cm

8 rectangle
sides 4 cm 7 cm

Use 1 cm squared paper.

9 Find as many rectangles as you can with an area of 18 cm². Work out the perimeters.

10 Find as many rectangles as you can with a perimeter of 20 cm. Work out the areas.

11 Draw a square with a perimeter of 24 cm. Work out the area.

B

1 Copy and complete the table, showing the measurements of rectangles.

Length (cm)	Width (cm)	Perimeter (cm)	Area (cm²)
9	3		
12		34	
	7		56
16			32
	10	60	
		26	42
	4		48
		40	75

For each of the following rectilinear shapes find:

a) the missing lengths x and y

b) the perimeter of the shape.

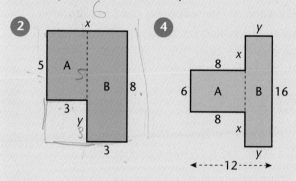

6 For each of the above shapes work out:

a) the area of rectangle A

b) the area of rectangle(s) B

c) the area of the whole shape.

C

For each of the following rectilinear shapes find:

a) the area

b) the perimeter.

All measurements are in centimetres.

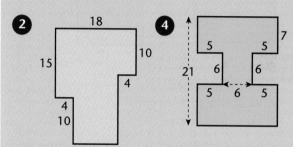

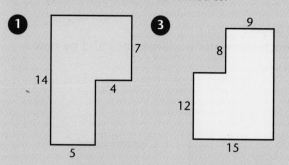

5 A playground has a length of 30 m and an area of 750 m².
What is the length of the railings around the playground?

6 A painting is 50 cm long and 40 cm wide. Its frame is 5 cm wide.

a) What is the perimeter of the framed painting?

b) What is the area of the unframed painting?

c) What is the area of the framed painting?

7 One quarter of this garden is a patio.

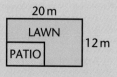

a) What is the area of the lawn?

b) Patio tiles are 50 cm by 50 cm. How many are needed to cover the patio?

c) What is the area of one tile? Write your answer in square centimetres and in square metres.

TARGET To calculate and compare the areas of squares and rectangles.

Examples

Which shape has the larger area and by how much?

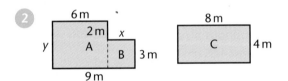

Area of A = (7 × 5) cm²
= 35 m²
Area of B = (6 × 6) cm²
= 36 cm²

The area of square B is 1 cm² larger than that of rectangle A.

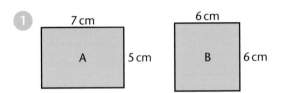

$x = 9\,m - 6\,m = 3\,m$
$y = 3\,m + 2\,m = 5\,m$

Area of A = (6 × 5) m²
= 30 m²

Area of B = (3 × 3) m²
= 9 m²

Area of irregular shape = 39 m²

Area of rectangle C = (8 × 4) m²
= 32 m²

The area of the irregular shape is 7 m² larger than that of rectangle C.

A

1 Copy and complete this table showing the measurements of rectangles.

Length	Width	Area
6 cm	4 cm	
8 cm	5 cm	
11 m		33 m²
9 m		54 m²
	8 cm	96 cm²
	10 cm	400 cm²
15 m		30 m²
	7 m	56 m²

For each of the following pairs of diagrams work out which rectangle has the larger area and by how much. All lengths are in centimetres.

2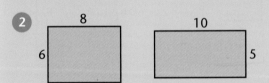

3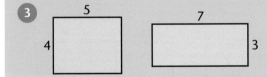

4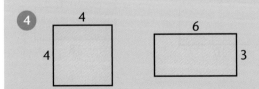

5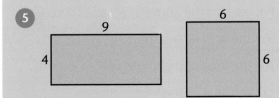

B

The following pairs of diagrams show the dimensions of rooms. For each pair work out which room has the larger area and by how much. All lengths are in metres.

1
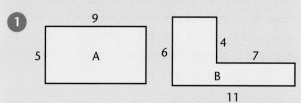

2
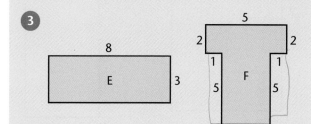

3
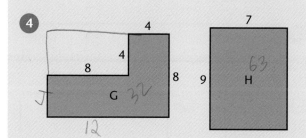

4
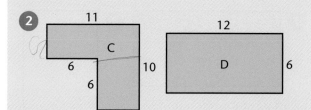

5
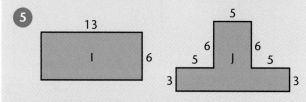

6
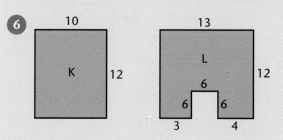

C

Each of the following pairs of diagrams shows two possible ways a shop might use its available floor space for display (yellow) and storage (pink). Work out which plan provides the larger display area and by how much.

All lengths are in metres.

1
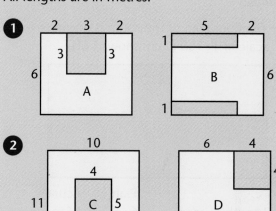

2
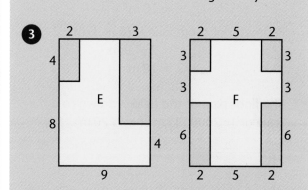

3
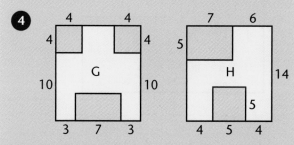

4
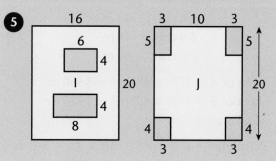

5

TARGET   To calculate areas and perimeters from scale drawings.

Examples

① The floor plan of this room is drawn to a scale of 1 : 100 (1 cm shows 1 m).

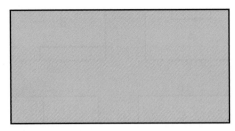

	Plan	Actual
Length of room	6 cm	6 m
Width of room	3 cm	3 m

Area of room = $(6 \times 3)\,\text{m}^2$
= $18\,\text{m}^2$

Perimeter of room = $2 \times (6 + 3)\,\text{m}$
= $2 \times 9\,\text{m}$
= $18\,\text{m}$

② The floor plan of this field is drawn to a scale of 1 : 2000 (1 cm shows 20 m).

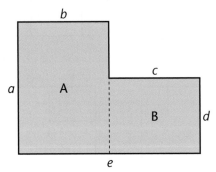

Side	Plan	Actual
a	3·5 cm	70 m
b	2·4 cm	48 m
c	2·4 cm	48 m
d	2·0 cm	40 m

Area of A = $(70 \times 48)\,\text{m}^2 = 3360\,\text{m}^2$
Area of B = $(40 \times 48)\,\text{m}^2 = \underline{1920\,\text{m}^2}$
Total area of field   = $5280\,\text{m}^2$

Perimeter = $(70 + 48 + 48 + 40 + 96)\,\text{m}$
= $302\,\text{m}$

These plans of rectangular fields are drawn to a scale of 1 : 1000. 1 cm shows 10 m. Copy each plan and label the actual length and width of the field in metres. Then work out:

a) the perimeter of the field

b) the area of the field.

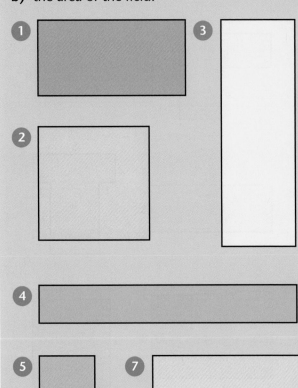

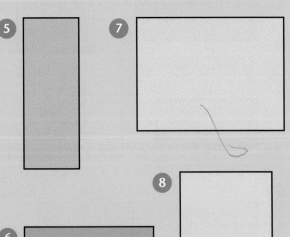

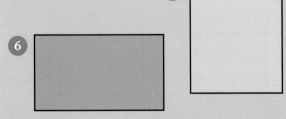

B

The following diagrams show the floor plans of buildings. They are drawn to a scale of 1 : 1000 (1 mm shows 1 m). For each diagram work out:

a) the perimeter of the building

b) the area of each room (A or B)

c) the area of the building.

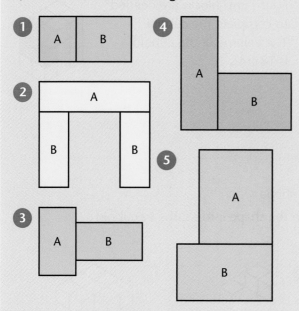

Use a scale of 1 : 200 (1 cm shows 2 m).

6️⃣ Draw the plan of a room with a width of 6 m and an area of 48 m². Label the dimensions (length and width) and work out the perimeter of the room.

7️⃣ Draw the plan of a room with a width of 5 m and an area of 60 m². Label the dimensions and work out the perimeter of the room.

Use a scale of 1 : 500 (1 cm shows 5 m). Design a bungalow to be built in a plot 20 m long and 15 m wide.

8️⃣ Draw the plan of your bungalow with a kitchen, a bathroom, a lounge and two bedrooms. Label the actual dimensions of each room. Work out the area of each room.

C

The following diagrams show the floor plans of buildings. They are drawn to a scale of 1 : 1000 (1mm represents 1 m).
For each building:

a) copy the diagram and label the building's actual dimensions

b) work out the area of the building.

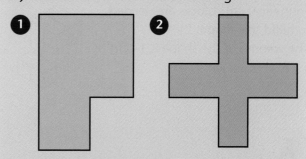

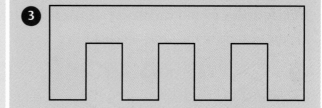

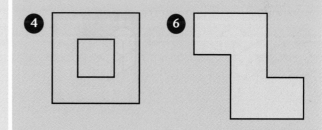

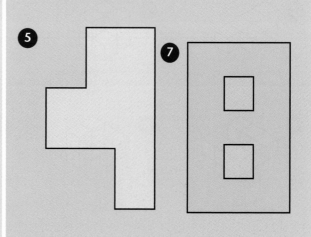

TARGET To recognise volume by using 1 cm³ blocks to build and visualise cuboids.

The volume of a shape is the amount of space it fills.
It is measured in cubic units, such as cubic centimetres (cm³).

Examples

Fourteen 1 cm³ blocks are needed
to build this shape.
The volume of the shape is 14 cm³.

Four 1 cm³ blocks are needed
to complete the cuboid.
The volume of the cuboid
is 18 cm³.

A

For each of the following shapes write down:

a) how many 1 cm³ blocks are needed to build the shape

b) how many more 1 cm³ blocks are needed to turn the shape into a cube or cuboid

c) the volume of the cube or cuboid.

1

5

9

13

2

6

10

14

3

7

11

15

4

8

12

16

B

For each of the following shapes write down:

a) the volume of the shape

b) the number of 1 cm³ blocks needed to turn the shapes into a cube or cuboid

c) the volume of the cube or cuboid.

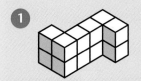 **1**

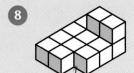 **8**

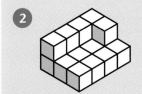 **2**

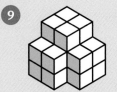 **9**

 **3**

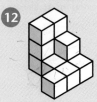 **10**

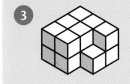 **4**

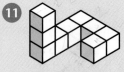 **11**

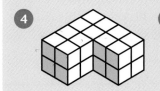 **5**

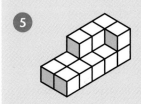 **12**

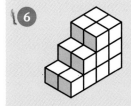 **6**

 **13**

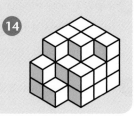 **7**

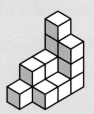 **14**

C

For each of the following shapes write down:

a) the number of 1 cm³ needed to cover the base of the cuboid

b) the number of layers of 1 cm³ needed to fill the cuboid

c) the volume of the cuboid.

1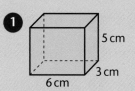
5 cm, 3 cm, 6 cm

5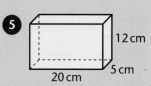
12 cm, 5 cm, 20 cm

2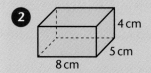
4 cm, 5 cm, 8 cm

6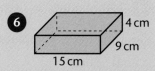
4 cm, 9 cm, 15 cm

3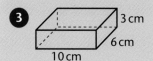
3 cm, 6 cm, 10 cm

7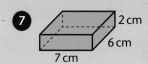
2 cm, 6 cm, 7 cm

4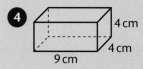
4 cm, 4 cm, 9 cm

8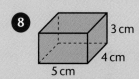
3 cm, 4 cm, 5 cm

9 The formula for the volume of a cuboid is:

VOLUME = LENGTH × WIDTH × HEIGHT

Use this formula to copy and complete the table.

LENGTH	WIDTH	HEIGHT	VOLUME
7 cm	2 cm	3 cm	42 cm³
25 cm	10 cm		3000 cm³
6 cm	4 cm	5 cm	
8 cm		4 cm	96 cm³
	8 cm	5 cm	480 cm³
9 cm	5 cm	6 cm	
15 cm	6 cm		360 cm³
10 cm	7·5 cm		450 cm³

10 What is the volume of a cube with 20 cm edges?

TARGET   To solve problems involving converting between units of time.

A

Copy and complete.

1. ☐ seconds = 3 minutes
2. 300 seconds = ☐ minutes
3. ☐ minutes = 7 hours
4. 120 minutes = ☐ hours

5. ☐ days = 2 weeks
6. ☐ days = 5 weeks
7. 21 days = ☐ weeks
8. 70 days = ☐ weeks

9. ☐ months = 4 years
10. ☐ months = 20 years
11. 60 months = ☐ years
12. 96 months = ☐ years

13. How many complete weeks and days are there in:
    a) April   b) May?

14. How many minutes are there in two and a half hours?

B

Copy and complete.

1. ☐ seconds = 1 minute 47 seconds
2. 500 seconds = ☐ minutes ☐ seconds
3. ☐ minutes = 2 hours 35 minutes
4. 419 minutes = ☐ hours ☐ minutes
5. ☐ hours = 5 days 17 hours
6. 100 hours = ☐ days ☐ hours
7. ☐ days = 2 weeks 3 days
8. 40 days = ☐ weeks ☐ days
9. ☐ months = 3 years 6 months
10. 70 months = ☐ years ☐ months

11. There are exactly 13 complete weeks in the first three months of a year. Is it a leap year?

12. A ship leaves port at 14:45 on Sunday. It returns at 09:20 on Wednesday. How long was the voyage in days, hours and minutes?

C

1. Adrian's marathon time is 2 hours 58 minutes and 39 seconds. This is 213 seconds faster than his previous best time. What was his previous best time?

2. It is Tuesday. There are 100 days until Christmas Day.
   a) What is the date that Tuesday?
   b) What day is Christmas Day?

3. Ivan leaves Moscow at 10:27 on 26th June. He arrives in Vladivostock at 16:05 on 2nd July. How long has his journey taken in days, hours and minutes?

4. A machine makes one bolt every second. How long will it take to make 10 000 bolts?

5. How many weeks and days are there in:
   a) the first 4 months of 2020
   b) the last 6 months of 2020?

6. How many hours are there in July?

TARGET   To calculate complements of one unit of measure.

Example   ☐ + 0·73 ℓ = 1 ℓ (litre)   Answer *0·27 ℓ*

A

Copy and complete.

1. 0·3 cm + ☐ = 1 cm
2. 0·5 cm + ☐ = 1 cm
3. 0·9 cm + ☐ = 1 cm
4. £0·15 + ☐ = £1
5. £0·65 + ☐ = £1
6. £0·75 + ☐ = £1

7. ☐ + 0·2 kg = 1 kg
8. ☐ + 0·8 kg = 1 kg
9. ☐ + 0·6 kg = 1 kg
10. ☐ + 0·05 m = 1 m
11. ☐ + 0·55 m = 1 m
12. ☐ + 0·35 m = 1 m

13. 1 cm − ☐ = 0·1 cm
14. 1 cm − ☐ = 0·7 cm
15. 1 cm − ☐ = 0·4 cm
16. £1 − ☐ = £0·85
17. £1 − ☐ = £0·25
18. £1 − ☐ = £0·95

19. 1 litre − 0·9 litres = ☐
20. 1 litre − 0·3 litres = ☐
21. 1 litre − 0·7 litres = ☐
22. 1 m − 0·45 m = ☐
23. 1 m − 0·05 m = ☐
24. 1 m − 0·65 m = ☐

B

Copy and complete.

1. 0·51 km + ☐ = 1 km
2. 0·27 km + ☐ = 1 km
3. 0·82 km + ☐ = 1 km
4. 0·09 kg + ☐ = 1 kg
5. 0·64 kg + ☐ = 1 kg
6. 0·78 kg + ☐ = 1 kg

7. ☐ + £0·45 = £1
8. ☐ + £0·93 = £1
9. ☐ + £0·16 = £1
10. ☐ + 0·39 ℓ = 1 ℓ
11. ☐ + 0·02 ℓ = 1 ℓ
12. ☐ + 0·85 ℓ = 1 ℓ

13. 1 m − ☐ = 0·63 m
14. 1 m − ☐ = 0·48 m
15. 1 m − ☐ = 0·71 m
16. 1 kg − ☐ = 0·06 kg
17. 1 kg − ☐ = 0·14 kg
18. 1 kg − ☐ = 0·67 kg

19. £1 − £0·52 = ☐
20. £1 − £0·98 = ☐
21. £1 − £0·21 = ☐
22. 1 ℓ − 0·36 ℓ = ☐
23. 1 ℓ − 0·89 ℓ = ☐
24. 1 ℓ − 0·13 ℓ = ☐

C

Copy and complete.

1. 0·205 kg + ☐ = 1 kg
2. 0·655 kg + ☐ = 1 kg
3. 0·015 kg + ☐ = 1 kg
4. 0·474 km + ☐ = 1 km
5. 0·737 km + ☐ = 1 km
6. 0·862 km + ☐ = 1 km

7. ☐ + 0·325 ℓ = 1 ℓ
8. ☐ + 0·295 ℓ = 1 ℓ
9. ☐ + 0·535 ℓ = 1 ℓ
10. ☐ + 0·941 kg = 1 kg
11. ☐ + 0·818 kg = 1 kg
12. ☐ + 0·696 kg = 1 kg

13. 1 km − ☐ = 0·975 km
14. 1 km − ☐ = 0·745 km
15. 1 km − ☐ = 0·385 km
16. 1 ℓ − ☐ = 0·422 ℓ
17. 1 ℓ − ☐ = 0·259 ℓ
18. 1 ℓ − ☐ = 0·104 ℓ

19. 1 kg − 0·065 kg = ☐
20. 1 kg − 0·305 kg = ☐
21. 1 kg − 0·835 kg = ☐
22. 1 km − 0·923 km = ☐
23. 1 km − 0·768 km = ☐
24. 1 km − 0·491 km = ☐

TARGET To multiply and divide measures by 10, 100 and 1000.

Examples
2·9 km × 100
Answer *290 km*

300 ℓ (litres) ÷ 1000
Answer *0·3 ℓ*

A

Write the answer only.

1. 3·8 cm × 10
2. 60·5 kg × 10
3. 0·19 litres × 10
4. 45·42 m × 10
5. 0·6 cm × 10
6. 7·31 km × 10

7. 504 kg ÷ 10
8. 197 m ÷ 10
9. 834·3 litres ÷ 10
10. 8 cm ÷ 10
11. 62 km ÷ 10
12. 1·5 m ÷ 10

13. 0·1 cm × 100
14. 5·87 kg × 100
15. 49·3 litres × 100
16. 28·49 km × 100
17. 0·24 m × 100
18. 4·6 kg × 100

19. 125 m ÷ 100
20. 780 litres ÷ 100
21. 30 cm ÷ 100
22. 1061 km ÷ 100
23. 17 m ÷ 100
24. 3240 kg ÷ 100

B

Write the answer only.

1. 0·169 litres × 1000
2. 0·002 m × 10
3. 7·6 km × 1000
4. 0·013 kg × 100
5. 3·957 litres × 10
6. 0·04 m × 1000

7. 28 km ÷ 100
8. 810 kg ÷ 1000
9. 0·05 litres ÷ 10
10. 3200 m ÷ 1000
11. 185·9 km ÷ 100
12. 27 kg ÷ 1000

Copy and complete.

13. 92·1 ℓ × ☐ = 92 100 ℓ
14. 0·344 km × ☐ = 34·4 km
15. 0·056 kg × ☐ = 56 kg
16. 0·93 m × ☐ = 9·3 m
17. 7·5 ℓ × ☐ = 750 ℓ
18. 1·48 km × ☐ = 1480 km

19. 60·7 m ÷ ☐ = 6·07 m
20. 400 kg ÷ ☐ = 0·4 kg
21. 1530 km ÷ ☐ = 15·3 km
22. 3·52 ℓ ÷ ☐ = 0·352 ℓ
23. 8089 kg ÷ ☐ = 8·089 kg
24. 50 m ÷ ☐ = 0·05 m

C

Copy and complete.

1. ☐ × 100 = 680 ℓ
2. ☐ × 1000 = 60 m
3. ☐ ÷ 10 = 0·471 kg
4. ☐ ÷ 1000 = 1·39 km
5. ☐ × 10 = 0·45 ℓ
6. ☐ × 1000 = 203 kg

7. ☐ ÷ 1000 = 61·616 km
8. ☐ ÷ 100 = 0·74 m
9. ☐ × 1000 = 200 cm
10. ☐ × 10 = 5·37 kg
11. ☐ ÷ 1000 = 0·8 ℓ
12. ☐ ÷ 100 = 0·041 m

13. ☐ × 1000 = 1964 km
14. ☐ × 100 = 22·9 ℓ
15. ☐ ÷ 10 = 3·67 m
16. ☐ ÷ 1000 = 0·023 kg
17. ☐ × 1000 = 18 820 ℓ
18. ☐ × 100 = 0·5 m

19. ☐ ÷ 10 = 0·6 km
20. ☐ ÷ 1000 = 0·1 cm
21. ☐ × 10 = 51·8 kg
22. ☐ × 1000 = 79 km
23. ☐ ÷ 100 = 49·2 ℓ
24. ☐ ÷ 1000 = 0·27 m

TARGET To multiply and divide measures mentally, converting between units.

Examples   400 g × 60 = ☐ kg   3 litres ÷ 5 = ☐ ml
              400 g × 60 = 24 000 g   3 litres = 3000 ml
              Answer *24 kg*   3000 ÷ 5 = 600 ml
                                          Answer *600 ml*

A

Copy and complete.

1. 50 cm × 8 = ☐ m
2. 700 g × 5 = ☐ kg
3. 30 mm × 12 = ☐ cm
4. 600 ml × 3 = ☐ litres
5. 200 m × 7 = ☐ km
6. 40 cm × 4 = ☐ m

7. ☐ g × 9 = 7·2 kg
8. ☐ ml × 10 = 6 litres
9. ☐ m × 6 = 5·4 km
10. ☐ cm × 2 = 2·2 m
11. ☐ ml × 11 = 5·5 litres
12. ☐ mm × 8 = 56 cm

13. 1·2 kg ÷ 6 = ☐ g
14. 28 cm ÷ 4 = ☐ mm
15. 6·3 litres ÷ 7 = ☐ ml
16. 0·4 km ÷ 10 = ☐ m
17. 4·5 m ÷ 9 = ☐ cm
18. 1·8 kg ÷ 2 = ☐ g

19. ☐ km ÷ 12 = 600 m
20. ☐ litres ÷ 5 = 80 ml
21. ☐ kg ÷ 11 = 300 g
22. ☐ m ÷ 3 = 70 cm
23. ☐ cm ÷ 8 = 40 mm
24. ☐ litres ÷ 6 = 600 ml

B

Copy and complete.

1. 90 g × 40 = ☐ kg
2. 30 m × 900 = ☐ km
3. 500 ml × 50 = ☐ litres
4. 800 × 60 cm = ☐ m
5. 700 × 20 g = ☐ kg
6. 30 × 80 ml = ☐ litres

7. ☐ m × 110 = 6·6 km
8. ☐ g × 300 = 33 kg
9. ☐ ml × 70 = 56 litres
10. ☐ mm × 120 = 10·8 m
11. ☐ cm × 600 = 240 m
12. ☐ ml × 900 = 18 litres

13. 28 kg ÷ 70 = ☐ g
14. 3·6 km ÷ 30 = ☐ m
15. 24 litres ÷ 1200 = ☐ ml
16. 4·5 m ÷ 50 = ☐ mm
17. 66 m ÷ 60 = ☐ cm
18. 22 litres ÷ 110 = ☐ ml

19. ☐ m ÷ 400 = 80 cm
20. ☐ kg ÷ 90 = 60 g
21. ☐ km ÷ 20 = 1200 m
22. ☐ litres ÷ 80 = 90 ml
23. ☐ m ÷ 700 = 70 mm
24. ☐ kg ÷ 120 = 50 g

C

Copy and complete.

1. 150 g × 12 = ☐ kg
2. 720 m × 3 = ☐ km
3. 560 ml × 4 = ☐ litres
4. 19 × 20 mm = ☐ m
5. 35 × 70 cm = ☐ m
6. 230 × 60 g = ☐ kg

7. ☐ g × 60 = 30 kg
8. ☐ m × 200 = 160 km
9. ☐ ml × 110 = 12·1 litres
10. ☐ g × 900 = 810 kg
11. ☐ m × 50 = 55 km
12. ☐ ml × 800 = 4800 litres

13. 14 × 110 m = ☐ km
14. 37 × 60 cm = ☐ m
15. 23 × 700 ml = ☐ litres
16. 56 × 120 g = ☐ kg
17. 75 × 40 mm = ☐ cm
18. 48 × 800 m = ☐ km

19. ☐ × 300 ml = 2400 litres
20. ☐ × 120 g = 36 kg
21. ☐ × 80 cm = 7·2 km
22. ☐ × 20 mm = 12 m
23. ☐ × 900 ml = 630 litres
24. ☐ × 50 m = 450 km

TARGET   To add metric measures using a formal written method.

Example

38·29 ℓ (litres) + 8·475 ℓ

Line up the decimal points.

$$
\begin{array}{r}
38\cdot29\ \ \ \ell \\
+\ \ 8\cdot475\ \ell \\
\hline
46\cdot765\ \ell \\
\end{array}
$$

A

Copy and complete.

1 cm
343·5
+247·8

2 m
43·67
+12·86

3 kg
271·9
+194·2

4 kg
63·58
+29·48

5 km
506·4
+125·9

6 km
41·56
+36·74

7 litres
352·3
+298·8

8 litres
70·97
+49·67

Set out correctly and work out.

9 357·5 kg + 154·6 kg

10 83·99 kg + 16·45 kg

11 248·6 cm + 225·9 cm

12 61·94 m + 48·37 m

13 566·8 ℓ + 337·3 ℓ

14 34·32 ℓ + 17·49 ℓ

15 471·7 km + 235·8 km

16 67·89 km + 45·67 km

B

Copy and complete.

1 m
26·38
+25·94

2 m
195·4
+187·6

3 litres
8·725
+39·7

4 litres
3·96
+2·384

5 km
476·53
+154·8

6 km
4239·3
+   6·761

7 kg
2·68
+195·77

8 kg
698·5
+2391·9

Set out correctly and work out.

9 10·76 ℓ + 9·895 ℓ

10 7·45 ℓ + 652·8 ℓ

11 285·9 m + 34·209 m

12 355·48 m + 1687·0 m

13 76·822 kg + 76·8 kg

14 47·39 kg + 4·85 kg

15 98·46 km + 205·577 km

16 1329·5 km + 84·536 km

C

Set out correctly and find the total of each list.

1 km
139·6
74·275
8·59

2 litres
4·682
12·85
3167·0

3 m
903·57
2326·2
0·563

4 kg
27·49
156·0
23·652

5 km
4·07
19·445
3·8
125·3

6 litres
1839
43·653
752·7
94·83

7 m
5·633
67·4
129·09

8 kg
6071·2
59·966
72·47

9 km
584·28
5·825
488·0

10 litres
40·199
167·86
325·2

11 m
68·74
29 306·0
7·395
147·2

12 kg
658·5
283·65
51·037
24·25

TARGET To subtract metric measures using a formal written method.

Example

13·25 kg − 6·385 kg

Line up decimal points.
Put in missing zeros.

$$\begin{array}{r} {}^{0}\!\!\!\!/1\overset{12}{\cancel{3}}\cdot\overset{11}{2}\overset{14}{5}\overset{1}{0}\text{ kg} \\ -\ 6\cdot385\text{ kg} \\ \hline 6\cdot865\text{ kg} \end{array}$$

A

Copy and complete.

1
```
   m
  3·73
 −2·46
```

7
```
 litres
  2·46
 −1·27
```

2
```
   cm
  54·8
 −39·2
```

8
```
   kg
  73·5
 −39·1
```

3
```
   km
  9·07
 −5·16
```

9
```
   m
  3·83
 −1·59
```

4
```
 litres
  46·2
 −13·5
```

10
```
   cm
  97·4
 −21·5
```

5
```
   km
  6·59
 −3·83
```

11
```
   kg
  4·16
 −2·33
```

6
```
   cm
  8·91
 −7·08
```

12
```
 litres
  84·5
 −47·9
```

13 A washing machine uses 54·2 litres of water during a long wash and 38·7 litres during a short wash. How much more water is used during the longer wash?

B

Copy and complete.

1
```
    m
  58·27
 −14·9
```

7
```
    m
  43·6
 −29·251
```

2
```
   kg
  21·4
 − 5·82
```

8
```
  litres
  95·209
 − 8·4
```

3
```
   cm
  176·3
 − 46·5
```

9
```
   km
  381·5
 −156·74
```

4
```
  litres
  8·39
 −0·837
```

10
```
   kg
  12·372
 − 8·49
```

5
```
   km
  64·05
 − 6·3
```

11
```
    m
  5·31
 −2·786
```

6
```
   kg
  77·1
 −29·49
```

12
```
  litres
  87·065
 −19·3
```

13 Julian throws a javelin 56·85 m. Travis throws 63·5 m. How much longer is Travis' throw?

14 A cake weighs 1·34 kg. 0·672 kg is eaten. How much is left?

C

Find the difference between each pair of measures.

1 525·4 kg   62·46 kg

2 7·908 km   33·1 km

3 9·238 ℓ   1·76 ℓ

4 41·65 m   31·895 m

5 0·939 kg   8·12 kg

6 42·8 km   67·06 km

7 14·265 ℓ   9·28 ℓ

8 3·287 m   7·13 m

9 23·42 kg   15·591 kg

10 45·84 ℓ   385·5 ℓ

11 2·915 km   140·6 km

12 241·68 m   75·9 m

13 The largest fish Peter had ever caught weighed 23·16 kg. His best catch this year weighed 18·593 kg. How much heavier was his best ever catch?

14 After one hour of a marathon Lindsay has run 13·04 km. After two hours she has run 25·785 km. How far did she run in the second hour of the race?

TARGET   To add/subtract metric measures using a written method.

Examples

43·54 km + 7·695 km

$$\begin{array}{r} 43\cdot54 \ \text{km} \\ + \ \ 7\cdot695 \ \text{km} \\ \hline 51\cdot235 \ \text{km} \\ \hline {\scriptstyle 1 \ \ 1 \ \ 1} \end{array}$$

95·8 m − 6·75 m

$$\begin{array}{r} {\scriptstyle 8 \ 1 \ \ 7 \ 1} \\ 95\cdot80 \ \text{m} \\ - \ \ 6\cdot75 \ \text{m} \\ \hline 89\cdot05 \ \text{m} \end{array}$$

A

Copy and complete.

1
```
    cm
  475·6
+ 263·8
```

2
```
   litres
   36·94
 + 15·29
```

3
```
    km
  293·8
+ 179·5
```

4
```
    m
  45·79
+ 37·83
```

5
```
    cm
  648·5
+ 284·5
```

6
```
    kg
  58·67
+ 18·94
```

7
```
   litres
   3·85
 − 1·37
```

8
```
    cm
  91·6
− 69·4
```

9
```
    km
  4·73
− 3·48
```

10
```
    kg
  70·9
− 23·2
```

11
```
    m
  5·28
− 2·45
```

12
```
    cm
  86·4
− 47·9
```

13 A fence is 8·75 m long. 4·28 m has been painted. How long is the unpainted fence?

B

Copy and complete.

1
```
    kg
  174·3
+ 57·77
```

2
```
    m
  5·294
+ 3·96
```

3
```
   litres
   38·6
 + 6·638
```

4
```
    km
  297·45
+ 47·6
```

5
```
    m
  43·95
+ 68·9
```

6
```
    kg
  86·58
+ 7·47
```

7
```
    km
  64·52
− 5·963
```

8
```
   litres
  38·109
− 14·85
```

9
```
    kg
  523·6
− 36·976
```

10
```
    m
  81·3
− 26·75
```

11
```
    km
  951·24
− 54·78
```

12
```
   litres
  17·947
−  4·999
```

13 A railway route between two cities is 532·3 km long. A tunnel would shorten the journey by 78·65 km. What would be the length of the new route?

C

Find the total of each list.

1
```
    kg
   9·37
  40·892
 257·4
```

2
```
   litres
   36·259
 1871·5
   46·38
    7·166
```

3
```
    m
   18·5
    9·463
 173·97
```

4
```
    km
   0·624
   5·48
 207·9
  12·375
```

Work out

5 284·3 m − 6·84 m

6 47·15 kg − 7·368 kg

7 60·527 ℓ − 51·49 ℓ

8 1526·4 km − 58·705 km

9 83·732 m − 16·8 m

10 95·06 kg − 48·466 kg

11 A full petrol tank holds 41·2 litres. There is 17·675 litres in the tank. How much petrol is needed to fill the tank?

12 A large turkey weighs 6·12 kg. A smaller one weighs 2·835 kg less. What is the weight of the smaller turkey?

TARGET To use mental methods to solve word problems involving conversion of units of measure.

Example

A full bottle of lemonade exactly fills eight 200 ml glasses. What is the capacity of the bottle in litres?

200 ml × 8 = 1600 ml
1600 ml = 1·6 litres
Answer *1·6 litres*

A

1. There is 3·6 litres of hot water in a bowl. 1·7 litres of cold water is added. How much water is in the bowl?

2. Felix weighs 37·2 kg. George weighs 1·5 kg less. What does George weigh?

3. Simone rides her horse 6·4 km four times in a week. How far has she ridden altogether?

4. Three identical boxes of cereal weigh 2·4 kg altogether. What does one box weigh?

5. A candle is 18 cm long. 7·4 cm is used. How much is left?

6. A suitcase weighs 3·5 kg. The clothes inside the case weigh 13·9 kg. What is the total weight of clothes and case?

B

1. A bottle holds 0·75 litres of water. 290 ml is drunk. How much water is left?

2. A football pitch is 91 m long. How far is it from the goal to the halfway line?

3. One can of peas weighs 0·35 kg. What do two cans weigh in grams?

4. A drainpipe is 2·8 m long. It is joined to a 65 cm length. What is the total length of the drainpipe?

5. Harry has 1·2 kg of flour. He uses 580 g. How much flour is left?

6. A square piece of card has a perimeter of 0·7 m. What is the length of one side in cm?

7. One scoop of ice cream is 0·08 litres. How much is six scoops in millilitres?

C

1. A pizza weighs 0·54 kg. It is cut into four equal slices. What is the weight of one slice in grams?

2. One pound is worth 1·46 US dollars. What is £20 worth in dollars?

3. At high tide the beach is 0·047 km wide. At low tide it is 225 m wide. How much of the beach is tidal?

4. Twelve identical sachets of shampoo hold 0·3 litres altogether. How much shampoo is in one sachet in millilitres?

5. A light bulb weighs 23 g. What is the weight of eighty bulbs in kilograms?

6. Ella makes a drink with 0·36 litres of water and 85 ml of orange juice. How much drink is there altogether?

7. Hugh swims fifty lengths of a pool. Altogether he swims 2·25 km. How long is one length in metres?

TARGET To solve word problems involving measures using decimal notation.

Example
Large cans of paint hold 2·65 litres
A small can holds 0·875 litres.
How much more paint is there in the large can?
Answer *There is 1·775 litres more paint in the large can.*

```
 1  15141
 2.650
-0.875
 1.775
```

A

1. Anita's father weighs 86·4 kg. Anita weighs half as much. How much does she weigh?

2. One cinema ticket costs £9·60. What do six tickets cost?

3. A washing machine uses 37·9 litres in the wash cycle and a further 18·6 litres in the rinse. How much water does it use altogether?

4. The temperature at 3 pm is 23·6°C. At 3 am it is 7·8°C. How much has the temperature fallen?

5. Ten pounds is 13 Euros. What is £1 in Euros?

6. A fence is 46·8 m long. 7·3 m of the fence needs repairing. How long is the undamaged fence?

B

1. A van is carrying freight weighing 276·8 kg. A further 69·54 kg is loaded on. What is the weight of the van's load?

2. A square courtyard has a perimeter of 55 m. How long is one side?

3. A shower uses 9·4 litres of water every minute. How much water is used in five minutes?

4. Sahil runs the 400 m in 51·36 seconds. The winner is 2·68 seconds faster. What is the winner's time?

5. Debbie works for five hours. She earns £76. How much does she earn each hour?

6. A tub of ice cream contains 2·5 litres. 1·685 litres is eaten. How much is left?

7. Shoe boxes are 10·8 cm tall. How tall is a stack of 7 boxes?

C

1. A rectangular garden is 12 m wide and has an area of 282 m².
   a) How long is the garden?
   b) What is its perimeter?

2. A carpet costs £17·90 per square metre. Debbie needs 26 square metres. How much will Debbie's carpet cost?

3. A Ferrari maintained an average speed of 159·4 km per hour throughout a race. A Renault was 2·79 km per hour slower. What was the Renault's average speed?

4. A boiling saucepan holds 2·25 litres of water. 0·476 litres evaporates. How much water is left?

5. One bag of flour weighs 1·45 kg. What do sixteen bags weigh?

6. Eight centimetres is 3·12 inches. What is one centimetre in inches?

TARGET   To solve number puzzles involving addition and subtraction.

In an addition pyramid, pairs of numbers are added together to make the number above them.

Example
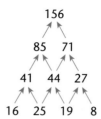

156
85 71
41 44 27
16 25 19 8

A

Copy and complete the addition pyramids.

1

□
□ □
□ 34 □
17 □ 29 22

2
183
96 □
□ □ □
□ 15 33 □

3
237
□ □
55 68 □
□ □ □ 19

4 | 7 16 18 21 |

Arrange the above numbers to form the bottom row of an addition pyramid with a top layer of 108.

5 Use the same four numbers. Find the largest possible top number.

B

Copy and complete the addition pyramids.

1
−7
□ □
□ −3 □
□ 3 □ −7

2
□
4·2 3·3
□ 2·3 □
□ □ □ 0·2

3
−5
1 □
□ 2 □
□ □ −5 □

4 | 0·6 1·7 1·9 2·2 |

Arrange the above numbers to form the bottom row of an addition pyramid with a top layer of 12.

5 Use the same four numbers. Find the largest possible top number.

C

Copy and complete the addition pyramids.

1
□
$2\frac{3}{4}$ □
$1\frac{1}{2}$ □ $\frac{3}{4}$
$\frac{1}{2}$ □ □ □

2
□
□ $1\frac{1}{5}$
$\frac{4}{5}$ $\frac{7}{10}$ □
□ $\frac{1}{2}$ □ □

3
□
□ □
□ □ □
$\frac{1}{4}$ $\frac{1}{12}$ $\frac{2}{3}$ $\frac{5}{6}$

4 | −6 −3 2 5 |

Arrange the above numbers to form the bottom row of an addition pyramid with a top layer of:

a) 2

b) −20

c) 12

TARGET To identify right angles and other multiples of 90°.

A quarter turn is 90°.
A half turn is 180°.

A three quarter turn is 270°

A whole turn is 360°.

A

Find the new time if the hour hand of a clock turns:

1. 90° from 9 o'clock
2. 180° from 3 o'clock
3. 360° from 12 o'clock
4. 90° from 3 o'clock
5. 180° from 6 o'clock
6. 90° from 12 o'clock
7. 360° from 6 o'clock
8. 180° from 9 o'clock.

How many degrees is the turn clockwise from:

9. S to W
10. W to E
11. E to S
12. N to S
13. W to N
14. S to N
15. N to E
16. E to W?

How many degrees is the turn anti-clockwise from:

17. W to S
18. N to S
19. E to W
20. S to E
21. N to W
22. S to N
23. E to N
24. W to E?

B

Find the new time if the hour hand of a clock turns:

1. 180° from 8 am
2. 90° from 1 pm
3. 360° from 6 pm
4. 270° from 5 am
5. 180° from 10 pm
6. 90° from 3 pm
7. 360° from 2 am
8. 270° from 11 am.

How many degrees is the turn clockwise from:

9. S to W
10. NE to SW
11. W to S
12. SE to SE
13. E to S
14. SE to NE
15. N to S
16. SW to NW?

How many degrees is the turn anti-clockwise from:

17. E to N
18. NE to SW
19. W to N
20. N to N
21. SE to SW
22. NW to SW
23. S to E
24. SW to NE?

C

How many degrees does the minute hand turn in:

1. 15 minutes
2. 5 minutes
3. 55 minutes
4. 10 minutes
5. 45 minutes
6. 20 minutes
7. 60 minutes
8. 35 minutes?

How many degrees is the turn clockwise from:

9. W to NW
10. S to SE
11. SW to N
12. NE to W
13. E to SW
14. NE to E
15. NW to S
16. N to NW?

17. Calculate the missing angles a–h.

TARGET To compare different angles.

acute angles < 90°   90° < obtuse angles < 180°   180° < reflex angles < 360°

A

Write each group of angles in order of size, smallest first.

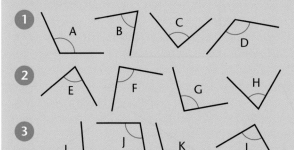

Place the angles in each shape in order, smallest first.

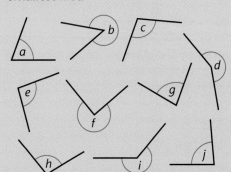

8) Decide if each of the above angles A–Z is:
a) acute **b)** right angle **c)** obtuse.

B

Write each group of angles in order of size, smallest first.

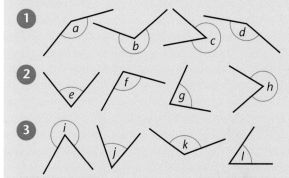

Place the angles meeting at each point in order of size, smallest first.

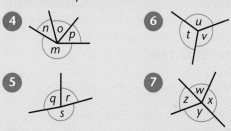

8) Decide if each of the above angles *a*–*z* is:
a) acute   **b)** obtuse   **c)** reflex.

C

1) Arrange these angles in order of size, smallest first.

Arrange the angles in each shape in order of size, smallest first.

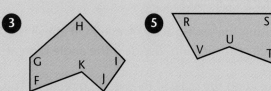

6) Decide if each of the above angles *a*–*j* and A–T is acute, obtuse or reflex.

TARGET   To measure angles with a protractor and to recognise acute, obtuse and reflex angles.

Angles measure the amount something turns or rotates. Angles are measured in degrees.

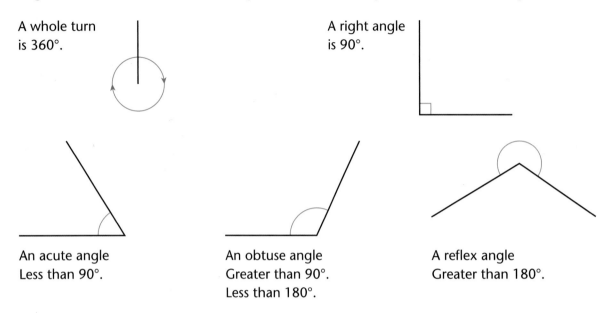

A whole turn is 360°.

A right angle is 90°.

An acute angle
Less than 90°.

An obtuse angle
Greater than 90°.
Less than 180°.

A reflex angle
Greater than 180°.

USING A PROTRACTOR

A protractor is used to measure or draw angles accurately. Most protractors have two scales, a clockwise outer scale and an anti-clockwise inner scale.
It is important to use the correct scale.

Examples

Outer Scale

$A\hat{O}B = 130°$

$A\hat{O}C = 25°$

$A\hat{O}D = 113°$

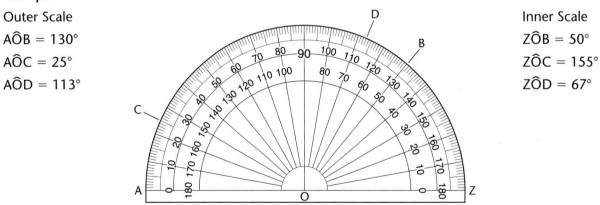

Inner Scale

$Z\hat{O}B = 50°$

$Z\hat{O}C = 155°$

$Z\hat{O}D = 67°$

COMMON MISTAKES

1 Using the wrong scale. Angle ZOB above is 50° and not 130°.
Before measuring, decide if the angle is greater than or less than 90°.

2 Reading the scale in the wrong direction. This mistake occurs more often when using the inner scale. Angle ZOD above would be incorrectly read as 73° and not as 67°.

A

Decide which is the correct angle from the two answers.

1 (70°, 110°)

2 (20°, 160°)

3 (50°, 130°)

4 (80°, 100°)

5 (45°, 135°)

6 (75°, 105°)

7 (85°, 95°)

8 (65°, 115°)

Give the measurement of each angle.

9 AX̂B 10   **17** ZX̂L 70

10 AX̂H 70   **18** ZX̂D 150

11 AX̂R 10   **19** ZX̂P 30

12 AX̂C 20   **20** ZX̂I 100

13 AX̂L 110 70   **21** ZX̂N 50

14 AX̂J 90   **22** ZX̂E 140

15 AX̂F 50   **23** ZX̂Q 20

16 AX̂N 130   **24** ZX̂G 120

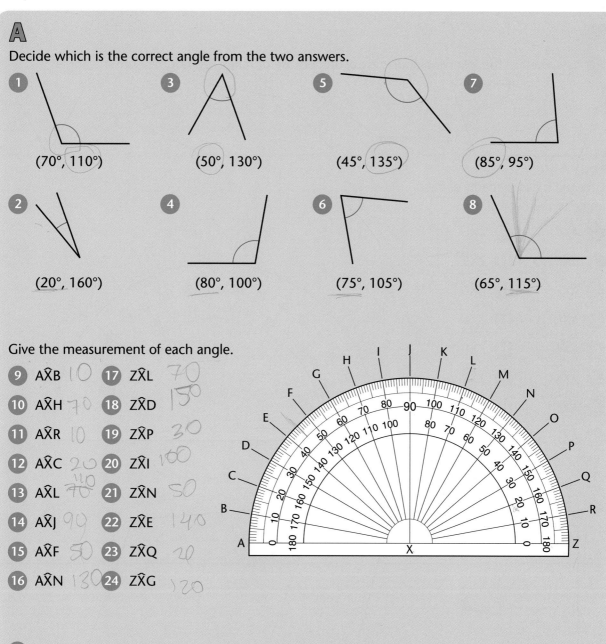

25 For each triangle write the angles in order of size, smallest first.

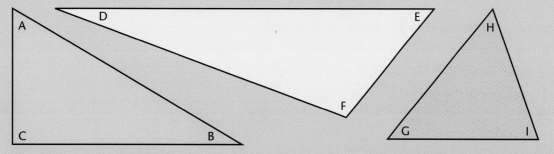

26 For each of the angles in the above triangles:

   a) say whether the angle is acute, obtuse or a right angle

   b) estimate the size of the angle to the nearest 10°

   c) measure the angle to the nearest 10°.

B

1 Say whether the following angles are acute, obtuse or reflex. Do not measure the angles.

Give the measurements of each angle to the nearest 5°.

2 AX̂C   **10** ZX̂L

3 AX̂F   **11** ZX̂B

4 AX̂I   **12** ZX̂D

5 AX̂H   **13** ZX̂N

6 AX̂E   **14** ZX̂F

7 AX̂M   **15** ZX̂K

8 AX̂G   **16** ZX̂H

9 AX̂J   **17** ZX̂C

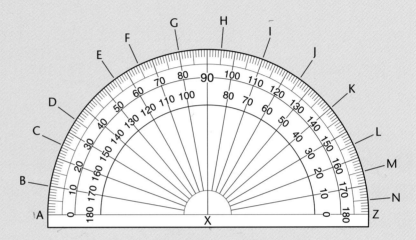

18 For each quadrilateral write the angles in order of size, smallest first.

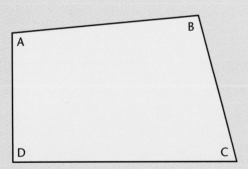

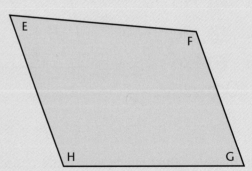

19 For each of the angles in the above quadrilaterals:

a) say whether the angle is acute, obtuse or a right angle

b) estimate the size of the angle to the nearest 5°

c) measure the angle to the nearest 5°.

Use 1 cm² paper

20 (0, 7), (2, 1) and (5, 2) are three vertices of a rectangle. Plot the co-ordinates and find the missing vertex. Complete the rectangle and use a protractor to check that the angles are 90°.

21 Plot the following co-ordinates and join up to form a triangle.

(5, 5) (6, 10) (10, 3)

Measure and label the angles of the triangle to the nearest degree.

C

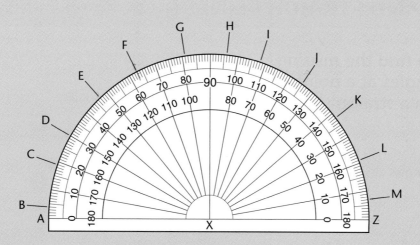

Give the measurement of each angle to the nearest degree.

1 AX̂C   **5** AX̂E   **9** AX̂G   **13** ZX̂E   **17** ZX̂B   **21** ZX̂F

2 AX̂K   **6** AX̂H   **10** AX̂L   **14** ZX̂J   **18** ZX̂K   **22** ZX̂L

3 AX̂F   **7** AX̂B   **11** AX̂D   **15** ZX̂G   **19** ZX̂D   **23** ZX̂C

4 AX̂M   **8** AX̂J   **12** AX̂I   **16** ZX̂M   **20** ZX̂H   **24** ZX̂I

25 Estimate the size of these angles and then measure them to the nearest degree. Use a 360° protractor. If you are using a 180° protractor, measure the inner angle and calculate the required angle.

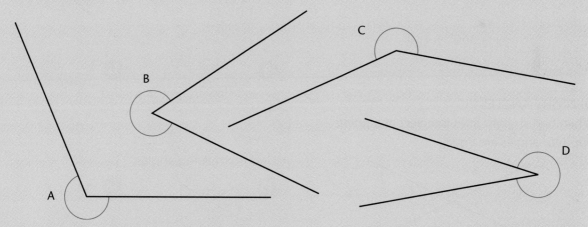

26 Use 1 cm² paper. Plot these co-ordinates and join up in the order given to form a quadrilateral.
(0, 0) (1, 3) (7, 7) (5, 0) (0, 0)
Measure the angles of the quadrilateral.

27 Draw a quadrilateral with a reflex angle. Measure and label the angles.

28 Use 1 cm² paper. Plot these co-ordinates and join up to form a triangle.
(1, 1) (2, 5) (7, 2). Measure and label the angles. Find the sum of the angles.

29 Draw five different triangles. Measure and label the angles.
Find the sum of the angles of each triangle. What do you notice?

TARGET To find the missing angles at a point and on a straight line.

Examples

ANGLES ON A STRAIGHT LINE
The sum of the angles at a point on a straight line is 180°.

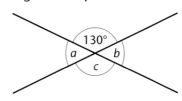

$$x = 180° - 65°$$
$$= 115°$$

ANGLES AT A POINT
A whole turn is 360°.

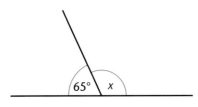

$$y = 360° - 130°$$
$$= 230°$$

OPPOSITE ANGLES
When two straight lines intersect at a point opposite angles are equal.

$$a = 180° - 130°$$
$$= 50°$$
$$b = 180° - 130°$$
$$= 50°$$
$$c = 360° - 130° - 50° - 50°$$
$$= 360° - 230°$$
$$= 130°$$

A

Find the missing angles.

1 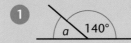 *a* 140°

4  145° *d*

2 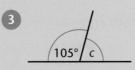 *b* 110°

5 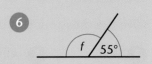 80° *e*

3 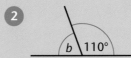 105° *c*

6 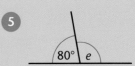 *f* 55°

Find the missing angles.

7 *g* 70°

10 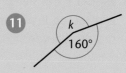 *j* 240°

8  *h* 330°

11 *k* 160°

9 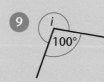 *i* 100°

12 50° *l*

Find the missing angles.

13  *n* 60° *m* *n*

16 70° *t* *t* *s*

14 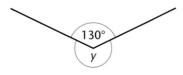 *p* *o* 140° *p*

17  *v* *u* 35° *w*

15 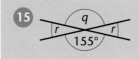 *q* *r* *r* 155°

18 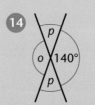 125° *x* *z* *y*

B

Find the missing angles marked with the letters.

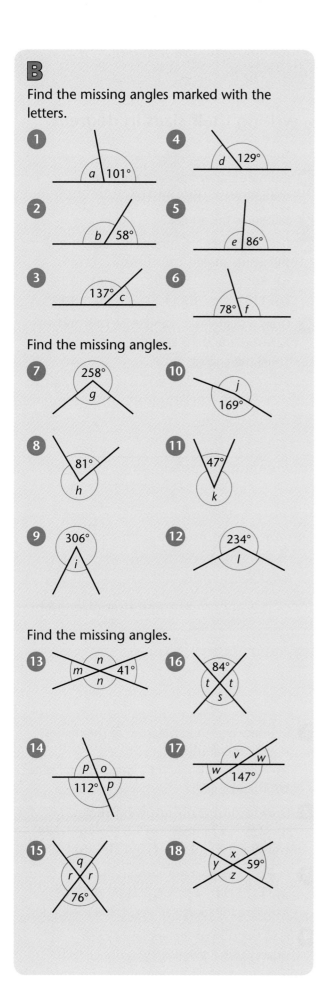

1 a 101°

2 b / 58°

3 137° / c

4 d \ 129°

5 e / 86°

6 78° / f

Find the missing angles.

7 258° / g

8 81° / h

9 306° / i

10 j / 169°

11 47° / k

12 234° / l

Find the missing angles.

13 m n n 41°

14 p o 112° p

15 q r r 76°

16 84° t t s

17 v w w 147°

18 x y z 59°

C

Calculate the missing angles.

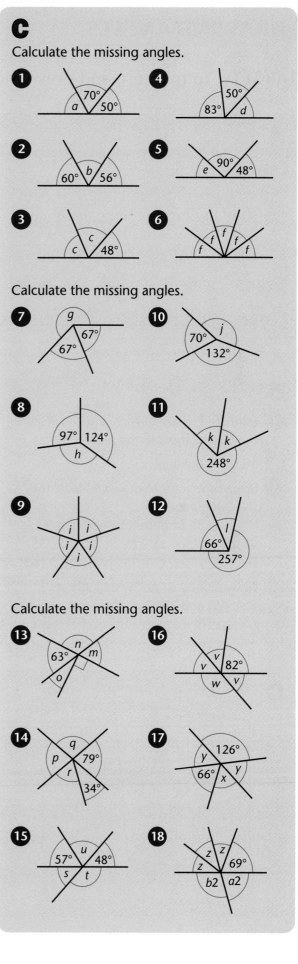

1 70° a 50°

2 60° b 56°

3 c c 48°

4 50° 83° d

5 e 90° 48°

6 f f f f f

Calculate the missing angles.

7 g 67° 67°

8 97° 124° h

9 i i i i i

10 70° j 132°

11 k k 248°

12 l 66° 257°

Calculate the missing angles.

13 63° n m o

14 p q 79° r 34°

15 57° u 48° s t

16 v v 82° w v

17 y 126° 66° x y

18 z z z 69° b2 a2

TARGET To measure and draw angles, writing their sizes in degrees.

A

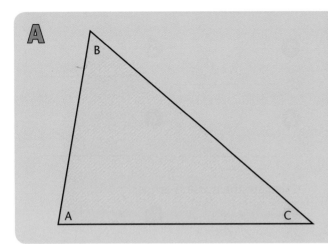

1. Estimate the size of each angle in the triangle to the nearest 10°.
2. Measures the angles.
3. Use a protractor to draw and label the following angles.

   a) 80° c) 20° e) 50°
   b) 110° d) 170° f) 140°
4. Draw a triangle with angles of 100° and 40°. Measure the third angle. Label the angles.

B

1. Estimate the size of each angle in the quadrilateral to the nearest 5°.
2. Measure the angles.
3. Use a protractor to draw and label the following angles. Write acute or obtuse by each angle.

   a) 65° c) 15° e) 35°
   b) 135° d) 95° f) 165°
4. Draw a quadrilateral with angles of 85°, 45° and 125°. Measure the fourth angle. Label the angles.

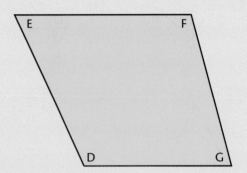

C

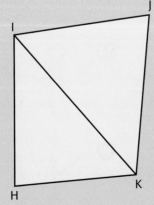

1. Estimate and then measure to the nearest degree the angles of:

   a) triangle HIK c) quadrilateral HIJK
   b) triangle IJK
2. Draw and label the following angles.

   a) 72° c) 159° e) 57° g) 224°
   b) 106° d) 23° f) 121° h) 278°
3. Draw a quadrilateral with angles of:

   a) 117°, 94°, 43° b) 38°, 202°, 67°
   Measure the fourth angles. Label the angles.
4. Find the sum of the angles of each quadrilateral. What do you notice?

TARGET   To use the properties of rectangles to find lengths and angles.

Examples

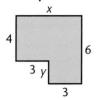

Find lengths x and y.
$x = (3 + 3)\,cm = 6\,cm$
$y = (6 - 4)\,cm = 2\,cm$

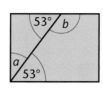

Find angles a and b.
$a = (90 - 53)° = 37°$
$b = (180 - 53)° = 127°$

Perimeters are rectilinear. (All lines meet at right angles.) All lengths are in centimetres.

A

Find the missing lengths, a–d.

Find the missing angles, e–h.

1

2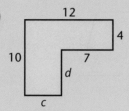

3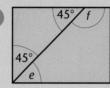

4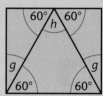

B

Find the missing lengths and angles.

1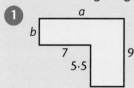

3

2

4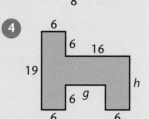

Find the missing angles, i–s.

5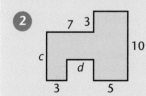

7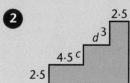

6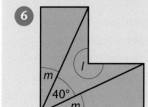

8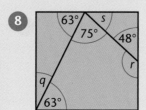

C

Find the missing lengths, a–h.

1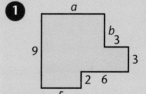

3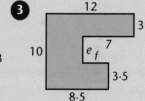

2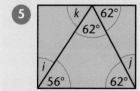

4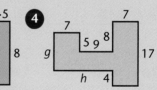

The sum of the angles of:

a) a triangle is 180°

b) a quadrilateral is 360°.

Use these facts to find the missing angles.

5

6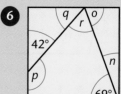

TARGET   To measure accurately with both ruler and protractor and to use conventional markings for right angles and parallel lines.

All lengths are in centimetres.

A

Construct the quadrilaterals. Show all right angles and parallel lines.

1 square
sides 3·5 cm

2 rectangle
sides 4·6 cm, 2·9 cm

3 square
sides 2·7 cm

4 rectangle
sides 1·3 cm, 3·1 cm

5
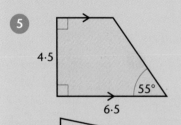

6
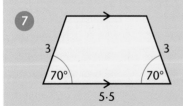

7
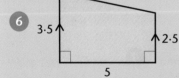

8
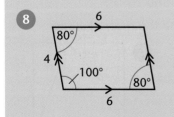

B

Construct the quadrilaterals. Measure and record all angles and lengths. Show parallel lines and right angles.

1
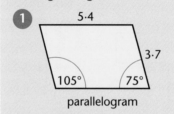
parallelogram

2
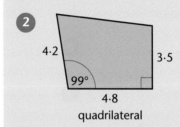
quadrilateral

3
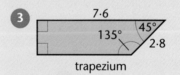
trapezium

4
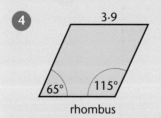
rhombus

5 parallelogram
sides 6·1 cm, 2·6 cm
angles 132°, 48°

6 rhombus
sides 4·3 cm
angles 97°, 83°

C

The sum of the angles of a quadrilateral is 360°. Use this fact to construct the quadrilaterals. Measure and record all angles and lengths. Show parallel lines.

1
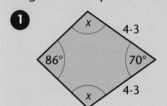

2
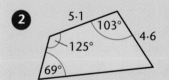

3
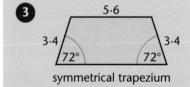
symmetrical trapezium

4
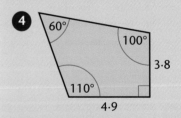

5 parallelogram
sides 5·7 cm, 1·8 cm
one angle of 111°

6 rhombus
sides 3·6 cm
one angle of 54°

TARGET   To recognise the properties of the diagonals of quadrilaterals.

DIAGONALS

Diagonal lines go from one vertex of a shape to another.

LINES WHICH BISECT

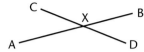

AX = BX
CX = DX

Bisect means cut in half. Lines which bisect cut each other in half.

PERPENDICULAR LINES

Perpendicular lines cross or meet at a right angle.

A

1. Use squared paper. Draw a square with sides of 3 cm. Draw on the diagonals.

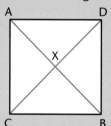

2. Measure the diagonals, AB and CD. Are they equal?

3. Measure AX and BX. Measure CX and DX. Do the diagonals cut each other in half?

4. Use a set square. Do the diagonals cross at a right angle?

5. Draw a square with 5 cm sides. Draw on the diagonals. Repeat questions 2 to 4 for this square.

6. Investigate the diagonals of rectangles.

B

1. For each of the quadrilaterals predict whether the diagonals:
   a) are of equal length
   b) bisect each other
   c) are perpendicular.

2. a) Copy the shapes onto squared paper and draw the diagonals.
   b) Check your predictions.
   c) Mark all parallel lines and right angles.
   d) Name each shape.

C

The following lines are the diagonals of quadrilaterals. For each pair of lines predict the properties of the shape.
a) Are any pairs of sides equal, parallel or perpendicular?
b) Are any angles equal?
c) Is the shape symmetrical? (Dashes show equal lines. Right angles are marked.)

7. a) Construct the shapes.
   b) Check your predictions.
   c) Mark all the right angles and parallel lines.
   d) Name the shapes.

TARGET To identify 3-D shapes from 2-D representations.

CURVED EDGES

These 3-D shapes
have curved edges.

cone
cylinder
hemisphere
sphere

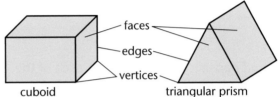

Cone

STRAIGHT EDGES

A 3-D shape with straight edges is called a polyhedron.
These shapes are some of the polyhedra.

cube   prisms: triangular
cuboid   pentagonal
square based pyramid   hexagonal
triangular based pyramid   and so on

faces
edges
vertices

cuboid   triangular prism

Look at the shapes A–J.
Write down the letters of all the shapes:

1 with curved faces

2 with a triangular face or faces

3 with curved edges

4 which are polyhedra.

Write down the letter of the shape
which has:

5 8 faces

6 6 edges

7 6 vertices

8 2 circular faces

9 18 edges

10 5 vertices

11 Which two shapes each have one
circular face?

12 Which two shapes each have eight
vertices?

13 Which two shapes each have five
faces?

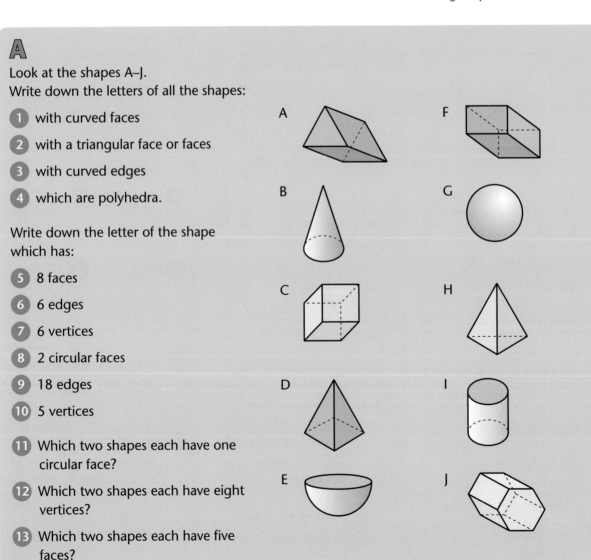

B

Copy and complete by matching the letters of the shapes in Section A to these names.

1 _____ sphere

2 _____ triangular prism

3 _____ square based pyramid

4 _____ cone

5 _____ cuboid

6 _____ triangular based pyramid

7 _____ cylinder

8 _____ cube

9 _____ hemisphere

10 _____ hexagonal prism

11 For each of the six polyhedra listed above, write down the number of faces, edges and vertices it possesses.

Example

triangular prism

5 faces, 9 edges, 6 vertices

12 Selina uses straws to build a 3-D shape. She uses nine lengths. Which shape has she made?

13 Hussein makes a 3-D shape by glueing together four flat pieces of card. Which shape has he made?

14 Danielle makes a 3-D shape by glueing together six identical flat pieces of card. What shape is each piece of card?

15 How many lengths of straw would be needed to build:

a) a pentagonal prism

b) a pentagonal based pyramid?

C

A prism is a polyhedron with two identical end faces and the same cross-section throughout its length.

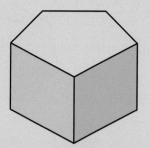

1 Look at the pentagonal prism. Write down the number of:

a) faces   b) edges   c) vertices.

2 Ahmed says a cuboid is a prism.

a) Is he right? Give a reason for your answer.

b) List all the shapes on page 122 which are prisms.

3 This is the end face of a prism.

a) How many faces would it have?

b) How many edges?

c) How many vertices?

4 A prism has 12 faces.

a) How many edges does it have?

b) How many vertices?

5 A pyramid has 10 edges.

a) How many faces does it have?

b) What shape is the base?

6 A prism has 24 edges.

a) How many vertices does it have?

b) What shape is the end face?

7 A pyramid has 7 vertices.

a) How many faces does it have?

b) What shape is the base?

TARGET To distinguish between regular and irregular polygons.

REGULAR POLYGONS

all sides equal
all angles equal

Example
a regular heptagon

IRREGULAR POLYGONS

all sides and all angles
not equal

Example
an irregular pentagon

A

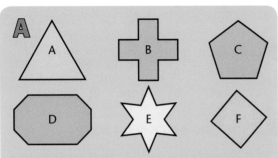

1 Give the letter and name of the above shapes which are regular.

2 Give a reason why each of the above irregular shapes is not regular.

3 Use squared paper.

   a) Draw a quadrilateral with equal angles which is not regular. Name the shape.

   b) Draw a quadrilateral with equal sides which is not regular. Name the shape.

B

1 An equilateral triangle has angles of 60°. Draw an equilateral triangle with sides 4·5 cm.

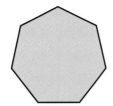

2 A regular hexagon has angles of 120°. Draw a regular hexagon with sides 2·5 cm.

3 Draw an irregular hexagon which has six 120° angles.

4 Find the missing angles *a*, *b*, *c* and *d*.

5 Construct the irregular hexagon shown in blue with all sides 3·2 cm.

C

1 Work out the equal angle *x* separating each pair of spokes.

2 Draw 5 spokes of equal length and with equal angles between them. Join up the ends of the spokes to draw a regular pentagon.

3 The angles of your pentagon should be 108°. Draw an irregular pentagon with all angles 108°.

4 Draw an irregular pentagon with all sides equal.

5 Draw a regular pentagon with sides 2·8 cm.

6 Use the spokes method to draw a regular polygon with:

   a) eight sides (octagon)

   b) nine sides (nonagon)

   c) ten sides (decagon).

TARGET   To identify and sketch the position of a shape following a reflection.

Examples

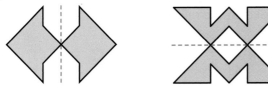

Use squared paper. Copy the shape and the mirror line. Sketch the reflection.

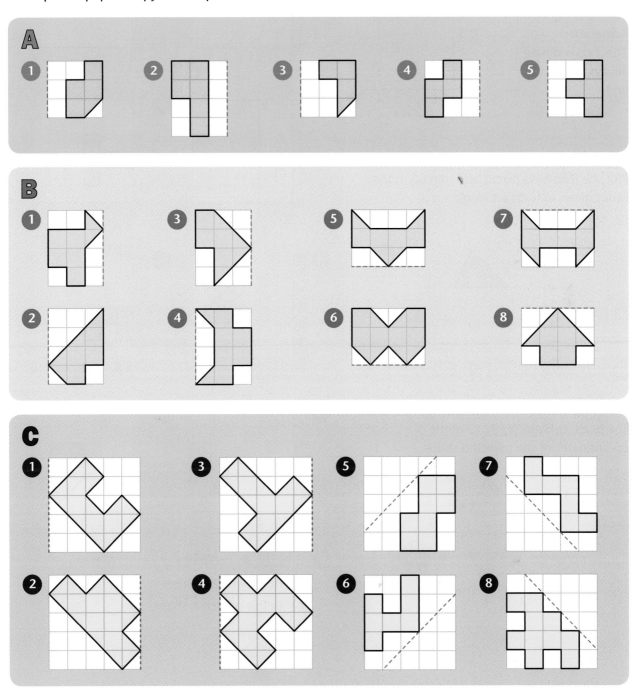

TARGET
To plot co-ordinates, to draw a shape and to predict its position following a reflection.

The position of a point on a grid is given by its *x* and *y* co-ordinates.

Examples

Point A is (1, 4).
Point B is (4, 1).
Remember:
The *x* co-ordinate always comes first.

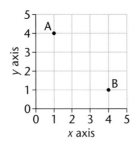

Example

Plot the following points and join up in the order given to form a triangle.

(2, 4) (4, 6) (5, 4) (2, 4)

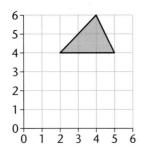

Sketch the reflection of the shape in a mirror line from (0, 3) to (6, 3). Give the co-ordinates of the reflected shape.

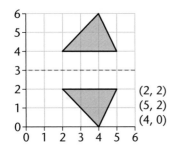

(2, 2)
(5, 2)
(4, 0)

Use squared paper.
Copy the grid, the shape and the mirror line.
Sketch the reflection.

1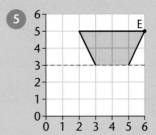

5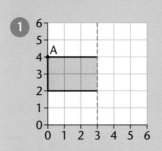

2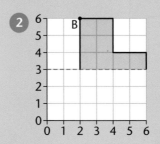

6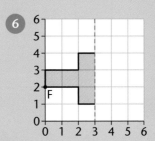

3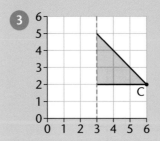

7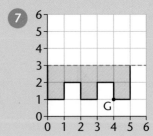

4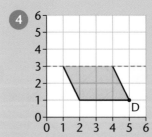

8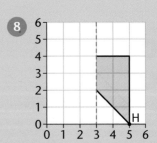

9 Give the co-ordinates of points A–H:

a) in the above shapes

b) in the reflected shapes.

B

Copy the grid, the shape and the mirror line.
Sketch the reflection.

1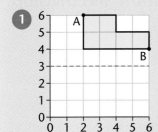

2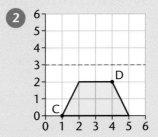

3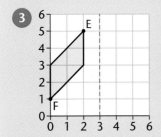

4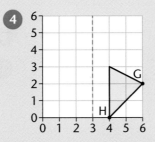

5 Give the co-ordinates of points A–H:

   a) in the above shapes

   b) in the reflected shapes.

Plot the co-ordinates for each of the following on a
6 × 6 grid and join them up in the order given to
form a shape. Draw the mirror line and sketch the
reflection.

6 (3, 4) (1, 6) (4, 6) (6, 4) (3, 4)

   Mirror line (0, 3) to (6, 3)

7 (0, 0) (0, 1) (2, 1) (2, 2) (3, 2) (3, 1) (4, 1)
   (4, 0) (0, 0)

   Mirror line (0, 3) to (6, 3)

8 (2, 1) (1, 1) (0, 3) (1, 5) (2, 5) (2, 1)

   Mirror line (3, 0) to (3, 6)

9 (4, 6) (6, 4) (5, 2) (4, 2) (4, 6)

   Mirror line (3, 0) to (3, 6)

10 (0, 6) (4, 6) (3, 5) (3, 4) (1, 4) (1, 5) (0, 6)

   Mirror line (0, 3) to (6, 3)

C

Copy the grid, the shape and the mirror
line.
Sketch the reflection.

1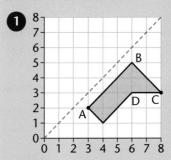

2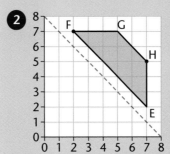

3 Give the co-ordinates of points A–H:

   a) in the above shapes

   b) in the reflected shapes.

Plot the co-ordinates on an 8 × 8 grid
and join them up in the order given to
form a shape. Draw the mirror line and
sketch the reflection.

4 (3, 2) (6, 5) (7, 4) (7, 1) (4, 1) (3, 2)

   Mirror line (0, 0) to (8, 8)

5 (1, 2) (1, 6) (3, 6) (5, 8) (5, 6) (1, 2)

   Mirror line (0, 0) to (8, 8)

6 (2, 8) (8, 8) (8, 2) (6, 4) (6, 6) (4, 6)
   (2, 8)

   Mirror line (0, 8) to (8, 0)

7 (1, 1) (1, 3) (0, 4) (0, 6) (1, 6) (6, 1)
   (6, 0) (4, 0) (3, 1) (1, 1)

   Mirror line (0, 8) to (8, 0)

TARGET To solve number puzzles involving multiplication and division.

Example
In a multiplication pyramid pairs of numbers are multiplied together to make the number above them.
Copy and complete the multiplication pyramids.

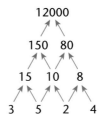

```
        12000
      150   80
    15   10   8
   3   5   2   4
```

A

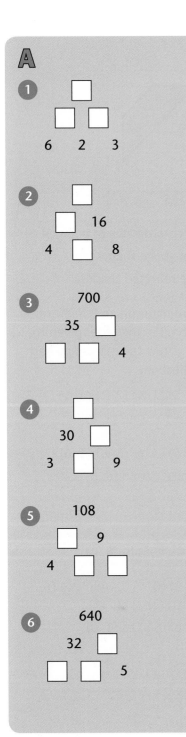

1
```
      □
    □   □
  6   2   3
```

2
```
      □
    □   16
  4   □   8
```

3
```
     700
   35   □
  □   □   4
```

4
```
      □
    30   □
  3   □   9
```

5
```
     108
   □   9
  4   □   □
```

6
```
     640
   32   □
  □   □   5
```

B

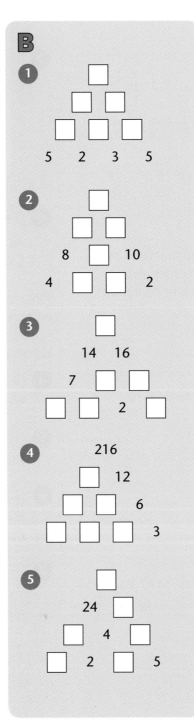

1
```
        □
      □   □
    □   □   □
  5   2   3   5
```

2
```
        □
      □   □
    8   □   10
  4   □   □   2
```

3
```
        □
     14   16
    7   □   □
  □   □   2   □
```

4
```
       216
      □   12
    □   □   6
  □   □   □   3
```

5
```
        □
     24   □
    □   4   □
  □   2   □   5
```

C

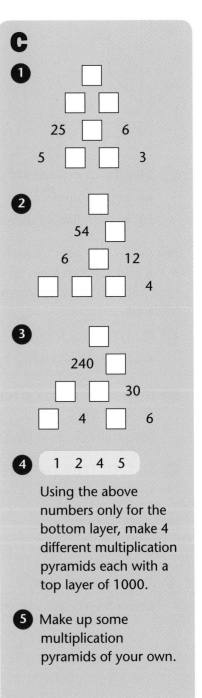

1
```
        □
      □   □
   25   □   6
  5   □   □   3
```

2
```
        □
     54   □
    6   □   12
  □   □   □   4
```

3
```
        □
     240   □
    □   □   30
  □   4   □   6
```

4   `1  2  4  5`

Using the above numbers only for the bottom layer, make 4 different multiplication pyramids each with a top layer of 1000.

5 Make up some multiplication pyramids of your own.

TARGET   To represent the position of a shape after a translation.

To translate a shape means to slide it into a new postion.

Examples

Translate the orange shapes as follows:

① R3 (right 3 squares)

② D2 (down 2 squares)

③ R1 D2 (Right 1 Down 2)

④ L3 U1 (Left 3 Up 1)

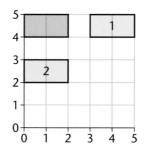

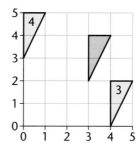

A

Copy the grids and the shapes. Translate each shape 3 times.

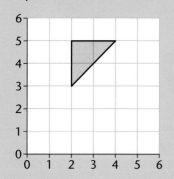

① L2   ② D3   ③ R2

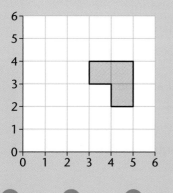

④ D2   ⑤ L3   ⑥ U2

B

① Copy the grid in Section A.
   a) Plot these points. (1, 6) (2, 4) (3, 6). Join them up to draw a triangle.
   b) Translate the triangle R2. Give the co-ordinates of the new position.
   c) Translate the original triangle D4. Give the new co-ordinates.

② Draw a new grid. Plot these points and join them up in the order given.

   (5, 0) (5, 2) (6, 3) (6, 1) (5, 0)

   Translate the quadrilateral:
   a) U3
   b) L2.

   Give the co-ordinates of the new positions.

C

① Draw a new grid.
   a) Plot these points and join them up to draw a triangle. (1, 2) (2, 4) (3, 1)
   b) Translate the triangle R2 D1. Give the co-ordinates of the new position.
   c) Translate the original triangle L1 U2. Give the new co-ordinates.

② Draw a new grid. Plot these points and join them up in the order given.

   (2, 4) (2, 5) (4, 3) (3, 2) (2, 4)

   Translate the quadrilateral:
   a) R2 U1
   b) L2 D2.

   Give the co-ordinates of the new positions.

TARGET
To identify and represent the position of a shape afer a translation.

To translate a shape means to slide it into a new position. The shape stays the same and is not rotated (turned).

Examples

1 Translate the blue hexagon Right 3 Up 2.
Give the co-ordinates of the new position.

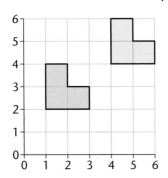

(4, 4) (4, 6) (5, 6) (5, 5) (6, 5) (6, 4)

2 Translate the blue triangle Left 1 Down 3.
Give the co-ordinates of the new position.

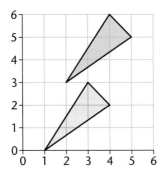

(1, 0) (3, 3) (4, 2)

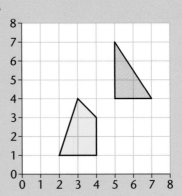

1 Copy the grid and the triangle.
Translate the triangle:

  a) Left 4 squares

  b) Down 3 squares.

2 Copy the grid and the quadrilateral.
Translate the quadrilateral:

  a) Right 2 squares

  b) Up 4 squares.

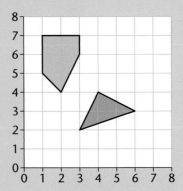

3 Copy the grid and the triangle.
Translate the triangle:

  a) Left 3 squares

  b) Up 2 squares.

4 Copy the grid and the pentagon.
Translate the pentagon:

  a) Right 3 squares

  b) Down 4 squares.

B

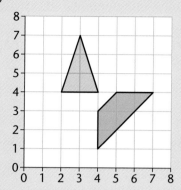

1 Copy the grid and the triangle.
Translate the triangle:

a) Left 2   Down 3

b) Right 4 Up 1

c) Right 3 Down 4.

2 Copy the grid and the trapezium.
Translate the trapezium:

a) Left 4   Down 1

b) Right 1 Up 4

c) Left 3   Up 3.

3 Draw a new grid. Plot these co-ordinates
and join them up in the order given.

(4, 6) (6, 6) (7, 4) (5, 4) (4, 6)

4 Translate the parallelogram:

a) Left 2   Up 2

b) Right 1 Down 3

c) Left 3   Down 4.

5 Draw a new grid. Plot these co-ordinates
and join them up in the order given.

(3, 1) (1, 3) (2, 4) (4, 4) (4, 2) (3, 1)

6 Translate the pentagon:

a) Right 3 Up 4

b) Right 4 Down 1

c) Left 1   Up 3.

7 Give the co-ordinates of the new
positions of the pentagon.

C

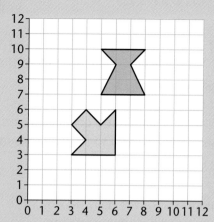

1 Copy the grid and the hexagon.
Translate the shape:

a) Left 3   Up 2

b) Right 2 Down 4

c) Left 5   Down 6.

2 Copy the grid and the heptagon.
Translate the shape:

a) Right 4 Up 2

b) Left 2   Up 5

c) Right 6 Down 2.

3 Draw a new grid. Plot these co-ordinates
and join them up in the order given.

(3, 7) (5, 9) (6, 8) (5, 7) (6, 6) (5, 5) (3, 7)

4 Translate the shape:

a) Right 5 Up 2

b) Left 3   Down 4

c) Right 2 Down 3.

5 Draw a new grid. Plot these co-ordinates
and join them up in the order given.

(6, 4) (7, 7) (8, 6) (9, 7) (8, 4) (7, 5) (6, 4)

6 Translate the shape:

a) Left 4   Up 5

b) Right 2 Up 4

c) Left 6   Down 2.

7 Give the co-ordinates of the new
positions of the hexagon which is not
symmetric.

TARGET To solve problems using information presented in a line graph.

A line graph consists of a series of points connected by straight lines. Line graphs are often used to show how something changes over time. To read the graph we need to locate points in relation to both axes.

Examples

This line graph shows the daily maximum temperature for one week in October.

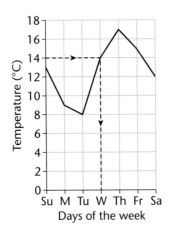

1 On which day was the temperature 14°C?

Answer *Wednesday (see graph)*

2 On which day was the lowest temperature recorded?

Answer *Tuesday*

3 How much higher was the temperature on Thursday than on Friday?

Answer *2°C (17°C – 15°C)*

4 On which day was there the largest fall in temperature?

Answer *Monday (4°C lower than Sunday)*

5 How much lower was the temperature on Saturday than on Friday?

Answer *3°C (15°C – 12°C)*

6 On how many days was the temperature below 10°C?

Answer *2 (Monday, Tuesday)*

 A

This line graph shows the daily maximum temperature for the first 12 days of March.

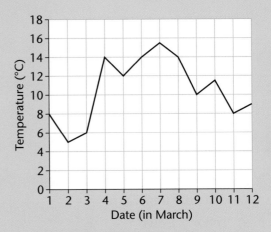

1 On which day was there:
a) the highest temperature
b) the lowest temperature?

2 What was the temperature on:
a) 6th March
b) 12th March?

3 On which day was the temperature:
a) 6°C
b) 10°C?

4 On which two days was the temperature 8°C?

5 How much higher was the temperature on the 8th than on the 9th?

6 How much lower was the temperature on the 5th than on the 6th?

7 On which day was there:
a) the largest rise in temperature
b) the largest fall in temperature?

8 On how many days was the temperature:
a) below 10°C
b) above 12°C?

B

This graph shows the number of boxes of cornflakes a supermarket has in stock recorded each morning before the store opens.

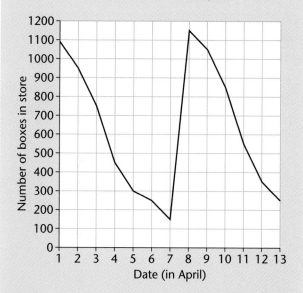

1. On which day is there a delivery of new stock?

2. How many boxes are there in stock at the start of:
   a) 7th April
   b) 5th April?

3. At the start of which day was the number of boxes in stock:
   a) 450
   b) 850?

4. How many more boxes were in stock on the 1st than on the 2nd?

5. How many fewer boxes were in stock on the 7th than on the 8th?

6. How many boxes were sold on:
   a) the 3rd
   b) the 9th?

7. How many more boxes were sold on the 10th than on the 11th?

8. How many fewer boxes were sold on the 5th than on the 6th?

9. One hundred boxes were sold on the 7th. How many boxes were delivered?

C

A High Street shop is open from 8 am to 6 pm on a Saturday. This line graph shows the number of customers in the shop recorded at hourly intervals.

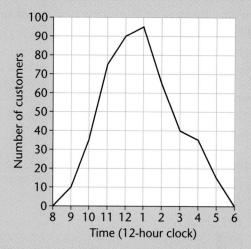

1. When was the shop most crowded?

2. How many customers were in the shop at:
   a) 2 pm
   b) noon?

3. At what time were there:
   a) 40 customers
   b) 75 customers?

4. How many more customers were in the shop at 4 pm than 5 pm?

5. How many fewer customers were in the shop at 9 am than 10 am?

6. Estimate the number of customers in the shop at:
   a) 10.30 am
   b) 1.30 pm?

7. In which hour was there:
   a) the largest rise in customers
   b) the largest fall in customers?

8. Between 11 am and noon 117 customers entered the shop. How many left?

9. Between 3 pm and 4 pm 56 customers left the shop. How many entered?

TARGET   To solve problems using information presented in a line graph.

A line graph consists of a series of points connected by straight lines. Line graphs are often used to show how something changes over time. To read the graph we need to locate points in relation to both axes.

Examples
This line graph shows the height above sea level of a hill walker measured every half hour.

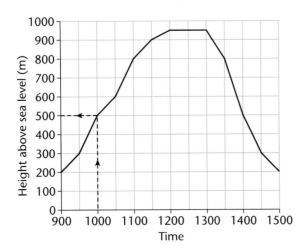

1. At what time does he begin his walk?

   Answer *09:00*

2. How high is he at 10:00?

   Answer *500 m (shown on graph)*

3. How much higher is he at 11:00 than 10:00?

   Answer *300 m (800 m – 500 m)*

4. How high is the hill?

   Answer *950 m*

5. How long is he above 800 m?

   Answer *2½ hours (11:00 to 13:30)*

A

This line graph shows the temperature of water being heated and then left to cool recorded every 2 minutes.

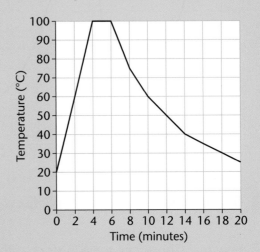

1. What is the temperature of the water before it is heated?

2. How long does it take the water to reach boiling point?

3. How much does the temperature rise in the first two minutes of heating?

4. How long is the water boiling?

5. How much does the temperature fall in the first two minutes of cooling?

6. As the water cooled at what time was the temperature:
   a) 50°C
   b) 35°C?

7. What was the temperature of the water after:
   a) 20 minutes
   b) 8 minutes?

8. At which two times was the temperature 60°C?

B

This graph shows the monthly sales of lawnmowers at a garden centre.

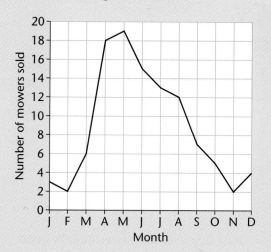

1 In which months were:
 a) most mowers sold
 b) fewest mowers sold?

2 How many mowers were sold in:
 a) March
 b) August?

3 In which month were:
 a) 4 mowers sold
 b) 15 mowers sold?

4 In which month was there:
 a) the largest rise in sales
 b) the largest fall in sales?

5 How many more mowers were sold in October than in November?

6 How many fewer mowers were sold in February than in May?

7 How many fewer mowers were sold in the first three months of the year than in the next three months?

8 In how many months were there:
 a) more than 10 mowers sold
 b) less than 5 mowers sold?

9 How many mowers were sold in the year altogether?

C

This graph shows the average daily maximum temperature recorded in Anchorage, Alaska, in one year.

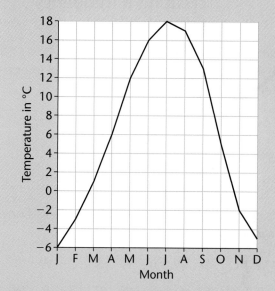

1 In which month was the highest temperature recorded?

2 What was the lowest temperature?

3 In which month was the temperature:
 a) 17°C
 b) −3°C?

4 What was the temperature in:
 a) June
 b) December?

5 In which month was there:
 a) the largest rise in temperature
 b) the largest fall in temperature?

6 How much higher was the temperature:
 a) in October than November
 b) in September than December?

7 How much lower was the temperature:
 a) in April than May
 b) in January than July?

8 In which months was the temperature:
 a) above 10°C
 b) below 0°C?

TARGET To organise data by creating a frequency table.

Example

The 60 children in Year 5 travel to school in one of four ways:

B   Bike

C   Car

S   School bus

W   Walk

This is how each of the 60 children travelled on one day.

W	C	S	W	B	W	S	C	W	S
S	W	S	C	S	W	C	S	B	W
C	W	B	S	C	W	S	W	W	C
W	S	C	W	S	W	B	C	S	W
B	W	S	B	W	C	S	W	C	S
S	C	W	S	C	B	S	W	S	W

A tally chart can be completed by counting in groups of five.

Travel Method	Tally
Bike	卌 II
Car	卌 卌 III
School Bus	卌 卌 卌 IIII
Walk	卌 卌 卌 卌 I

The data can be presented in a frequency table.

Travel Method	Number of children
Bike	7
Car	13
School Bus	19
Walk	21
Total	60

A

1 The children in Class 5 were asked to choose a flavour of yogurt to take on a trip for lunch time. The flavours available were hazelnut, orange, peach and strawberry. These are the choices.

S	P	H	O	P	S	H
H	O	P	S	H	O	P
P	H	S	P	H	P	O
S	P	O	H	S	P	H

a) Copy and complete the tally chart.

Flavour	Tally
hazelnut	卌 III
orange	
peach	
strawberry	

b) Present the data in a frequency table.

2 These are the ages of the 36 children in the school chess club.

9	11	10	8	9	11	9	10	11
10	8	9	11	8	9	10	11	9
8	9	11	10	10	8	11	9	10
11	10	9	11	9	10	9	8	11

a) Copy and complete the tally chart.

Age	Tally
8	卌 I
9	
10	
11	

b) Present the data in a frequency table.

B

1 A football team played 50 matches in one season. These are the number of goals the team scored in each match.

1	3	2	0	1	1	2	4	2	1
2	1	0	3	2	3	1	0	1	2
0	4	2	1	1	2	0	2	3	1
1	2	0	1	0	3	2	1	0	4
2	3	1	2	2	1	1	0	2	1

a) Make a tally chart to find the total for each number of goals scored.

b) Present the data in a frequency table.

c) Check that the sum of the totals is 50.

2 A shop sells baseball caps in four different colours: black, red, white and yellow. In one day the following caps were sold.

B	W	Y	B	W	W	R
Y	B	W	R	Y	W	B
W	R	Y	W	B	R	W
B	W	R	B	Y	W	Y
R	B	Y	W	R	B	W
Y	W	R	W	B	W	Y

a) Make a tally chart to find the total for each colour of cap.

b) Present the data in a frequency table.

c) Check that the sum of the totals matches the number of caps sold.

C

1 The depth of a river was recorded each week for a year. These are the results rounded to the nearest metre.

6	5	5	4	6	5	4	4	3
5	5	4	3	4	3	3	2	3
2	3	2	2	3	3	2	4	3
4	3	2	2	4	3	2	4	3
5	4	3	3	4	5	3	4	5
6	4	4	6	5	4	6		

a) Make a tally chart to find the total of weeks for each depth.

b) Check that the sum of the totals matches the number of weeks.

c) Present the data in a frequency table.

2 The 60 employees of a firm voted to choose the restaurant they would go to for their annual Staff Meal. The five restaurants large enough to cater for the group were Chinese, English, French, Italian and Thai. The votes were:

I	C	E	F	I	T	E	C	I	F
C	F	C	I	E	C	T	F	E	I
I	E	T	C	I	F	I	E	T	C
T	I	F	E	C	E	T	C	F	I
E	F	C	I	F	T	E	I	C	I
C	T	E	F	I	C	T	F	I	E

a) Make a tally chart to show the total of votes for each restaurant.

b) Check that the sum of the totals matches the number of employees.

c) Present the data in a frequency table.

TARGET   To read and interpret information in a table.

This table shows the planets in our solar system in order of distance from the Sun.

Planet	Number of moons	Year length (Earth days/years)	Day length (Earth hours\days)	*Diameter (miles)	Temperature	
					Max. (°C)	Min. (°C)
Mercury	0	88 days	59 days	3031	430	−184
Venus	0	225 days	243 days	7521	464	464
Earth	1	365 days	24 hours	7926	57	−89
Mars	2	687 days	24·6 hours	4222	20	−120
Jupiter	67	11·9 years	9·8 hours	88729	−110	−110
Saturn	62	29·5 years	10·2 hours	74600	−140	−140
Uranus	27	84·1 years	17·9 hours	32600	−197	−197
Neptune	13	164·8 years	19·1 hours	30200	−204	−204

*The diameter of a planet is a straight line from one side to the opposite side passing through the centre of the planet.

Examples

What is the diameter of Mars?
Answer   *4222 miles*

Which planet has days 10·2 hours long?
Answer   *Saturn*

 A

1 How many moons does Mars have?

2 How long is a year on Mercury?

3 What is the diameter of the Earth?

4 What is the temperature on Saturn?

5 How long is a day on Uranus?

MARS

The solar system

6 Which planet has a maximum temperature of 20°C?

7 Which planet has 67 moons?

8 Which planet has a year 29·5 years long?

9 Which planet has a diameter of 30 200 miles?

10 Which planet has a day 59 times longer than a day on Earth?

B

Look at the table on page 138.

1 Which planets are moonless?

2 In the table year lengths are rounded to the nearest whole day. Give the actual length of Earth's year correct to 2 decimal places.

3 Which planet is closest to the Earth:
   a) in size (diameter)
   b) in length of day
   c) in length of year?

4 Which planet is:
   a) furthest from the Sun
   b) closest to the Sun?

5 Which planet is:
   a) coldest
   b) hottest?

6 Which planet has:
   a) the longest day
   b) the shortest day?

7 Which two planets have a diameter approximately four times that of Earth?

8 What is the difference between the maximum and minimum temperatures:
   a) on Mercury
   b) on Earth
   c) on Mars?

9 How many planets have:
   a) a shorter year than Earth
   b) a shorter day than Earth?

C

Look at the table on page 138.

1 Which planet has a day longer that its year?

2 What is the difference in maximum temperature between the hottest planet and the coldest planet?

3 Which planet takes the least time to orbit the Sun?

4 How much longer does it take Mars than Earth to:
   a) rotate on its axis
   b) orbit the Sun?

5 Give the total number of moons in our solar system.

6 On which planets would it be impossible to drink a glass of water? Give an explanation for your answer.

7 List the planets in order of:
   a) size, largest first
   b) length of day, shortest first
   c) minimum temperature, lowest first.

8 In 2046 you are the first astronaut to make use of space/time wormhole portal technology to explore the planets orbiting a distant star. Give information about the planets of that solar system in a table.

TARGET To complete, read and interpret information in tables.

Example

At a multiscreen cinema there are four performances daily at each of the five screens. This table shows the size of audience for each performance on one Saturday.

Screen	Performance			
	3 pm	5 pm	7 pm	9 pm
1	240	180	70	20
2	190	210	250	110
3	80	70	120	90
4	140	170	130	80
5	50	90	160	230

1. What was the audience in Screen 2 at 9 pm?

   Answer *110*

2. Which performance in Screen 1 had an audience of 180?

   Answer *5 pm*

3. What was the combined audience for the first two performances in Screen 4?

   Answer *310 (140 + 170)*

4. Which performance had an audience of 120?

   Answer *7 pm performance in Screen 3*

5. At 7 pm how many fewer people were in the audience in Screen 1 than in Screen 2?

   Answer *180 (250 − 70)*

6. How much larger was the audience in Screen 5 for the 9 pm performance than the 7 pm?

   Answer *70 (230 − 160)*

 A

At regular intervals in the Autumn Term the children in a class were given 60 mental calculations and five minutes to answer as many as they could. These are the scores of the children on one table.

Name	Test 1	Test 2	Test 3	Test 4
Kay	18	28	26	35
Gill	28	29	37	42
Zain	26	34	41	53
Lori	19	21	25	37
Ruja	25	27	43	44
Tim	23	22	34	39

1. How many did Tim score:
   a) in Test 1
   b) in Test 4?

2. Who scored 34:
   a) in Test 2
   b) in Test 3?

3. Who had the highest score:
   a) in Test 1
   b) in Test 3?

4. In which test did:
   a) Lori score 37
   b) Gill score 37?

5. In which Test did Kay make her greatest improvement?

6. How many more was scored in Test 4 than Test 1 by each of the children?

This table shows the number of bottles of milk sold in a supermarket.

Size	Red top	Green top	Blue top
1 litre	82	49	54
2 litres	46	78	39
3 litres	17	25	32

1 How many of these bottles were sold?

a) 1 litre bottles of red top

b) 2 litre bottles of blue top

c) 3 litre bottles of green top

2 How many more 2 litre bottles were sold of green top than red top?

3 How many fewer 1 litre bottles were sold of green top than blue top?

4 How many more 2 litre bottles of red top were sold than 3 litre bottles of red top?

5 How many fewer 2 litre bottles of blue top were sold than 1 litre bottles of blue top?

6 Give the total number of 3 litre bottles sold.

7 Give the total number of blue bottles sold.

8 Copy and complete the table.

Type of milk	Number of bottles sold	Number of litres sold
red top		
green top		
blue top		

This table shows the number of cars entering and leaving the 3 levels of a car park hourly after its 08:00 opening. Cars entering are shown in black. Cars leaving are shown in red.

Hour	Level 1		Level 2		Level 3	
1st	54	0	12	0	5	0
2nd	35	13	61	2	18	0
3rd	59	52	44	37	31	3
4th	48	65	25	39	26	29

1 How many cars entered the car park in:
a) the 1st hour   **b)** the 2nd hour?

2 In the first two hours how many cars entered:
a) Level 1   **b)** Level 3?

3 How many cars left the car park in:
a) the 2nd hour   **b)** the 4th hour?

4 How many more cars left Level 1 than Level 2 in:
a) the 3rd hour   **b)** the 4th hour?

5 In the second hour how many more cars entered Level 2 than:
a) Level 1   **b)** Level 3?

6 At the end of the second hour how many cars were on:
a) Level 2   **b)** Level 1?

7 Copy and complete the table showing the number of cars on each level at the end of each hour.

Time	Number of cars		
	Level 1	Level 2	Level 3
09:00			
10:00			
11:00			
12:00			

TARGET To read and interpret information in timetables.

	BUS 1	BUS 2	BUS 3	BUS 4	BUS 5
Ashwell	07:00	08:35	10:50	13:25	16:20
Basley	07:20	09:00	11:10	13:45	16:45
Cowthorpe	07:35	09:15	11:25	14:05	17:05
Downford	07:50	09:25	11:35	14:15	17:20
Eastbank	08:15	09:45	11:55	14:35	17:45
Foxhill	08:40	10:05	12:15	15:00	18:05

Example
How long is the journey on Bus 1 from Basley to Eastbank?

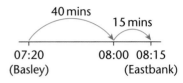

Answer *55 minutes*

A

1 At what time does Bus 1 leave Ashwell?

At what times does Bus 1 stop at:

2 Cowthorpe

3 Eastbank

4 Foxhill?

How long is the journey on Bus 1 from:

5 Ashwell to Cowthorpe

6 Eastbank to Foxhill

7 Basley to Downford?

How long is the journey on Bus 4 from:

8 Ashwell to Basley

9 Downford to Foxhill

10 Cowthorpe to Downford?

11 Nathan is meeting a friend at Cowthorpe at 8:00 am. He takes Bus 1 from Ashwell. How long will he have to wait at Cowthorpe?

B

At what time would you reach:

1 Basley on Bus 3

2 Eastbank on Bus 5

3 Cowthorpe on Bus 2

4 Foxhill on Bus 1

5 Downford on Bus 4

6 Eastbank on Bus 3?

How long is the journey:

7 on Bus 2 from Ashwell to Cowthorpe

8 on Bus 5 from Downford to Eastbank

9 on Bus 3 from Cowthorpe to Downford

10 on Bus 4 from Basley to Foxhill?

11 Which bus would you take from Ashwell if you need to be at Foxhill by:
a) 4:00 pm
b) 11:00 am
c) 6:00 pm?

C

1 How long does each bus take to travel from Ashwell to Cowthorpe?

2 How long does each bus take to complete the journey from Ashwell to Foxhill?

Which bus should someone take from Ashwell if they need to be:

3 in Cowthorpe at 11:00 am

4 in Foxhill at 1:30 pm

5 in Downford at 9:00 am

6 in Eastbank at 2:00 pm?

At what time would you catch a bus at Basley to be at:

7 Eastbank at 10:00 am

8 Downford at 5:30 pm

9 Downford at 2:30 pm

10 Cowthorpe at 2:00 pm?

TARGET   To practise using a timetable to find information.

Newcastle	08:15	09:53	11:27	–	14:02
Darlington	08:48	10:26	12:00	–	14:35
York	09:27	11:05	12:39	13:58	15:14
Leeds	09:55	11:33	13:07	14:26	15:42
Huddersfield	10:16	11:52	13:26	14:45	16:01
Manchester	10:54	12:30	14:02	15:23	16:39
Warrington	–	12:53	–	15:46	–
Liverpool	11:31	13:08	–	16:04	17:16

Example
How long does it take the
14:35 from Darlington to
reach York?

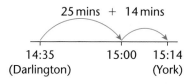

Answer   *39 minutes*

A

1. How long does it take the 08:15 from Newcastle to reach Darlington?

2. At how many stations does the 14:02 from Newcastle stop?

3. At what time does the 11:27 from Newcastle reach:
   a) York
   b) Manchester?

4. If you had to be in Liverpool by 12:30 which train would you catch from Newcastle?

5. You arrive at Newcastle at 11:05. How long do you have to wait for the next train to Leeds?

6. The 09:53 from Newcastle runs 10 minutes late. At what time will it reach:
   a) Huddersfield
   b) Warrington?

B

1. How long does it take the 09:53 from Newcastle to travel to:
   a) Darlington
   b) Leeds
   c) Liverpool?

2. At how many stations does the 15:14 from York stop before it reaches Liverpool?

3. At what time does the 10:26 from Darlington reach Warrington?

4. If you had to be in Manchester by 3:00 pm which train would you catch from Leeds?

5. You arrive at Newcastle at 10:45. How long do you have to wait for the next train to Huddersfield?

6. The 08:15 from Newcastle runs 15 minutes late. At what time will it reach:
   a) Manchester
   b) Liverpool?

C

1. How long does it take the 13:58 from York to travel to:
   a) Huddersfield
   b) Liverpool
   c) Manchester?

2. At what time does the 11:33 from Leeds reach Manchester?

3. If you had to be in Huddersfield by 2:00 pm which train would you catch from Darlington?

4. You arrive at Newcastle at 13:26. How long do you have to wait for the next train to Leeds?

5. You catch the 11:27 from Newcastle. How long do you have to wait at Manchester for the connection to Liverpool?

6. The 09:27 from York runs 46 minutes late. At what time will it reach Liverpool?

Write in words.

1. 80 026
2. 307 400
3. 791 005
4. 200 873
5. 429 608
6. 150·009
7. 97 301·2
8. 6605·04

Write down the value of the underlined digit.

9. 3<u>1</u> 728
10. 850 <u>9</u>46
11. 19<u>2</u> 387
12. <u>5</u>06 490
13. 323 8<u>6</u>5
14. 9<u>4</u>7 261
15. 8<u>9</u> 632
16. <u>7</u>65 170
17. 2105·1<u>9</u>
18. 78·05<u>3</u>
19. 60 <u>4</u>92·6
20. 4513·0<u>8</u>

Write these numbers in order, starting with the smallest.

21. 2209 2902 2290 2099
22. 116 011 61 606 66 016 110 611
23. 575 527 557 255 577 255 552 775
24. 393 344 349 439 344 993 349 399

What number do you reach?
Count on

25. six 1000s from 705 340
26. four 10 000s from 183 019
27. nine 100s from 372 653
28. seven 1000s from 597 428

Count back

29. eight 10 000s from 256 179
30. five 100s from 819 036
31. seven 1000s from 905 294
32. four 10 000s from 634 807

Round to the nearest:

100
33. 2392
34. 35 174
35. 468 045
36. 772 953

1000
37. 521 368
38. 43 807
39. 859 523
40. 267 289

10 000
41. 56 138
42. 103 724
43. 92 547
44. 169 025

100 000
45. 391 210
46. 748 009
47. 462 836
48. 853 742

Round to the nearest 100 and estimate.

49. 7462 + 3827
50. 12 937 + 5593
51. 8253 − 2446
52. 20 384 − 4871
53. 5864 × 4
54. 3629 × 7
55. 5073 ÷ 3
56. 17 954 ÷ 5

Write in Arabic numbers.

57. CCCLXV
58. DCCXXIII
59. CCLVII
60. CMLXXX
61. DIX
62. CXCIV
63. DCCCLXXIX
64. CDXLVIII

Write in Roman numerals.

65. 617
66. 975
67. 562
68. 496
69. 754
70. 208
71. 130
72. 829
73. 371
74. 403
75. 685
76. 999

Write in order, smallest first.

1 $\frac{2}{3}, \frac{1}{3}, \frac{1}{6}, \frac{1}{2}$

2 $\frac{1}{2}, \frac{4}{5}, \frac{7}{10}, \frac{2}{5}$

3 $\frac{5}{8}, \frac{3}{8}, \frac{3}{4}, \frac{1}{2}$

4 $\frac{2}{3}, \frac{1}{4}, \frac{7}{12}, \frac{5}{12}$

Write as mixed numbers.

5 $\frac{11}{2}$ **9** $\frac{14}{9}$

6 $\frac{15}{4}$ **10** $\frac{29}{6}$

7 $\frac{9}{7}$ **11** $\frac{10}{3}$

8 $\frac{43}{10}$ **12** $\frac{31}{12}$

Write as improper fractions.

13 $4\frac{2}{5}$ **17** $5\frac{2}{3}$

14 $5\frac{7}{8}$ **18** $6\frac{1}{4}$

15 $2\frac{4}{11}$ **19** $1\frac{5}{12}$

16 $3\frac{1}{6}$ **20** $3\frac{4}{9}$

Work out

21 $\frac{2}{6} + \frac{1}{12}$ **25** $\frac{3}{4} - \frac{7}{12}$

22 $\frac{1}{3} + \frac{5}{12}$ **26** $\frac{11}{12} - \frac{1}{6}$

23 $\frac{3}{4} + \frac{5}{8}$ **27** $\frac{7}{8} - \frac{1}{2}$

24 $\frac{1}{2} + \frac{7}{10}$ **28** $\frac{4}{5} - \frac{3}{10}$

Work out

29 $6\frac{4}{7} \times 2$ **33** $3\frac{2}{3} \times 6$

30 $4\frac{3}{4} \times 3$ **34** $7\frac{3}{5} \times 2$

31 $1\frac{5}{9} \times 8$ **35** $1\frac{8}{11} \times 5$

32 $5\frac{7}{10} \times 4$ **36** $2\frac{7}{8} \times 4$

Work out, writing remainders as fractions.

37 $\frac{3}{8}$ of 48   **41** $\frac{1}{10}$ of 74

38 $\frac{4}{5}$ of 60   **42** $\frac{1}{4}$ of 39

39 $\frac{5}{6}$ of 54   **43** $\frac{1}{3}$ of 17

40 $\frac{2}{9}$ of 63   **44** $\frac{1}{7}$ of 58

Write as a decimal.

45 $\frac{34}{100}$ **49** $27\frac{65}{100}$

46 $\frac{918}{1000}$ **50** $1\frac{573}{1000}$

47 $13\frac{2}{10}$ **51** $\frac{6}{100}$

48 $\frac{6}{1000}$ **52** $\frac{92}{1000}$

Write as a mixed number.

53 $2 \cdot 408$ **57** $0 \cdot 83$

54 $0 \cdot 76$ **58** $4 \cdot 06$

55 $0 \cdot 015$ **59** $0 \cdot 007$

56 $6 \cdot 1$ **60** $9 \cdot 309$

Give the value of the underlined digit.

61 $1 \cdot 2\underline{5}1$ **65** $35 \cdot \underline{4}8$

62 $0 \cdot 9\underline{6}$ **66** $3 \cdot 01\underline{4}$

63 $\underline{8} \cdot 5$ **67** $12 \cdot \underline{7}$

64 $0 \cdot 63\underline{2}$ **68** $0 \cdot 02\underline{6}$

Write $<$ or $>$ in the box.

69 $0 \cdot 37 \,\square\, 0 \cdot 317$

70 $0 \cdot 828 \,\square\, 0 \cdot 882$

71 $1 \cdot 16 \,\square\, 0 \cdot 661$

72 $0 \cdot 054 \,\square\, 0 \cdot 14$

Copy and complete.

73 $0 \cdot 52 + \square = 1$

74 $0 \cdot 75 + \square = 1$

75 $1 - \square = 0 \cdot 09$

76 $1 - \square = 0 \cdot 36$

77 $4 \cdot 5 + \square = 5 \cdot 2$

78 $\square + 0 \cdot 8 = 3 \cdot 7$

79 $7 \cdot 3 - \square = 6 \cdot 8$

80 $\square - 0 \cdot 9 = 1 \cdot 2$

Write as a percentage.

81 $\frac{1}{2}$ **85** $0 \cdot 27$

82 $\frac{19}{100}$ **86** $0 \cdot 4$

83 $\frac{3}{4}$ **87** $0 \cdot 06$

84 $\frac{9}{10}$ **88** $1 \cdot 0$

Write as:

a) a fraction in its lowest terms

b) a decimal.

89 47%   **93** 31%

90 25%   **94** 70%

91 60%   **95** 96%

92 8%   **96** 50%

Find:

97 25% of £7

98 10% of 4·9

99 30% of £120

100 75% of 5

Copy and complete.

1 1 m = ☐ + 0·35 m

2 1 m = ☐ + 0·71 m

3 1 km = 0·48 km + ☐

4 1 km = 0·63 km + ☐

5 £1 − ☐ = £0·84

6 £1 − ☐ = £0·09

7 1 kg − 0·57 kg = ☐

8 1 kg − 0·12 kg = ☐

Write the answer only.

9 0·19 m × 1000

10 0·058 litres × 10

11 2·06 km × 100

12 7·034 kg × 1000

13 16 m ÷ 100

14 82 litres ÷ 1000

15 4·7 km ÷ 10

16 5·3 kg ÷ 100

Copy and complete.
(≈ means in
approximately equal to)

17 6 inches ≈ ☐ cm

18 3 feet ≈ ☐ cm

19 5 yards ≈ ☐ m

20 100 miles ≈ ☐ km

21 8 oz ≈ ☐ g

22 5 kg ≈ ☐ lb

23 2 pints ≈ ☐ litres

24 10 gallons ≈ ☐ litres

Write the measurement
shown by each arrow.

25

26
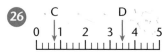

For each shape find:

a) the area

b) the perimeter.

27 rectangle
sides 16 cm, 8 cm

28 square
sides 20 cm

29 rectangle
sides 50 m, 30 m

30 square
sides 14 m

For each shape find:

a) the perimeter

b) the area.

31
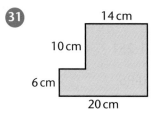
14 cm
10 cm
6 cm
20 cm

32
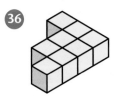
4 cm   4 cm
3 cm   3 cm
5 cm   5 cm
12 cm

33 A square has an area
of 400 m². What is its
perimeter?

The floor plans of these
rooms are drawn to a scale
of 1 : 1000 (1 mm shows
1 m).

For each plan work out:

a) the area of each room

b) the difference in the
area of each room.

34
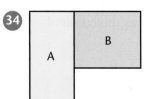
A   B

35
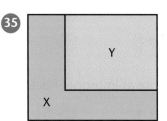
Y
X

For each shape find:

a) how many 1 cm³ cubes
are needed to build the
shape

b) how many more are
needed to turn it into a
cuboid.

36
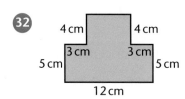

37
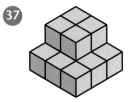

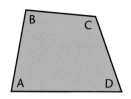

1 Write acute or obtuse for each angle of the quadrilateral.

2 Measure each angle to the nearest degree.

Draw the following angles. Label each angle acute, obtuse or reflex.

3 137°   7 63°

4 262°   8 191°

5 29°   9 158°

6 306°   10 44°

Find the new time if the hour hand of a clock turns:

11 180° from 10 am

12 90° from 11 pm

13 360° from 4 pm

14 180° from 7 pm.

How many degrees is the turn clockwise from:

15 E to S

16 NW to NW

17 SW to NE

18 SE to SW?

Place the angles meeting at each point in order of size, smallest first.

19
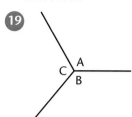

20
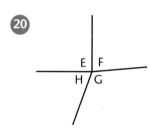

Construct and identify these shapes. (Lengths in cm)

21   22
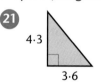

23
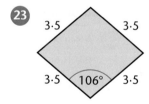

These lines are the diagonals of quadrilaterals. Construct and identify each shape. (Dashes show equal lines.)

24   26

25   27

Identify each shape and write the number of faces, edges and vertices each has.

28   31

29   32

30   33

Plot each set of co-ordinates on a 6 × 6 grid and join up the points in the order given. Draw the mirror line and sketch the reflection of the shape.

34 (1, 0) (2, 2) (4, 2) (5, 0) (1, 0)
Mirror line (0, 3) to (6, 3)

35 (4, 3) (4, 6) (6, 2) (4, 3)
Mirror line (3, 0) to (3, 6)

36 Draw a new 6 × 6 grid. Plot these co-ordinates and join them up in the order given
(3, 2) (4, 4) (5, 3) (3, 2)

37 Translate the triangle:
a) Left 3 Up 2
b) Right 1 Down 2

38 Give the co-ordinates of the new positions of the triangle.

TEST 1

1. Multiply 50 by 400.

2. What is 0·09 less than 1?

3. What needs to be added to 58 to make 111?

4. A rectangle is 8 cm long and has an area of 48 cm². What is its width?

5. Round 123 519 to the nearest thousand.

6. Find the difference between 8² and 3².

7. Add 42 000 to 163 219.

8. Write two hundred and ninety thousand and sixty-two in figures.

9. Find the lowest common multiple of 9 and 12.

10. Write eight thirds as a mixed number.

11. One parcel weighs 1·6 kg. Another weighs 740 g. What is their combined weight in kilograms?

12. Write down all the prime numbers between 50 and 60.

13. Subtract 2700 from 300 000.

14. Give the value of each of the eights in 11.818.

15. Write 847 in Roman numerals.

16. How many eights are equal to 720?

17. What is 3009 more than 100 847?

18. What is the sum of a quarter and seven twelfths?

19. What is 13 multiplied by 21?

20. Find five sixths of 24.

21. What distance is 1000 times greater than 0·025 km?

22. Find the new time if the hour hand of a clock turns 180° from 7 pm.

23. Which number squared gives 121?

24. What number is 100 times greater than 620?

TEST 2

1. What is 900 times 7?

2. Divide 164·5 by 100.

3. Write 964 in Roman numerals.

4. What needs to be added to 0·63 to make 1?

5. Find the highest common factor of 30 and 75.

6. Add 283 and 76.

7. Lee spends £3·57. He pays £10. How much change is he given?

8. Write 508 037 in words.

9. Which number multiplied by 12 makes 840?

10. There are 32 chess pieces. Three eighths have been taken. How many pieces are left on the board?

11. Find the twentieth multiple of 6.

12. What is 90²?

13. What is 3800 more than 14 675?

14. Find one tenth less than four fifths.

15. Round 362 450 to the nearest hundred thousand.

16. A square has an area of 400 cm². How long is each side?

17. Write 9% as a decimal.

18. What is the difference between 10 000 and 4982?

19. Write three and two fifths as an improper fraction.

20. Holly walks 1·35 km. Tania cycles 1·8 km further. How long is Tania's journey?

21. Take 5500 from 401 740.

22. How many degrees is the turn clockwise from SE to SW?

23. What is 10 cubed?

24. A bottle holds 5 litres of water. 1·25 litres is used. How much is left?